The

Fruit

Machine

*

The

Fruit

Machine

Twenty Years of Writings

on Queer Cinema

THOMAS WAUGH

Foreword by John Greyson

Duke University Press

Durham and London, 2000

© 2000 Duke University Press
All rights reserved
Printed in the United States of America on acid-free paper ∞
Typeset in Scala by Wilsted and Taylor Publishing Services
Library of Congress Cataloging-in-Publication Data
appear on the last printed page of this book.

FOR ROSS,

who's been there the whole time

and put up with a lot of bad movies

Contents

Foreword

John Greyson

*   *   *   *   *

The author and John Greyson (left), ca. 1984.

*   *   *

When Tom sent me the manuscript of *The Fruit Machine* last spring, our semiweekly emails became limericks. No big reason: we were maybe bored with haiku or something. Every half-dozen chapters or so, I'd stop reading to zap off another five-line effort. For instance, I once rhymed *Tommy, bonhomie*, and *salami*; he responded with *Greyson, kyrie eleison*, and *d'être raison* (You be the judge).

> Remember that movement called gay lib?
> Its convictions were occasionally très glib,
> But now we're a nice bunch—
> No more demos, we do brunch.
> Oh Mary, could we use a gay squib!

Reading this two-decade collection of Tom's reviews and articles, I'm struck by his squibbishness: by how much this volume is also a record of an evolving movement, and an evolving language. (The fact that we don't say "movement" anymore with any confidence is telling. We certainly don't say "liberation." We don't even say "we.")

Another more pedestrian critic may someday pen a homogenizing account of how the earnest documentaries and Eurofaggy art cinema of the gay lib seventies gave way to the activist videos and pomo narratives of the ACT UP eighties, devolving grotesquely into the Don't Ask Don't Tell Kiss Me Guido comedies of the nineties. That'll be another book, written from a safe historical distance. Tom can't and won't homogenize: he was there. This book consists of his critical missives from the front lines, insistent on the geography and community and moment that he was living through, in all its vernacular specificity. His early chapters (articles for *The Body Politic* and *Jump Cut*) make me embarrassingly nostalgic for a time when a combative and diverse gay Left (when exactly did this term become so hopelessly quaint?) picketed *Cruising* and thus forever changed our passive relationship to dominant cinema. His later chapters remind me how a decade later, in the epicenter of the pandemic, my queer film class watched *Cruising* with uncritical awe; for them it was an ethnographic account of a distant culture that had gone with the wind. How do you homogenize that? Give me Tom's subjectivity any day.

The Fruit Machine takes me back to my first tentative steps out of the closet as a fag and as an artist, early baby steps when everyone was trying to figure out what a radical gay culture might look like, taste like. Tom's writing, then as now, was special: quivering with excitement, laced with irony, tumescent with the passions and contradictions of our very queer subjectivities. His Eisenstein article changed my life: it sent me running off to see if there really was a gay subtext in *Potemkin* (oh yeah!), and ten years later I featured Sergei as one of my reluctant dead fags and dykes in my film *Urinal*.

In his introduction Tom describes how the Mounties in the sixties developed a so-called Fruit Machine to weed out security risks from the civil service. Basically, they'd show suspected homos slides of naked men and measure their responses (dilated eyeballs, sweaty palms). These poor dilated and sweaty souls would then be fired or arrested. Needless to say, the Mounties' Machine was a crock: after a decade of breathtaking inaccuracy, it was consigned to mothballs. In contrast, Tom's *Fruit Machine* is a dazzling success. It works. He shows us celluloid pictures of naked (and clothed) men (and sometimes women) and measures *his own* responses. In the process he proves to even the most resistant reader how central, how fun, how *interesting*, the desiring gaze can be, the queer desiring gaze, to the production and consumption of cinema. I echo oh-so-hetero Andrew Sarris here, who credits pioneering gay film critic Parker Tyler with legitimizing his "passionate pursuit of the cinema through an eroticism of the heart."[1] Tom may swoon over methodical Monty or sing a heartfelt aria to Rainer: he's always happy to tell us who turns him on. However, the *why* is his true passion and profound subject, as he takes us from Quentin Crisp to Midi Onodera. Why do we *need* our differences on the screen? How do we *learn* our differences from the screen? Don't they produce us, just as we produce them?

Tom's two decades of film writing also track a singular journey through the ever-changing landscape of media criticism, from the early days of positive images through the current revelations of queer theory. With characteristic vigor, he has *fruitfully* and idiosyncratically engaged with various strands of poststructuralist thought that have impacted cinema studies. As significantly, he has critically embraced the work of a new generation of queer video and film artists (myself included), as well as supported the lesbian and gay film festival movement, contributing much-needed commentary to an emerging field. His engagements are neither tokenist nor fashionable. Indeed, of Tom's many critical and theoretical voices, the one I most value is his mode of self-interrogation, featured prominently in the introductions that contextualize each article. He has the enviable ability to wonder, to question, to doubt his previous convictions. His questions trigger our own: why did we all hate *Sebastiane* when it first came out? Where does Almodovar find himself in our affections? Why is Tom *still* so wrong about Lothar Lambert?

Eisenstein (who signed a cartoon published in the *St. Petersburg Gazette* with the pseudonym "Sir Gay" on the eve of the Bolshevik Revolution) had this to say about a related medium: "Books burst open like ripe fruit in my hands, and fold back their petals like magic flowers, bearing a fertilizing line of thought, a stimulating word, a corroborating quotation, a convincing illustration. I have loved them so much that they have finally begun to love me back."[2]

The films and tapes that Tom describes on these pages burst open like ripe fruit. His love of moving images spills down his chin, as he savors the sweet juices, revels in the sting of citrus, sinks his teeth deep into the fleshy pulp. He writes with his saliva ducts turned up full blast. His Fruit Machine is on: prepare to get sprayed.

Notes

1 Parker Tyler, *Screening the Sexes: Homosexuality in the Movies*, new foreword by Andrew Sarris, new afterword by Charles Boultenhouse (New York: Da Capo, 1993), xiv.
2 Sergei Eisenstein, *Immortal Memories* (Boston: Houghton Mifflin, 1983), 184.

Acknowledgments

*   *   *   *   *

In the original writing of the pieces in *The Fruit Machine* and in the production of the book, I have many debts of gratitude: to Concordia University and the Quebec Fonds pour la formation de chercheurs et l'aide à la recherche for generous financial and institutional support; to Duke University Press and my editor Richard Morrison for their warm and professional support; to the press's anonymous readers for incisive and constructive feedback; to the artists and distributors, too numerous to mention, who have cooperated with this bothersome critic in the past and for the purpose of this volume; to the Museum of Modern Art Film Stills Collection and other generous providers of illustrations; to my research and technical assistants, especially Marisa Rossy and Christine Harkness; for reprint permission from Pink Triangle Press, *Jump Cut, Cinéaste*, former editors of *Le Berdache* and *Rites* Jean-Michel Sivry and Gary Kinsman respectively, the Concordia University Faculty of Fine Arts, La Cinémathèque québécoise, University of Toronto Press, the Banff Centre for the Arts, University of Minnesota Press, and Lorraine Johnson and Toronto Photographers Workshop; to many commissioners and editors over the years, especially *The Body Politic*'s Ed Jackson, Stephen MacDonald, Rick Bébout, and the others on the Collective, consummate unpaid professionals, and to *Jump Cut*'s John Hess, Chuck Kleinhans, and Julia Lesage, coeditors and gurus, all of whom *believed* in what they were doing; to John Greyson for his kind foreword and subversive complicity through the years, as well as my first starring role; to Richard Dyer for friendship, mentorship, and shopping tips; to two decades worth of loyal proofreaders and resourceful consultants, especially Steve Kokker, Ross Higgins, and indefatigable challenger José Arroyo.

Introduction

*   *   *   *   *

This collection of reviews and essays about cinema and visual culture, piled up over more than twenty years, has several objectives. I would like to make available works and perspectives from the past and recent past that are now hard to find. My aim is to bring them together in coherent, chronological form, both for readers who are too young to remember even *Longtime Companion* let alone *A Very Natural Thing* and for readers who remember them all too well but would like to reconsider and resynthesize two decades of queer film culture. Tracing the context and trajectory of one person's responses, ideas, feelings, and arguments about movies will, I hope, lead to a rediscovery of certain films and filmmakers from the past and, perhaps more important, to a rediscovery of cultural and political frameworks that might have bearing on today's images and issues. Assembling all of this has already led to much personal remembering and introspection, the discovery of a voice I sometimes don't recognize and one I sometimes recognize much too well, a voice coming out of many places.

Genes

My father and grandfather were preachers, and my brother followed in their footsteps. My mother and grandmother were teachers. When I reread these texts that I've produced with such monastic single-mindedness over the last two decades, I think the moral fervor and didactic bent might be in my genes. They're certainly never very far below the surface, even in my most licentious and narcissistic writing about sex. From my crusades against negative stereotypes to those against censorship, from my persistent class-analysis of queer culture to my queer-analysis of straight culture, from my early haranguing of *The Advocate* for selling out, to my more recent badgering of lawyers and editors, it's all there. In the classroom, however, I seldom subject my students to moral uplift; rather I think I'm known for lis-

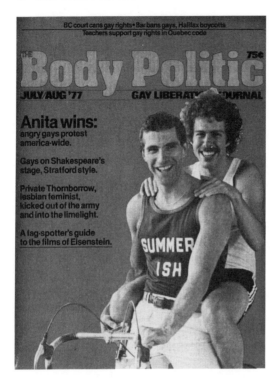

The Body Politic: Toronto's
radical tabloid, 1977.

tening to every side. So undoubtedly it's as a critic and scholar that my
genetic destiny of preaching and teaching comes out.

Of course the atmosphere of permanent crisis that has been the backdrop
to these twenty years of film writings has encouraged the homiletic/peda-
gogical tone. Starting out writing for an activist community paper like *The
Body Politic*, rooted in the leftist branch of gay liberation, or a "radical" journal of media criticism like *Jump Cut*, borne out of the marriage of Marxism
and feminism, certainly imprinted a habit of seeing movies, images, and
the world politically. There was the naive assumption in the air in the late
seventies that the feeling of urgency—the Anita Bryant crisis, the Toronto
prosecution of *TBP*, the Montreal bar raids, the Briggs Initiative in California—wasn't going to last. We assumed that unmasking and challenging the
system would, if not bring it to its knees, at least nudge the world in the
right direction.

But in fact, twenty years after Anita and thirty years after Stonewall,
those of us stumbling into our fifties, who have survived *Cruising*, Clause

28, Oregon, Colorado, Alberta, and Maine, not to mention the Pandemic and all the rest, would be surprised to wake up one morning and not hear new alarms on the horizon. But with aging, with getting used to the atmosphere of permanent crisis, with the realization that we might have failed to transmit the hard-learned wisdom of the sixties and seventies to the young, the rhetoric has changed—at least *mine* has. The result has been not only the longer, more comprehensive pieces (enabled also by leaving the newspaper milieu behind, for better or worse). There has also been a changed tone, less reactive, hopefully more profound, less prescriptive, more tolerant, more willing to see pleasure and contradiction in cultural forms. But maybe this is wishful thinking: is the sermonizer still lurking behind the aspired to urbanity?

The political atmosphere of urgency shows no sign of dissipation as the nineties come to an end. As films like *Licence to Kill*, Arthur Dong's document of the murder of gay people, remind us, it has only evolved. But no one could deny that the cultural environment has indeed been transformed. At least in terms of queer-defined representation. A film like *Licence*—sober, sturdy, and provocative—is one of dozens of features that move every year through the circuit of queer film and video festivals—on every continent now!—and occasions a dutiful but short-lived admiration that is a contrast to the major paradigm shift it would have effected two decades ago, as the 1977 epic documentary and collective self-portrait *Word Is Out* did (see "Films by Gays for Gays"). It's all about visibility. It's one of the things we film critics clamored for in the seventies, and do we ever have it now! Our banal omnipresence in the mainstream media is paralleled by such a lively and diverse universe of queer-defined media that the queer festival hordes and *Advocate* readers take it for granted. How did our culture of urgency and desperate scarcity evolve into a culture of excess, amnesia, complacency, and satedness? Now the cultural critic, at least in urban centers throughout the North—and thankfully I am no longer one—has a much bigger job on his or her hands, must navigate through the flood and indulge in the luxury of high standards of selection and evaluation.

At times, while editing this volume, I found myself regretting that in recent years I have abandoned the pulpit of the reviewer for the keyboard of the man of letters, or rather the fruit of images. It is not that the academic vocation is any harder. For I found reviewing to be a very tough and exacting discipline, a constant struggle for accessibility, tone, conciseness, insight, and wit, not to mention the precise format of plot synopsis and description, evaluation, and extension that is part of the job. We academics would do well to polish these skills, for I find I have grown rusty at keeping things short and snappy now that I no longer have those fanatical editors at *The Body Politic* to keep me on my toes.

As I was moving from famine to feast, and as I moved away from criticism (paradoxically, now that there was so much out there to criticize and so many people doing it so badly), I was moving also from a rigid essentialism to an ambivalent relativism, from cinephile auteurism to pomo eclecticism, from "positive image" Stalinism to a benign indifference to doctrines of social harm caused by negative stereotypes (in part because the antipornography movement's doctrine of social harm has permanently devastated our already shaky constitutional guarantees of freedom of speech in Canada [see "Archaeology and Censorship"]). I have also been taken over almost entirely by my academic writing, represented here by "Kiss of the Maricon," "Erotic Self Images in the Gay Male AIDS Melodrama," and "Walking on Tippy Toes," etc. This full-time enterprise has all of the institutional support and cultural status that unpaid writing for community left tabloids never had. In this esoteric subculture that is scholarly work in film and cultural studies, there are dangers of suffocation. It is a daunting challenge to make cultural reflection lucid and exciting for the nonspecialist, to build your interface with the outside world, to maintain a voice and an integrity in the face of the pernicious trendiness of academe. Here one is rewarded for quoting one brand-name deconstructionist theorist yesterday and another postcolonial high priestess tomorrow but punished for publishing in nonrefereed journals. Very few meet the challenge, and I admittedly have often lost sight of the activist intellectual role that was envisaged by that pioneering generation—Michael Lynch, Jonathan Katz, Allen Bérubé, John D'Emilio, Jane Rule, and the others—who insisted on writing for that still lamented and now crumbling newsprint rag from Toronto.

With the shifts in political and cultural environments have come a different audience and a different sense of audience. At *Jump Cut* and *The Body Politic*, if there was a feeling of preaching to the converted, leftist academics and gay activists respectively, and if there wasn't always as much feedback and dialogue as I would have liked, there was a sense of belonging and pertinence that animated the writing. A minority of pieces in *Fruit* were aimed for straight—or rather mixed—audiences ("Films by Gays for Gays"; "Gays and Straights"; "Film and the Left"; "Montgomery Clift Biographies"; "The Kiss of the Maricon"; "Beauty and the Beast, Take Two"; "We're Talking, Vulva"; and "Archeology and Censorship"), and all but the last one now seem to me slowed down by the uncertainty about shared ground. I remember the feeling I've sometimes had, presenting queer work at predominantly hetero academic affairs, of dropping it all into a deep dark well of polite indifference, especially with male listeners. It's strange: I spend most of my waking hours teaching groups of predominantly heterosexual students, apparently successfully, yet my writing seems to struggle with ghettos and walls. Have we failed to establish a place for queer studies at the center, all the hype notwithstanding? Perhaps the hordes of young queer grad students who have come of age in the nineties will succeed where my generation has failed—if they get the jobs that their queer work may be disqualifying them for! With this collection of work aimed originally, in many cases, at queer readers, will there be, the second time around in recycled form, a crossing over the walls and out of the ghetto?

Pages

This book doesn't look like what I thought it would. I considered several options before locking into the simple chronological organization of thirty-five articles, short and long, shallow and deep, accessible and academic, topical and abstract. Early on, committed to producing a book that you could comfortably hold in one hand (at the prodding of my publisher, admittedly), I became resigned to omitting several of the longer academic pieces I consider "major," my articles on documentary ethics, gay narrative structures, Warhol, etc. These are easily available in existing anthologies, even though their absence creates several gaps in the political and intellectual history before your eyes. A major omission is my long article on gay pornography, for example, an intervention in the porn and sex wars between 1982 and 1985, now twice anthologized and in a sense the germ of my book *Hard to Imagine: Gay Male Eroticism in Photography and Film from Their Beginnings to Stonewall*. Another gap is all the pieces from 1983 onward that were little chunks of *Hard* in embryonic form, the testing ground for the research methods and insights that would get honed later and see print in 1996. Yet another gap is many of the pieces that intersect with my specifically Canadian/Quebec context: although a few pieces in print in Canada are included simply because they travel well and are less available elsewhere, most of the dyed-in-the-wool local color was deselected, unfortunately too full of national references to be accessible to "international" readers (i.e., Americans). We Canadians are used to the imperial politics of this, but we never tire of railing against New Yorkers who identify more with the valley of the Loire than with that of the St. Lawrence.

At one point the idea of separating a collection of "reviews" from longer in-depth articles was considered but dropped. I have ended up liking *Fruit*'s eclectic mixture and chronological peripeteia. This refusal to separate the academic from the topical community stuff was a basic principle of film studies and queer studies in their founding moments that we have too easily forgotten. Surely, writing about cultural forms, above all that hybrid eclectic cannibalistic art form that is the cinema, requires constant adjustment in tone, language, and audience orientation. I hope that *Fruit* readers will find the lurches back and forth between four-letter vulgarity and scholarly pretention invigorating rather than jarring. As for the editing of the individual pieces, the process has been quite minimal, mostly consisting of translation and minor corrections, in order to retain the flavor of the original texts. (Readers will forgive me for having lost some of the original references from newspapers, where the policy was that footnotes were distracting and elitist.)

A word about the title *The Fruit Machine* may well be in order, since it may mean something different to American readers than it does to my compatriots. The uninitiated non-Canadian reader will hopefully, as I intended, read into this phrase a sense of the cinema as a special queer technology. Historically and culturally, how much the moving image has been entangled in our subcultural networks, as well as personal dynamics of identification, longing, desire, and pleasure! No accident that so many gay men in the pre-Stonewall period loved Fellini and worshiped Judy Garland or that perhaps two of the most important pre-Stonewall English-language magazines were the closety but blatant *Films and Filming* and *After Dark*. No accident either that, after Stonewall, we queer film critics instinctively found the movies so life-and-death and that queer film and video festivals are among our most thriving community institutions twenty-five years later. Even the other generalized film festivals (like the Montreal monstrosity I endlessly had to write about in these pages), artificial hothouses of offbeat films rejected by Cannes and distributors, often look like carnivals of queer cinephilia. I guess this volume, then, is also a document of my own personal entanglement with the technology of the fruit, like Charlie Chaplin turning round and round in the cogs and belts of some giant lavender projector (or vcr), wrench in hand.

However, there is more to the title *The Fruit Machine*, a Canadian angle. A decade or so ago Canadian gay historians stumbled on a weird, symptomatic page from our Monty Pythonesque national history that sociologist Gary Kinsman has been fleshing out through dogged detective work ever since.[1] In the late fifties and early sixties our very own Mounties, ever conscious of security threats, had commissioned research into mechanical devices for detecting homosexuality, inspired by similar research in the States where McCarthyism and the sex panics had created a market for such paranoid and lunatic pseudoscience. The idea was to unmask perverts by measuring involuntary pupillary dilations and other physiological reactions to pictures and words. Dubbed "the fruit machine" by terrified straight Mounties who didn't want to be the guinea pigs and whose security was already threatened, the technology came in several proposed models. One involved perspiratory responses to vocabulary with homosexual meanings like *queen, circus, gay, bagpipe, bell, whole, blind, mother, punk, queer, rim, sew, swing, trade, velvet, wolf, blackmail, prowl, bar, house, club, restaurant, tea room,* and *top men* [sic]. Several others involved showing subjects pictures of seminude men, taken from high art or physique magazines, alongside "normal" images, like *Playboy* nudes, and measuring eye movements or attention spans. The project was eventually abandoned because of a lack of cooperative volunteers and any semblance of real results. When I reappropriated the homophobic moniker of the fruit machine from the rcmp for a retrospective of Canadian lesbian and gay film and video, curated for the Cinémathèque Ontario in 1994, the name rang so true that I felt there was more mileage in it yet. What better title for a book that registers ocular reactions to images that are all too often involuntarily physiological, reactions to images that define identity, threaten security, and elicit associations with both pleasure and danger!

Canons

My *Fruit Machine* film list must not be mistaken for a kind of canon of the queer cinema of the last two decades. Who could imagine what that would even look like? Richard Dyer's *Now You See It*, a study of lesbian and gay–authored work ending in 1980, was a daunting task, but at least a feasible one because it covered a half century of relative scarcity. Would it even be *possible* to come up with a similarly representative but selective intercultural narrative of queer-authored cinema over the last two decades (not to mention the larger canon, including those significant queerish works whose relationship to queer authorship is negligible or unknown, like *Lethal Weapon* and *The Taste of Cherries*, or complex, like *Philadelphia*)? Recent volumes like Raymond Murray's and Jenni Olsen's are encyclopedically inclusive and indiscriminate rather than evaluative or prescriptive, hence their great use-value as reference books.[2] Would a distillation of the post-1980 film deluge into a canonical form predicated on *value* or *significance* be possible at this short distance? It is clear, for example, that Arthur Bressan's *Buddies* is one of the most "important" queer feature films of the eighties, despite its total lack of availability (often the deciding factor in canon formation), but will *Mrs. Dalloway* still look like one of the dullest queer features of the nineties a decade from now? If possible, would such a canon be even *desirable*? Some of my queer students think not and suspect me of a generational chauvinist conspiracy through my exposing them to *Death in Venice* and *Querelle*, thereby offending their postmodern ahistoric nonjudgmental sensibilities. Their attitude stems partly from their disaffection with what we used to call the "art cinema," the refuge for so much gay and lesbian identification of the sixties and seventies that is now one more heritage package (mostly by dead white men) that leaves them cold. The art-film culture that gave birth to queer-film culture in the sixties seems more and more like a museum piece, the cultures of VCRs and queer festivals notwithstanding. Does anyone care about Cocteau and Visconti out there? Do my students secretly feel that I love *Death in Venice* so much because I identify with that antediluvian old queen in the film? Not that I have abandoned this pedagogical challenge—far from it.

On the other hand, my students may well be reacting to the contradiction between my commitment to an often esoteric art cinema favored by my middle-class background and intellectual formation, and the popular cultural forms, from Garland to Pee-Wee Herman, from *Rope* to *An Early Frost*, prioritized by my ingrained sense of the class politics of culture and the cultural politics of class. If so, they are on to something, of course, and the taste of seventies feminists for Marguerite Duras and of New Lefters for Jean-Luc Godard is equally problematic. With a lively third stratum of community media work having entered the scene and in fact sustaining the queer festival circuit in no small part, the mainstream/art binary is less immobilizing than it once was, but the negotiation of canons becomes all the more tricky.

A canon is the signature of a cultural constituency at a given historic moment, its collective memory. Since it implies coherence, if not monolithic conformity, perhaps the queer dispersion of the rainbow nineties—our fear of nouns like *community*, as well as the indifference to history that is by no means the unique property of queer people at this global conjuncture—means that our generation will forgo canons and revel somewhat longer in the glut before a canon-making imperative returns.

In any case, the present selection is everything but. The eclecticism of the stream of objects I have written about goes hand in hand with the eclecticism of language, tone, and audience positioning and is no doubt suitable pomo anticanon fodder. The reader will find nary a whisper let alone a major article on many of the epochal films and personalities of queer film history since the seventies. *Taxi zum Klo, Maurice, Kiss of the Spider Woman, Law of Desire, Parting Glances*, and indeed *Buddies* and *Querelle* are all here. But what are *Porky's* and *Caligula* doing in place of *La Cage aux folles* and *Outrageous, Swoon* and *Poison, Looking for Langston* and *Savage Nights?* I can't believe there is no piece here on John Waters/Divine or on John Greyson (I did write a long piece on the latter once, published in French, but the final cut had no room for this strained explanation of queer English-Canadian art video to straight Québécois academics for whom *queer, English-Canadian*, and *art video* were all equally mysterious).

It is tempting to retroactively construct an argument about the importance of writing illuminatingly on minor and peripheral work, of writing against the canon—which I firmly believe in, incidentally. But in point of fact the present attention to the jetsam of film history happened rather accidentally. The big movies like *La Cage aux folles* were usually snapped up by TBP's Toronto staff writers close to the ghetto pulse, and my career as a critic was usually otherwise shaped by chance or the whims of distributors and editors. At the same time, not always inspired by the *Victor Victorias* that everyone else was writing about, I did consciously think of my mission as the introduction of minor but interesting works that no one else had discovered: hence the space taken up in this volume by *By Design* and other titles guaranteed never to be seen by any reader. Was I writing evocatively and above all relevantly enough on *Born a Man . . . Let Me Die a Woman* to engage a reader, not in the rediscovery of a justifiably forgotten film but in the weighing of the issues it raised twenty years later, without the reader's having ever seen the film? If so, then I will have accomplished an important objective for this book.

Finally, my inclusion of lesbian materials needs a mention because it is inconsistent. Over the twenty years, I have oscillated between the delicately negotiated division of the world between the two gender-determined *chasses gardées* (boys talk about boy stuff, girls talk about girl stuff) and the reckless pragmatism of covering interesting lesbian texts that my male readership should know about, those that overlapped the gender divide (like *Word Is Out*), or those that lesbian critics were overlooking. I think the formerly rigid walls, not only based on gender but on other essential categories as well, may be crumbling, but should middle-class white males be chipping away at them? Yes.

Selves

Though I have always tried to write openly and in the first person, hating to have to hide behind the academic veneer, I wonder to what extent the reader will find *The Fruit Machine* a personal trajectory, as well as a professional and intellectual one. Though I am no doubt just as good as my United Church of Canada father at avoiding personal feelings, there may be a confessional reading of this book leaping out at the reader. No doubt many quirks and fetishes will be unwittingly unveiled, as well as those continuities of personal sensibility that are impossible to separate from cultural perspectives: my strong autobiographical identification with the genre of narratives about teachers (at least a half dozen of them treated in this volume—not counting *Porky's*!), my erotic tastes that will seem to have developed little beyond *Physique Pictorial*, my voyeuristic disposition that will seem even more unremitting than that of most cinephiles and critics, my striving for love and approval that all writers must feel, my romantic idealization of coupledom. . . .

Perhaps the latter can be traced to the eleven-year primary relationship I lived between Almodovar's *Labyrinth of Passion* and his *Kika* (does anyone else measure out their sentimental lives in movies?). One resolution of the climate of urgency during the sex'n'porn wars of the early eighties was not an academic one: a work and strategy session aimed at the Trudeau government's scary threat of antisex, antigay obscenity legislation was my first date with a fiery young McGill economics student and movie buff named José Arroyo. The two of us called ourselves the Emergency Committee of Gay Cultural Workers Against Obscenity Laws, showed up with a brief at the hearings, and were quoted in the final government report (not that the surprisingly progressive 1985 "Fraser Commission" report on Pornography and Prostitution in Canada did any good, as the Tories had been swept into power the previous year). It turns out José and I both had other strategies in mind as well, and we ended up spending the next decade together. I suspect that connubial bliss had a certain impact in dissipating the sense of emergency, cultural work, and obscenity in my work during those years, and I do know that José certainly made me clarify my arguments.

As our relationship drew to a close, and as *Hard to Imagine* neared the printers, do I detect a sense of generational angst coming to the surface? In 1990, in Washington, where José and I were both delivering papers (he on Almodovar, I on gay narrative), I first began to take seriously the buzz of queer studies and queer grad students networking, flirting, and taking off. People were beginning to talk about the New Queer Cinema, as well, though I have never understood exactly what was meant, other than an amnesiac semantic construction of the music video generation, because the queer cinema had been in a process of flux and accelerando since the late seventies and was anything but New. I also heard myself quoted an embarrassing amount, and felt old. Do the midlife crises that followed enter into *The Fruit Machine*'s final episodes, perhaps in my nostalgic revisiting of the seventies in "Walking on Tippy Toes," or in the increasingly autobiographical discourse, both here and in *Hard*? The *Fruit* reader shall decide. I am not Roland Barthes nor Eve Sedgwick, two great cultural critics whose personal lives are inseparable from their work. But they have been right in affirming, or at least implying, that for the queer critic especially, the element of personal desire is at the center of his or her vision and work. You can't take the fruit out of *The Fruit Machine*.

Did any of my ancestors love their own sex? Did any love movies? Not to my knowledge, in answer to both questions. Unlike a recent boyfriend, whose family tree is gnarled with knots, I know that any queer ancestors I might have hid their tracks. As for movies, my professional grandparents lived in God-fearing small towns and probably never got a chance, and my working-class urban grandparents with seven kids probably couldn't afford the time or money. However, I do have a vague childhood memory of seeing *The Robe* and *The Greatest Show on Earth* in drive-ins when I would have been four or five, together with some unclear configuration of grandparents (the former set would have approved of *Robe*, and the latter might have enjoyed *Show*). It might even have been a double bill (is my flash of Cornel Wilde's bulging white tights from the latter due to false memory syndrome brought on by latter-day film stills, or was I already a trapeze queen?). Despite this evanescent memory, I can't trace my cinematic culture to my genes: it has been shaped genetically only insofar as I still love hymn movies (*If . . .* , *Distant Voices, Still Lives*, and *Places in the Heart*, for example). My route through my passionate engagement with my queerness and my movies has been my own personal construction, and I have no one to blame for their inextricable linkage but myself. I now invite the reader of *The Fruit Machine* to navigate this route, with proper forewarning, with moral uplift, and, hopefully, with pleasure.

Notes

1   Gary Kinsman, "Spooks in the Canadian State: Heterosexual Hegemony," *Canadian Dimension* (Winnipeg), May–June 1994, 21–23; " 'Character Weaknesses' and 'Fruit Machines': Towards an Analysis of the Anti-Homosexual Security Campaign in the Canadian Civil Service," *Labour/Le Travail* 35 (spring 1995): 133–161; "The Textual Practices of Sexual Rule: Sexual Policing and Gay Men," in Marie Campbell and Ann Manicom, eds., *Knowledge, Experience, and Ruling Relations: Studies in the Social Organization of Knowledge* (Toronto: University of Toronto Press, 1995), 80–95.

2 Raymond Murray, *Images in the Dark: An Encyclopedia of Gay and Lesbian Film and Video* (Philadelphia: TLA Publications, 1994); Jenni Olsen, *The Ultimate Guide to Lesbian and Gay Film and Video* (New York: Serpent's Tail, 1996). The books do contain some canonizing discourse. Murray spotlights the following post-Stonewall directors: Chantal Akerman, Pedro Almodovar, Lindsay Anderson, Kenneth Anger, Gregg Araki, Emile Ardolino, Paul Bartel, Lizzie Borden, Arthur Bressan, James Bridges, Lino Brocka, James Broughton, Terence Davies, Eloy de la Iglesia, Robert Epstein and Jeffrey Friedman, Rainer Werner Fassbinder, Su Friedrich, Constantine Giannaris, Marlene Gorris, Barbara Hammer, Todd Haynes, Colin Higgins, Marc Huestis, Jaime Humberto Hermosillo, Derek Jarman, Beeban Kidron, George Kuchar, Lothar Lambert, Curt McDowell, Ismail Merchant and James Ivory, Robert Moore, Paul Morrissey, Ulrike Ottinger, Jan Oxenberg, Sergei Paradjanov, Pratibha Parmar, Pier Paolo Pasolini, Wolfgang Petersen, Tony Richardson, Marlon Riggs, Ken Russell, Greta Schiller, John Schlesinger, Werner Schroeter, Monika Treut, Gus Van Sant, Luchino Visconti, Rosa von Praunheim, John Waters, Franco Zeffirelli. This incomplete and problematic list fudges the issue of gay or lesbian authorship through including straights, closet cases, subtexters, and disavowers, among others, and omits the eligible Canadians, as usual, and even the French. Still it's a fine, admirably cosmopolitan start.

Films by Gays for Gays:

A Very Natural Thing, Word Is Out,

and *The Naked Civil Servant*

*   *   *   *   *

I still remember my quavers about publishing this, my coming-out piece in academia. I had just begun my new job teaching at Concordia University and would not be up for tenure until 1981, but plowed ahead fearlessly. I must have felt pretty confident about my place at Concordia and don't remember any reactions from my colleagues. Twenty years later I should perhaps acknowledge my gratitude and affection for this carnivalesque institution, with its erratic escalators, nurturing networks, and safe places for risky scholarship (I won't get into that nasty business about same-sex spousal benefits at the end of the eighties, when, when it came to actual money, a conservative faculty union and the inertia of a liberal institution came together to hesitate just a little too long for my liking). I also have a debt to the Jump Cut *coeditors, Chuck Kleinhans, Julia Lesage, and John Hess, who encouraged me on this first brazen venture, then not blinking, eventually got me on the board of this immeasurably influential rad tab, where I would continue to publish major work over the next decade. This indefatigable pinko media rag is celebrating its twenty-fifth birthday as we go to press.*

All three of the films discussed in this article have entered the nineties gay canon, thanks as much to their availability on video as to their centrality to our cultural history. None has lost its power to move and astonish. I still cry at Word Is Out. The Naked Civil Servant *I think I understand better now, less as a serendipitous fluke in a vacuum than as a logical outcome of a British tradition that had provided space for almost two decades for such images of queer dignity.*

A Very Natural Thing remains the most precarious of the three but still may not have deserved the disproportionate ideological thrashing I gave it. No doubt my defensiveness reflects a lot about the atmosphere in the cultural wing of the North American New Left, about my sense of mission caught in the middle be-

tween the straight Left, who didn't understand identity politics, and the gay-lib mainstream, who denied class. Whether or not the late editor David Goodstein of The Advocate *really deserved comparison to the fascist Chilean dictator is another question. But categorical moral judgments were the flavor of the day. Plus ça change . . .*

*   *   *

Will Homosexuals Be Admitted to the Classless Society?

The prospect of writing on a few gay-oriented films for *Jump Cut* has caused me a few tremors of hesitation. There are obvious dangers in blowing one's professional cover (i.e., coming out) in academia in 1977. But there are worse places to come out in than a faculty of Fine Arts, like a Faculty of Engineering, for example (to indulge in a little of what is called interdisciplinary retaliatory stereotyping). And if a friend of mine in an English department was able, just last year, to seize tenure from the jaws of a board of Catholic priests, things are looking up indeed. There are other more important reasons for my hesitation, which I would like to outline briefly before I get started.

Dialogue between gay leftists and straight leftists is not a new phenomenon, but until recently it was never conducted equitably or constructively. As a rule, most serious leftists now give at least token support to the issue of gay civil rights, as they do to one variation or another of the feminist analysis— you just can't keep opportunism in the closet these days. Nevertheless, gays still occasionally get expelled from left party formations; the Venceremos Brigade still won't let us go to Cuba with them; an enthusiastic gay contingent gets ignored and insulted at last summer's Fourth of July Coalition, Anti-Bicentennial Rally in Philadelphia; and one still has to deal with such provocations as a position paper recently published by a California-based splinter group that states unequivocally that "homosexuals cannot be communists."[1]

As a teacher, I occasionally run into a few other variations of this old song and dance. Two recent examples: a claim that "There won't be any homosexuals in the classless society" and a reference to the Nazi extermination of homosexuals as an "isolated atrocity."

Adherents to the robust and rapidly growing gay left movements in North America and Europe constantly run into that kind of bigotry within the Left. Ironically, this more often comes from middle-class intellectuals than from workers themselves, as the experiences of lesbians in working women's groups and of gay men and women in various unions have revealed. The attitudes of these pseudoradicals usually boil down to, "We think you should have job security even if you are sick and leave the revolution to us." In the face of all of this, many gay radicals have simply resorted to organizing and consciousness raising within the gay community itself. Others refuse to leave the revolution to the straights—for this courageous minority, the model provided by contemporary East Germany is an important one: it can hardly be a coincidence that the most liberal of the socialist states with regard to sexual minorities is also the one in which gays participated most actively in prerevolutionary party formations.[2]

To return somewhat closer to home, even a journal as progressive in its sexual politics as *Jump Cut* needs to examine its own record. The most obvious blot in this record came late in 1974, when a *Jump Cut* reviewer casually passed on one of the oldest and most libelous stereotypes going.[3] A lot of water has flowed under the bridge since then, but the offending article, a discussion of the Clint Eastwood vehicle *Thunderbolt and Lightfoot*, wittily entitled "Tightass and Cocksucker," needs to be given a decent burial. One of the few critics around to have confronted the homoerotic subtext of the "buddy" genre head-on, the author, Peter Biskind, correctly points to a fabric of sly allusions and suggestive imagery beneath the surface of the film but then turns his perception in a direction so perverse and reductionist that it is hard to follow. The gist of the argument is that there must be some connection between this latent gay motif and the film's much more blatant misogynist sensibility (surely a conventional feature of the genre). But the connection posited by the article is that, as everyone knows, homosexuals hate women. Behind the film, in fact, lies a conspiracy of woman-hating homosexuals with the intent of denigrating heterosexuality. This seditious intent is no doubt realized by the total suppression of overt gay references; by the prurient, mocking, and exploitative tone of the gay subtext; and by the startlingly original idea of having the protogay character stomped to death. The film is no less antigay than it is antiwoman—in fact it is antisex and about as subversively homoerotic as a frat party drag show or a barroom fag joke. Thanks a lot—we could pull off a better conspiracy than that anytime. (Just think of how skillfully we seduce your children.) The mind boggles over how a jumble of sly fag jokes tossed about by presumably straight filmmakers can be read as progay propaganda and, furthermore, how gays can get blamed for the antiwoman attitudes that accompany them. You can't win. For me the film is definitive proof of the intrinsic identity between homophobia and sexism.

If *Jump Cut's* single such slipup is easily atoned for, a more general homophobia-by-default is less easy to repudiate, or to define. Any faggot or dyke worth his or her salt knows that silence is one of the first symptoms of advanced homophobia, and in this sense *Jump Cut* is clearly suspect (although the silence of other radical film mags, from *Cinéaste* to *Screen*, is deafening in comparison—without even considering the latter's adherence to certain latently homophobic aspects of Lacanian psychoanalysis).

Jump Cut's most recent attempt to deal with the "buddy" movies, Arthur Nolletti's "Male Companionship Movies and the Great American Cool,"[4] was so anxious to block and repress a crucial aspect of the films under discussion—that is, the obvious homoerotic undertone of most of them—that it left a trail a mile wide. Except for a single passing reference, the article's avoidance of the love that dare not speak its name was as conspicuous as that of the films themselves.

It is true, however, that *Jump Cut* has been inching forward in this area. I was so excited to see the two open lesbians among the contributors to last summer's special issue that I nearly stopped hating women for a moment. And the two pieces on *Dog Day Afternoon* in the same issue at least recognized the relevance of the film to the gay problematic, although neither went beyond the call of duty.

Okay, it is in this context that I hesitate in writing this piece. Given the lingering homophobic tendency of the straight Left, does it not amount to treachery to criticize fellow gays (which I am about to do), to provide fuel for existing antigay stereotypes within the *Jump Cut* readership, to wash the gay movement's linen in front of a possibly unsympathetic audience? Just what the movement needs!

What it really needs, I believe (as does an increasingly articulate segment), is a recognition of its stake in all revolutionary struggles and a firmer commitment to its natural alliance with radical and feminist causes. And not only this. What it also needs is dogged and determined spokespeople within the straight Left loudly refusing to down one or more ounce of shit from the closet bigots therein and defiantly insisting that any Marxist analysis or feminist analysis that ignores the gay struggle is an incomplete analysis. And they must persistently remind the Left that we are planning to turn out in full force, in our habitual percentage, for the classless society.

A Very Natural Thing

When Christopher Larkin's *A Very Natural Thing* first appeared in early 1974, the gay movement had every reason to be encouraged. *Serious* and *first* were the two words everyone used to describe this feature-length color narrative that dared to deal with gay male life from a gay perspective and in a nonporno framework. And it is true that its seriousness and its innovativeness both guarantee its place as a milestone in gay film history, despite its many obvious shortcomings.

There had been gay films before. After all, by the seventies the concentrated, profitable market of young, urban gay males was a well-tested commercial reality. Everyone from the Mafioso gay-bar entrepreneurs to haberdashers had long since cashed in on this ghettoized market, and filmmakers, at first primarily pornographers, were no different. (During the early seventies the gay porno industry was well ahead of its hetero counterpart in technical and stylistic sophistication.) Even Hollywood would wake up to the economic reality of this market, which gay publications such as *The Advocate* and *After Dark* (respectively the largest open-gay and the largest closet-gay magazines) made clear to their advertisers was composed of free living, big spending young bachelors with sophisticated tastes. However, until *A Very Natural Thing*, the nonporno films that catered to this market seemed relics of that pre-Stonewall past that gays wanted to forget. Two fairly competent such films had appeared in 1970, for example (the year after the New York Stonewall riots, which symbolically introduced the era of gay lib), and both reflected the gay perspective of gay subject matter: *The Boys in the Band*, a quite faithful Hollywood version of a gay-authored play, slightly enervated for general consumption by director William Friedkin, and *Sticks and Stones*, a more modest, independent treatment of a similar theme, directed by Stan LoPresto. Both of these films, however, embodied an anachronistic defeatism, a morbid, self-directed hatred that surely reinforced homophobia within their straight audiences, curious but still powerfully destructive artifacts of an era when "gay" translated onto the screen meant "trivial, tragic, and tormented."

What was different about A Very Natural Thing was that it deliberately attempted to escape the traditional rituals of self-loathing. Here was a film that so many of us wanted to call our own that many of us did so without thinking, not in the least because of one specific feature of the film that had vast symbolic importance—its happy ending.

Digression: Why Gay Endings Aren't Always Happy
The happy ending is a convention that Hollywood and its foreign competitors have traditionally reserved for films about straight people. Gay characters traditionally drop off like flies, with clockwork predictability, at the service of dramatic expediency and the sexual anxiety of the dominant culture. Nineteen seventy-four, for example, saw, in addition to A Very Natural Thing, the successful release of Truffaut's *Day for Night*. Truffaut's gay audiences were momentarily transported when the film's leading man, Jean-Pierre Aumont, was revealed to be gay and to have a beautiful young lover to boot. But they should have known that it was too good to be true. Truffaut's knee-jerk liberal impulse, on introducing such a fine affirmative image, was to have Aumont and his lover summarily wiped out by the most freakishly gratuitous highway accident in film history. Two more faggots bite the dust as Truffaut's warm, humane, joyous tribute to filmmaking tidies up its loose threads in the last reel.

As I've said, Truffaut was in traditional company. Death by unnatural causes has been the standard device used by the bourgeois cinema to finish off any token minority member who doesn't know his or her place—blacks and sexually forward or independent women, as well as gays. Remember the dozens of gruesome deaths inflicted on poor Sidney Poitier by fifties liberalism and the hundreds of saloon prostitutes finished off so that Henry Fonda, or whoever, could end up with the virtuous, submissive girl from the East? The deaths reserved for lesbians and gay men have been particularly mechanical, however, and often fiendishly ingenious. If Shirley MacLaine's dangling from the ceiling in *The Children's Hour* and Ratzo Rizzo's glazed eyeballs in the Miami bus in *Midnight Cowboy* are perhaps the images imprinted most indelibly on our collective unconscious, death by gunshot has been by far the favorite recourse of screenwriters looking for a tidy ending. Sal Mineo in *Rebel without a Cause*, Stéphane Audran in *Les Biches*, Don Murray in *Advise and Consent*, and Rod Steiger in *The Sergeant* head this list of the departed. The prizes for the most original deaths go to Mark Rydell for the tasteful way he had Sandy Dennis struck down by a falling tree in *The Fox* and to Ken Russell for Richard Chamberlain's magnificent demise in *The Music Lovers*, cholera-induced convulsions in a vomit-laced tub of boiling bathwater.[5]

Even as superficially progressive a film as *Sunday, Bloody Sunday* left poor Peter Finch alone with his stoic courage at the end as his handsome lover jetted off to the New World—a transatlantic flight providing a more discreet way out for seventies chic than the suicide or freak accident that would have been Finch's lot in any other era.

In any case, the flourishing gay audience of the seventies, fed up with all this gore, was bound to get its happy ending sooner or later. Larkin stepped in to fulfill the historical role of providing it for them. And happy it was!

A Very Natural Thing: Why Happy Endings Aren't Always Gay
Larkin's conclusion to *A Very Natural Thing* was the fulfillment of generations of suppressed and sublimated gay male fantasy: a dazzlingly sunny, climactic beach sequence, with the film's hero and his new-found, not-quite lover running hand in hand, naked, through the surf, penises flinging about with carefully revealed spontaneity, in slow motion, of course, with swelling romantic music (tasteful brass) filling the screen, the theater, and ten million ravaged hearts.

It was a sequence that sent its original audiences out into the dark homophobic world with a euphoric, utopian energy, those sunny slow-motion shots undoing generations of bullets and falling trees (the sequence also provides the standard publicity still used by the distributor). The ending left California critic Lee Atwell equally elated, and he closed what was probably the most intelligent review of the film (reserved but encouraging) with Larkin's own description of the slow motion coda: "expansive with pure joy, playful, free, intimate, passionate—symbolizing the effort of every person who seeks a life informed by beauty, intelligence and love."[6]

A Very Natural Thing (1974): sexual liberation in a presocial paradise. Museum of Modern Art Film Stills Library.

If the sequence did in fact capture the mood of a whole generation of gay men who had discovered the freedom and beauty of their own bodies, each other, and the world outside the closet door, it is also true that the pure joy, etc., on the beach had very little to do with the anxious, reflective tone of the rest of the film and in fact blocked some of the insights that Larkin was groping for but never managed to articulate fully.

The story follows a year or so in the life of a young New York schoolteacher who has his fantasies of monogamous felicity rudely shattered in the first half of the film by a doomed relationship with a straight-identified young businessman. In the second half, the hero meets Mr. Right but this time manages to keep his cool and resolves to play it by ear. Mr. Right is of course the other frolicker in the surf.

The story builds, then, on a recognition of the inadequacy of traditional romantic patterns for gay lifestyles: the first relationship is destroyed by possessiveness and inflexible expectations based on received heterosexual models. But this recognition, which even the film's gratingly earnest hero, David, seems on the verge of articulating, is ultimately undercut by the sun, the sand, and the pair of gleaming asses in the waves.

This pattern of conflicting loyalties is pure Hollywood: give literal surface allegiance to the correct ideological formation (matrimony and family in the case of classical Hollywood and gay lib's ideal of nonstereotyped sexual roles in Larkin's case), but devote all your visual and dramatic energies to the values you really feel deep down (in Hollywood's case, the strictly nondomestic eroticism that props up the box office and, in Larkin's, the conventional hetero romantic fantasies). Larkin is certainly aware of the limitations of David's pathetic Hollywood-derived expectations—he forces lover Number One to say "I love you" and to roll through the autumn leaves with him—but Larkin can no more get his sights on an alternative to the old model than can David. Larkin is confined by the very problematic he seeks to resolve. Having dutifully said "no" in the script, Larkin indulges in his slow-motion coda, which drowns out that "no" with every fleck of surf and overdetermined flash of crotch.

The final sequence points to other serious limitations in Larkin's insight as well. The beach, naturally, is deliriously empty for Larkin's farewell image. The endless vista of sand and sea could be part of a Bahamas travel ad if both figures had bathing suits on, one being a bikini. Now I do not mean to be too hard on a sequence that moved me no less than it did many others in the original audience and fulfilled a specific historical function in 1974, but the emptiness of it all had disturbing implications. It is as if the two naked figures were gamboling in some presocial paradise, like the plaintive fantasy of Blake's young chimney sweeps,[7] and such an image unfortunately expresses the social perspective of all too many gay ideologists. It is the ultimate delusive myth of a certain middle-class core of the gay community that sexual liberation would be no problem if we all had our private beach to play on.

It is no accident that the deserted beach is also a stock image from the pages of *The Advocate*, the California-based biweekly organ of the nonpoliticized gay community. Here we find the consumerized, middle-class co-optation of the gay movement expressed in its most blatant terms. *The Advocate* millionaire publisher, David Goodstein, the General Pinochet of gay lib, delivers regular polemics against the unrespectable, "unkempt" troublemakers (i.e., radicals) in the movement who hog the limelight and threaten his projected image of the respectable, winter-in-Hawaii, middle-class gay. Much of his space is devoted to features on closeted and straight showbiz celebrities, who all assure their interviewers that some of their best friends are gay. There is even an investment counseling column.

To be sure, Larkin is to be credited with showing slightly more awareness of the social realities than *The Advocate*. He does show all three main characters, for instance, in their occupational milieus (although Goodstein would approve heartily of each one): the hero teaching poetry to a class of girls, Lover Number One carrying his attaché case to and from his office and ordering a female secretary around therein (I couldn't tell whether this potentially provocative insight was intentional on Larkin's part), and Mr. Right, a self-employed photographer, wielding his camera with all the artistic sensitivity to be expected of a gay man. Regrettably, this is as far as it goes. Although, for example, we learn that David cannot come out because of his teaching job, the movie communicates little sense of the dynamics of this oppression—perhaps the most palpable for gays of David's class and profession—and the way it confines him and his businessman lover to their schizophrenic lives and their isolated, fearful ghetto. And, of course, there is little sense as well that most New York gays do not have smart West Side apartments, cozy fireside dinners à deux, Deutsch Grammophon records, and Fire Island summers, with no persecution from landlords, police, thugs, and Salem ads. The New York of the film is that clichéd paradise for lovers from the pages of *The Advocate* and *After Dark*, revolving around Central Park, the West village, Lincoln Center, and Fire Island, a fantasy as sanitized and phony as any Hollywood set in spite of Larkin's skilled use of location shooting and an unknown cast. It goes without saying that there is no sense whatsoever of the affinity between gays and other oppressed groups such as that felt in the work of some European gays, like Fassbinder and Pasolini, and even in that of Americans such as the Warhol/Morrissey and John Waters/Divine duos.

One or two scenes built on David's interactions with his equally ghetto-ized friends have satiric, even critical potential, which Larkin seems to be aware of without being able to exploit fully. In one dinner party sequence, for example, the camera repeatedly catches the host's gleaming silver services and seems equally drawn to one of the guest's working-class Puerto Rican lover, silent and painfully out of place. This scene suggests a potential analysis of class structures within the gay ghetto à la Fassbinder, but this is never fully realized.

One of Larkin's most intelligent choices was to intercut his story with some documentary footage and interviews taken during the 1973 Christopher Street Liberation Day Parade. In one sense this choice compensates partly for the empty societal backdrop in the rest of the picture. The image of real lesbians and gay men being themselves and talking to the camera are lively and refreshing (the interviews provide the film's keynote and title in one lesbian's comment that gayness is "a very natural thing"). But even here, the atmosphere has a somewhat overstated, euphoric edge to it and the title a strained, idealist ring as well. Seeing the film now, in retrospect, one can too easily find the lurking implication that it is no less easy to talk of liberation and natural things when surrounded by one's gay sisters and brothers in a collective demonstration than it is to frolic slow motion on a deserted beach.

In 1974, however, it seemed certain that Larkin's was a voice to be heard from in the future. Despite the awkwardness and ideological naiveté of his first effort, it seemed possible that he was on the verge of asking important questions. *A Very Natural Thing* itself still appears from time to time: it played in Montreal for a few weeks last summer in ironic juxtaposition to the mass arrests of gays being carried out at the same time by officials who apparently considered gayness A Very Dirty Thing to be swept under the carpet for the Olympics. Meanwhile, Larkin has apparently no plans for a follow-up film. Reportedly disillusioned and bitter about his first bout behind the camera, he has recently produced a commercially successful musical, *Boy Meets Boy*, which has run in several of the major gay ghettos. Another product for *The Advocate* market, *Boy Meets Boy* is a gay updating of thirties musicals conventions, consummated presumably with another happy ending.

Word Is Out

It seems as if North American gay men will have to look elsewhere for a serious expression of their reality, filmic or otherwise. One possible direction in

which to look, incredible as it may seem, is the television screen. I'm not referring to the much-touted presence of a few token gays in network sitcoms
last fall.[8] It would be unrealistic to expect more from such tokenism than
blacks got from *Julia*. After all, the portrayal of Walt Whitman in the PBS special last winter was so innocuous and whitewashed that the uninitiated audience no doubt concluded that the great gay poet was persecuted for his
long hair and that harmless-looking young man he picked up in a taxi and
lived with for twenty years but never touched let alone kissed was his roommate. (The only person Walt did touch in the whole hour of the histrionics
and verbosity was his retarded brother.) So even if *Mary Hartman, Mary
Hartman* does go one step beyond this, it's still not enough.

The question of whether establishment TV can go far enough (in case anyone is still wondering) will no doubt be answered more definitively when
Word Is Out,[9] a documentary by and about lesbians and gay men, is finally
finished and broadcast on public television sometime in the (ambiguous)
future.

In the works for almost four years, the project was initiated by a West
Coast documentarist, Peter Adair, whose major previous credit is a documentary on a snake-handling Protestant sect. That film made a modest impression a decade ago. The subject matter this time is somewhat closer to
home. Otherwise the film has been a collective endeavor, and now working
on the final stages of the film are Adair's sister Nancy, Andrew Brown, Rob
Epstein, Veronica Selber, and Lucy Phenix (who was associated with the
prestigious radical documentary *Winter Soldiers*).

The collective's fifty-fifty composition of women and men reflects their
determination to redress the invisibility of lesbians in the public image of
the gay movement (Item: *A Very Natural Thing*, where the only important
female part was Mr. Right's heterosexual ex-wife). More generally, the aim
of *Word Is Out* is simply to answer that basic question posed by the working
title, *Who Are We?*

This answer has proven to be more elusive, however, than the group at
first expected. In fact, the impossibility of the project—the sheer ludicrous-
ness of the job of defining filmically a community of twenty million lesbians
and gay men that not even social scientists have been able to define to anyone's satisfaction (not that straight social scientists are particularly inter-

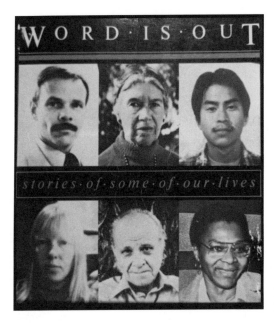

Word Is Out (1977):
paradigm-shifting self-
portrait.

ested)—may prove to be the film's undoing. As with *A Very Natural Thing*, its ultimate importance may be as a symbolic milestone rather than for any intrinsic aesthetic or political virtue.

Simply the very fact of being confronted with a gallery of cinéma vérité portraits of real, actual people, lesbians and gay men, rather than the fantasies and dramatic pretexts of sitcoms, the soap operas, and the skinflicks— real people describing real situations and experiences to the camera—this fact alone will be an important breakthrough for a minority that has never controlled its own image before.

The conception of the film has been in a constant state of flux since the outset. For one thing, the number of subjects to be presented has risen steadily as the collective has attempted to represent more and more elements within the gay community. When I encountered some of them last summer, they were in search of an East-Coast Third-World Young Male and were collecting video tests of an East-Coast White Student Activist and an East-Coast Lesbian Activist, among others.

Fault will inevitably be found with the spectrum of subjects finally chosen by the group. It will be impossible to please everyone, or maybe even anyone. The criticism they had encountered so far in the course of trial projections came from every direction. Too many monogamous couples (shades of *A Very Natural Thing*). Not enough "effeminate" men. Too many "effeminate" men. What about drag queens?

One of the interviewees, a lesbian around thirty, tells of her bitter memories of institutionalization as a teenager and then conducts the camera around her wilderness retreat as she chops down trees, in flannel shirt, jeans, and boots. Is that woman a negative stereotype (escapist and alienated) or a positive one (resourceful and independent), or is she simply a real person with an important historical testimony to offer?

If twenty subjects are necessary to suggest the diversity of the gay community, will the resulting portraits be too sketchy and superficial? The baffling range of reactions to the work in progress no doubt reflects the range of presuppositions about what the finished film should try to do. Would it be most valuable if aimed at straights? at open gays? at closet gays? The emphasis was at first to find positive role models for the gay audience on either side of the closet door, but the possibly conflicting tendency to reflect a legitimate cross section of the gay community seems present also. Naturally, there are radically opposing views on what constitutes a positive role model and what constitutes a legitimate cross section depending on whether you read *The Advocate* or not.

One strategy of the collective that seems fairly definite and that many radical gays have found dismaying is the soft-pedaling of explicit political rhetoric and analysis in the interviews—in short, according to some critics, censorship.

Adair believes that such rhetoric will alienate nonpoliticized gays and prevent them from coming out and that films like *Hearts and Minds*, with its explicit political viewpoint, talk down to their audiences from a position of righteousness. Even if this approach may ultimately be the only realistic way to get on the air, such logic is not likely to placate the radical critics of the project, who see the systematic suppression of political aspects of the subjects' lives as a vicious betrayal. They point to the case of the well-known activist lawyer from San Francisco who was presented in the trial version of the film without the slightest mention of his political life.

Yet when I saw that version along with a small New York audience that included several of that city's most respected gay radicals, as well as a larger number of prospective small investors and other gays, the tears flowed abundantly, and there could be no question of the compelling power of the document on its way to completion.

Whatever may be the situation by the time the collective arrives at a release version (their response to feedback seemed so conscientious that the final shape of the project is hard to predict), it is likely that any radical content will arise from an extension of the film's documentary ontology itself rather than in the views articulated by any of the subjects or the exemplary nature of their lives as seen on the screen. I mean this in the same way that the early feminist films, modest records of ordinary women talking about their lives, proved invaluable as a consciousness-raising tool in the women's movement, regardless of the level of awareness reached by the subjects on the screen. If the lively debate triggered by the trial version is matched on a larger scale when *Word Is Out* is finally broadcast, the collective and radical gay community will have no cause to complain.

If, on the other hand, radical gays want films directly answering our needs as organizing tools and the needs of the gay community as a whole, films incorporating radical discourse and offering clearsighted analysis, it is hardly news that we cannot expect these films from the establishment media but must look to alternative media resources instead, the way the feminists and the straight Left have been learning to do for some time.

The Naked Civil Servant

Another television film produced recently, in England this time, *The Naked Civil Servant*, also appears as a model, encouraging in many respects, of the best we can expect from the establishment media. A Thames Television International production directed by Jack Gold, *The Naked Civil Servant* is a three-part dramatization of the autobiography of one Quentin Crisp, a British gay in his seventies who, since the film came out last year, has become something of a cult figure for the British movement.

Crisp is a "Queen" (or "graceful," as Olympic sportscasters say of certain male figure skaters)—in effect, defiantly and flamboyantly "effeminate." As we see him in a brief introductory appearance at the start of the film, delicately poising his teacup for the camera, and as the record of his fifty-year struggle demonstrates fully, Crisp is in every way worthy of the regal conno-

Positive image? John Hurt (right) as Quentin Crisp (left) in *The Naked Civil Servant* (1975). Museum of Modern Art Film Stills Library.

tation of the term *queen*, as well as the vernacular one. In fact, Crisp's story serves as much as an exemplary history of resistance to societal oppression over the years as it does as a personal memoir.

Crisp, as enacted by John Hurt, with his wildly fluffed and henna-ed hair and his Cowardly intonation, comes across somewhat like Maggie Smith. Both *The Body Politic* and *Gay Left*, the Canadian and British journals of radical gay lib, respectively, expressed reservations about the ultimate effect the Crisp image would have in confirming existing stereotypes among the straight and closet gay public (surprisingly, since it is more typical of *The Advocate* to be concerned about being butch in public).[10] I think however that any potential damaging affect is fully offset by the film's defiant embrace of the "queen" stereotype and its success in fleshing out that stereotype dramatically and historically. It is no mean accomplishment for Gold and Hurt to have realized a popular dramatic work in which an "effeminate" man, the traditional outcast of the more respectable elements of the gay community as well as of the outside world, should enlist such as a strong identification from a general audience, as the Crisp character seems to do, without any of the usual shortcuts of sentimentality, condescension, or martyrology.

The Naked Civil Servant is remarkably tough-headed. It manages to avoid a feeling of the bland, affirmative image making that gay media critics often seem to be demanding and of which *A Very Natural Thing* is the ultimate expression. It does this by retaining the personal specificity of Crisp's story and exploiting the sharp sense of self-awareness that apparently marked the original memoirs. Furthermore, the script, using a first-person voice-over narrative and pointedly ironic intertitles, has effected a layer of analytic counterpoint above the story itself, commenting at one point, for example, on the self-destructive, exhibitionist urges that seem to motivate Crisp's struggle as much as any more conventional heroic impulse.

As I've said, the film has considerable value as a historical document, a record of an aspect of contemporary history that I daresay straight people (and many young gays) know very little about: the ubiquitous, systematic homophobia of traditional bourgeois society. Once the young Crisp leaves the oppressively middle-class parental home (typical breakfast-time ice-breaker: "Are you going to get a job today?"), his picaresque journey takes him a lot of places. There are various entries into the job market, where he briefly occupies a few of those artistic positions available to discreet members of his caste: he tries his hand as a commercial artist and a tap-dancing teacher, for example. Although his adventures take place at every level of the social ladder, he invariably returns to one of the two ghettos that pre-Stonewall society permitted the uncloseted gay, the lumpen underworld and the upper-class salon circuit of the bohemian-chic intelligentsia. Along the way Crisp runs into every kind of persecution offered to the discriminating gay (most of which is still available) by punks, queer-bashers, police, judges, psychiatrists, clergymen, landlords, neighbors, soldiers, psychopaths, liberals, and the upper-class gays who coldly exclude such a tactless brother from their club. Crisp defies one and all to do their worst. He stubbornly refuses through all of it to surrender his chosen identity and lifestyle. His ultimate survival—and triumph, even, as "one of the stately old homos of Britain"—is a happy ending that, in contrast to Larkin's romp through the surf, resounds with inspiration, integrity, and realism.

Humor is one important way *The Naked Civil Servant* is able to sharpen its analysis of the social and psychological dynamics confronted by Crisp. The film is wonderfully funny. It is paradoxical, and no doubt significant, that *A Very Natural Thing* and many other gay films make virtually no use of this formidable device. I say "paradoxical" because humor has always been the gay resource par excellence—virtually the only refuge and weapon we had during those eons in the closet. I would even venture to say that it often had the same kind of liberating function in the pre-Stonewall gay community that music and Christianity are said to have for blacks under slavery (and is equally likely to interiorize society's hatred and serve the oppressor by virtue of its sublimatory function). Both *Boys in the Band* and *Sticks and Stones*, as rooted as they are in preliberation ideology, have delightful comic moments. Even if the comic predisposition has resulted in the addition of "bitchery" and "camp" to the faggot stereotype, I think it has often served us well. This makes it all the more amazing to me that, of the ten or so major gay filmmakers I could list, most are unredeemably solemn: the belly laughs are few and far between, for example, in the films of Eisenstein, Murnau, Cocteau, Visconti, Pasolini, and Fassbinder. Apart from the somewhat special case of Laurel and Hardy, and without considering the latter-day lumpen-camp genre of Warhol/Morrissey and Waters/Divine, Lindsay Anderson is the only significant exception I can think of.

But to return to Quentin Crisp, the irreverent wit with which he assails every target within the bourgeois order is devastating. As examples, the portrait of the army psychiatrist who crumbles before the task of deciding whether this effete young man in his underwear and nailpolish is competent to serve King and Country, or Crisp's version of London gays' patriotic contribution to the war effort in the form of recreational facilities for the GIS ("Never in the history of sex was so much offered to so many by so few"). When it comes to the protagonist's own internalized oppression, the narrator is no less keen. Crisp's persistent fantasy of "the great dark man whose love I will win" is continually played within the intertitles until finally he wakes up to the delusion of this fantasy, and the viewer is assaulted with the title to end all titles: "There is no great dark man." Class structures within the gay community and the economic bases of ghetto, closet, homophobia, and the political function of psychiatry are all treated with the same clarity and dispatch.

Crisp's chronicle is a history, as I've said, that must be kept alive. No bourgeois historians are going to bother with it, any more than they bother noting our "isolated atrocity" at the hands of the Nazis. But at the same time, this history needs to be made complete by the qualifications that Crisp is likely an exception—many of his contemporaries not gifted with the resources of his courage, tenacity, social connections, sense of humor, and luck no doubt have succumbed to the bleak terrors of prison, asylum, closet, ghetto, and repression. Homophobia is not a gratuitous quirk of bourgeois society but an integral link in a chain of sexism and economic exploitation. The ultimate victory cannot be won outside of society or despite it, as Crisp's was, but *through* it, by changing it, and this is a lesson *The Naked Civil Servant* stops short of articulating, for all its merits.

But this analysis will never be found on establishment television. We will only see it on the screen when we ourselves control our own distribution and exhibition systems, as well as the camera triggers that gay activists are using more and more in the eighth year of the Stonewall era. In any case, now that we have our happy endings, this next step has been pointed to all the more clearly.

Jump Cut, no. 16 (1977): 14–18

Notes

1   "Position Paper of the 'Revolutionary Union' on Homosexuality and Gay Liberation," reprinted in *Toward a Scientific Analysis of the Gay Question* (Los Angeles Research Group), Cudahy, Calif. Also included in this piece of hate literature are the insights that "because homosexuality is rooted in individualism it is a feature of petty bourgeois ideology which puts forth the idea that there are individual solutions to social problems" and that gay liberation "can lead us only down the road of demoralization and defeat."

2   Jim Steakley, "Gays Under Socialism: Male Homosexuality in the German Democratic Republic," in *The Body Politic* (Toronto), no. 29, December 1976–January 1977.

3   Peter Biskind, "Tightass and Cocksucker," *Jump Cut*, no. 4 (Nov.–Dec. 1974). Biskind is a personal friend of mine, and I can vouch that he has come a long way since 1974, has agreed to serve as whipping boy in this article, and has been invaluable in keeping me in touch with my latent heterophobia over the years.

4   Arthur Nolletti Jr., "Male Companionship Movies and the Great American Cool," *Jump Cut*, no. 12/13 (Dec. 1976).

5 For a more complete sense of this macabre tradition, see "Those Were the Gays," *Gay News* (London), no. 101 (August–September 1976), an unsigned compilation of over 250 gay roles in the commercial cinema since 1960, with a capsule summary of each one, that reads like a list of the fallen at a veterans' memorial service.

6 Lee Atwell, *"A Very Natural Thing," Gay Sunshine, a Journal of Gay Liberation* (San Francisco), no. 23 (Nov.–Dec. 1974).

7 ". . . And by came an Angel who had a bright key,
And he open'd the coffins and set them all free;
Then down a green plain leaping, laughing, they run,
And wash in a river, and shine in the Sun.
Then naked and white, all their bags left behind,
They rise upon clouds and sport in the wind. . . ."
(Blake, *The Songs of Innocence*, "The Chimney Sweeper")

8 Bill Barbanes, television reviewer for *The Body Politic*, summarized his response to the new gay presence on TV in this way (no. 28 [November 1976]): "If a trend toward honest depiction of gay people isn't in the near future, we get back to the question of gay exposure on television. Do we want it? I think so. It boils down to this: the price we pay for a little elbow room on the tube is a lot of limp wristed jokes. At this point, the jokes can't hurt that much and, by sheer mathematical odds, a show will occasionally happen that portrays homosexuality sympathetically and, who knows, as a healthy alternative."

9 In my original article I used the film's working title, *Who Are We?*

10 *The Body Politic* (no. 27 [October 1976]) wondered whether *The Naked Civil Servant* was not open to "Serious misinterpretation" in its review by Robert Trow: "There are enough stereotypical notions of the gay experience in this film that would allow it to be viewed in much the same manner as *Boys in the Band*. For example, the film dwells just enough on Crisp's loneliness and inability to find a stable relationship that these two clichés can and will be trotted out once again as part of the 'sad truth' of gay life. Similarly, Crisp's exhibitionism and flamboyant appearance will be seen as the perverse defiance of an unstable mind, rather than a gay man's courageous assertion of his right to lead his own lifestyle. Like *Boys in the Band*, this picture invites a response of compassion and pity from the liberal consciousness, while it tacitly reasserts the superiority of heterosexual life."

Gays, Straights, Film, and the Left:

A Dialogue (with Chuck Kleinhans)

*   *   *   *   *

This interview seems primitive now in its list of the references that I seemed to be getting steamed up about in the late seventies, from Bertolucci to Barbra, an era of increasingly visible, increasingly banal homophobia in Hollywood film culture. Now perhaps I would stress more the visibility than the homophobia, but that's another story. The bibliography I appended to the interview was a mixed bag, some of the pioneering gay historians who were already making their mark—James Steakley, John Lauritsen, and Jonathan Katz, my old buddy from a New York study and zap group called Gay Socialist Action Project—plus an assortment of pamphlets from various American and British leftist groups with names like "The Lavender and Red Union." Those were the days. Reprinting this dialogue twenty years later is above all an homage to Chuck, whose friendship I value more and more with each decade.

*   *   *

The following dialogue condenses several letters exchanged between us during the evolution of this Special Section on "Gays and Film" and supplements it with excerpts from a taped discussion we had in Montreal in July. We thought it important to bring out some points the articles and reviews only briefly touched on in the special section.

TOM: As you can see, and as I think I forewarned you, your suggested article on *A Very Natural Thing* has expanded considerably. I felt it would be unpolitical to trash one gay film without semipraising, or at least encouraging, two others at the same time. I also felt the four page introduction was an important part of the article even though it isn't about the film, for reasons you will see when you read it. If you like the film part and not the intro, we will have to talk about it. I'm particularly anxious to know if you think it sounds

Julia Lesage, the author, and prohibition, Montreal 1976; Chuck Kleinhans, the author, and dessert, Cardiff, 1996.

querulous, self-righteous, belligerent, etc. . . . The last issue looked great; the *Lifeguard* cover was a real turn-on. Real *Advocate* butch. I'm sure your sales skyrocketed.

CHUCK: I'm sending your article around the editorial board, and we should have a discussion in a month or so. It was terribly flattering to have your article come in with the introduction you wrote: obviously you trust us, and that kind of comradely engagement is all too rare sometimes and something to treasure when it happens. I don't think the tone was wrong, though I can't speak for others on the ed board. I think the intro sets the article and also is exactly the kind of ongoing process that *Jump Cut* or any other decent political work has to be. We learn; we change.

In the area of general observations about the intro: I think that you single out Peter, whereas I am at least as culpable. I thought about the particular headline of his article for a bit of time and changed my mind several times about printing it or not, and finally decided that the irony of the stereotypes was heavy enough to anyone who read the article to make it clear Peter was critical of the stereotypes. That's not a justification (I agree with your criticisms) but an explanation. But, of course, the reader never knows what went on in the editor's head. In short, we would have, having made the mistake, been absolutely ready to print any (or any number of) outraged replies . . . that is, our consciousness was high (though not high enough to avoid the mistaken headline to start with). There is a certain vicious circle effect here.

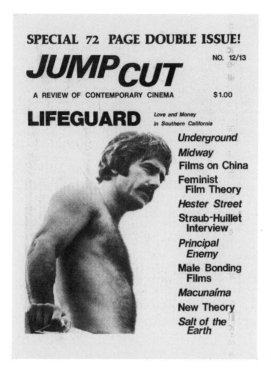

Marx plus beefcake: *Jump Cut's* hot *Lifeguard* cover, no. 12/13 (1976).

Even if you keep using little formulas like we do in a lot of our editorials and our advertising such as, *"Jump Cut* recognizes the struggles of workers, women, Third World people, gays and lesbians," that still doesn't connect up with reality—people don't always realize that we're desperately trying to get material. But, why should a gay write for *JC*, which hasn't published anything by or on gays, etc.? So, the articles don't come in, so you don't print them, etc. I think we're breaking through now (though our track record on racism is a lot worse than on sexism . . . failure to consider it a priority, inertia, etc.).

I would make one criticism of your intro (though I don't mean by this that you should change it) which is that I think pointing out that gay men are not by definition women haters, you avoid the problem that some are and that it is no more tolerable or justifiable than when found in straight men. Perhaps it's more noticeable (being less "natural" than routine sexism against women) by often being a ghettoized cultural expression of defensive responses to oppression. I have a hard time dealing with that when it pops up among men I know. Ageism is a similar thing in some parts of the gay culture that I'm critical of.

I talked with John Hess on the phone and since we also have an article on the image of gays in film noir by Richard Dyer in England, we thought of printing the two articles together, perhaps with the review you sent on the Fassbinder film from *Gay Left*. What do you think of that? We could even make a special section. Do you have any other leads on articles? . . . Of course the real solution is to get all these gay left film people who haven't been writing to start sending us manuscripts. I'm thinking of keeping the section to gay men. I don't like the idea of sticking in a lesbian writer just for the token value, and because lesbian criticism is very close to feminist criticism, it makes sense to separate gay male and female views, as individuals and organizations in fact have.

TOM: A possible section on gays and film is a great idea and I'll do anything I can to help out. Here are some possible articles and reprints. . . .

I certainly agree that ageism and misogyny are no more tolerable in gay culture than in the dominant culture, and it's interesting that you find it more "noticeable" in gay culture for the reasons you mention. However, I still don't feel obligated to do a heavy mea culpa number about it for a straight public. I think these problematic elements in gay culture are simply echoes of the same thing, institutionalized and omnipresent, in the dominant culture, and unpoliticized gays can't be held accountable for them any more than can blacks or other minorities. We have no choice since we live within a certain society but to use the cultural and political environment of that society as the raw material for our cultural expression. Until you can show me that *Blueboy* is demonstrably more sexist than *Playboy*, I've got other things on my mind. In any case, thank you for your candor, your sensitivity, and your return.

CHUCK: I'm enthusiastic about the Special Section because it's important for *JC* to get involved in developing gay criticism and fighting sexism within the left. As you point out in your article, some parts of the left have a totally reactionary attitude and dismiss or attack gays as "decadent." We have to struggle against that and fight for gay liberation as part of a total left perspective and program. Today you can't call yourself a leftist and not take into account the struggle against sexism by women's, lesbian, and gay liberation—just as you must deal with racism. Right now in the left, at least in the States, there's a lot of liberalism about gay issues. People will just pay lip service and say, "Yes, that's important," but not go any further. Hopefully the Special Section is a starting point for straight people to see what a gay film criticism is and see how they can incorporate it into their own criticism and teaching.

TOM: It's only in the last ten years that the left has reevaluated its attitude towards women. Similarly, until now the left's attitude towards gays has reproduced the attitudes of the dominant institutions in the most retrogressive ways. For that reason, most gay leftists have more or less disassociated themselves from the left movement and worked only in the gay movement, often abandoning the left after years of scrapping and humiliation. Leftists at best often see the gay struggle as a civil rights struggle and nothing more, and fail to see the connection between the oppression of gays and that of women and minorities and the working class.

CHUCK: It's often very hard for any of us to understand the systematic nature of our oppression . . . that it is understandable only as a system and not just as what happens to us as individuals. Both gay and straight men have to understand sexism, as a system of oppression, as part of patriarchal capitalist society, not just in terms of how it affects them psychologically or materially but also how it affects women. I'm critical of the film *Men's Lives* (Josh Hanig and Will Roberts, 1975) for not making that connection. While it's very good at showing the surface level oppression of men, it never connects that to the oppression of sexism within our whole capitalist culture. It fails to see that all men benefit from the oppression of women, whether they want it or not. We need to move to a much more comprehensive analysis and political action. Straight men have to be active in fighting in the interests of gay men; and both gay and straight men have to understand and fight against the oppression of straight women. And all of us have a stake in replacing capitalism with socialism. Whatever our immediate priorities, we have to realize we're fighting a whole system of exploitation.

In examining my own attitudes, I realize that in the past few years I've tended to think of gays in terms of those who are able to live a relatively open gay lifestyle in several hip professional areas in Chicago. Because those men are "visible," I've tended to think of gay issues more in terms of lifestyle and also to assume that indeed there has been a gradual improvement in the situation—that gays are accepted, or at least tolerated. I remember saying that about a year ago to John Hess and he strongly disagreed. At the time he was teaching a course called "Men's lives," learning a lot himself, and was more sensitive to gay oppression than I was. Now with the Anita Bryant campaign against gays, I've had to see that was a pretty superficial attitude. I was really wrong. The depth of the problem is more apparent, and from what I've seen in Chicago, I think gays and straights who had counted on gradual reform are rethinking their politics.

TOM: There was a lot of illusory "progress" in the early seventies. What really happened was not so much a liberalization of social attitudes, but an accelerated ghettoization of the gay community in large urban areas where there was a kind of anonymity and defense in numbers. These were ghettos with a definite economic and cultural vitality which led to a false sense of well-being, a kind of complacency on the part of middle-class, unpoliticized gays. People failed to see that the gay community extended far beyond those ghettos and that the liberation of the ghetto was every bit as tenuous as the security in the closet. You're right that Bryant has really shown us how premature the euphoria of "ghetto-liberation" really was.

Movies made in the atmosphere of so-called liberation might have shown us the same thing; that the new hip tolerance was really a form of homophobia. I get the feeling that Hollywood and European filmmakers who openly and frankly portray gays really think they're being liberated. It's as if the new frankness about rape in a film like *Lipstick* actually made that film a progressive one. Or as if the brazen effrontery it took to make all of the villains in *The Deep* black indicated a progressive attitude towards race. It's incredible: popular films like *Scarecrow, Slapshot, Funny Lady, Cross of Iron, The Man Who Fell to Earth, Barry Lyndon*, etc., instead of being liberal in their use of gay characters, actually perpetuate the most vicious of stereotypes.

Look at *Slapshot*. The movie comes across as hip, realistic, and liberal because of all the "freak" homophobic language in the script and the introduction of a "sensitive" lesbian character (actually an insidious stereotype—all she needed was to be satisfied in bed by Paul Newman). But the antigay language of the hockey players, which the scriptwriter probably thought would be taken ironically, as a sign of macho sexual fear or whatever, actually caters to homophobia. Audiences lap it up. They think it's cute and original to be able to queer-bait openly and without guilt. When Paul Newman tells a widowed businesswoman that she better toughen up her preteenaged son or else she'll find him with a cock in his mouth, one of the oldest stereotypes in the book is confirmed, legitimized because it's said by hip, liberal Newman.

CHUCK: I think there's a similar danger within the left, within *Jump Cut*, that we'd run this Special Section on gays and then congratulate ourselves and in effect ghettoize gays by either stopping at that point or saying, "Well, now we have some people who will write about gay films and we'll run them from time to time," rather than really dealing with issues of sexism and gay struggles in all of our criticism. It would reproduce the way men have sometimes dealt with the women's movement, saying, "Well, we'll have a women's page," or letting women write feminist criticism and acting as if that absolves men from dealing with their own sexism or with sexism in the films they make, write about, or teach.

TOM: You're right that that's a dangerous kind of tokenism, but film culture hasn't even gotten to the stage of tokenism yet. There are all kinds of areas which should be impossible to discuss without dealing with the gay question. But it's never dealt with; it's politely ignored.

I'm not talking only of films like *Dog Day Afternoon*, where the subject is obvious. But those areas where a gay reference is obviously suppressed or visible just below the surface. Male buddy films, for example, and most male action genres. I'm not saying such films have consciously touched on any truths about homosexual components of male-to-male relationships, but the fear of such truths is usually clearly articulated; those films show the repression of such truths, whatever they may be.

Another area where the gay question is a crucial one but is always suppressed is that whole stream of European cinema which expresses a kind of "decadent" or androgynous sensibility, regardless of whether it deals explicitly with gayness. I'm thinking of the Italians of course—Fellini, Bertolucci, Visconti, Zeffirelli, Pasolini, but also of Fassbinder, Daniel Schmid, Losey, Ken Russell, Jansco, and Roeg, etc., etc. Questions of gayness are never raised in criticism of those films, leftist or otherwise. The fact, for example, that *The Conformist* is positing some vague and ambiguous connection between fascism and homosexuality is never interrogated in any criticism of Bertolucci that I've seen.

The erotic cinema and pornography are another area where the gay perspective is suppressed. I thought it was shocking when *Cinéaste* magazine ran their survey on "Pornography and the Left,"[1] and they invited comments from five or six "authorities" and it never occurred to them to ask an openly gay person for his or her opinion. Particularly since the gay pornography industry is such a huge one and pornography has had such a formative influence on gay culture, a progressive influence even, according to many people.

CHUCK: Progressive in what sense?

TOM: Before the days of an openly visible gay movement, the only way for many gay people to discover and explore their own homosexuality was through pornography. That's how they recognized certain things about themselves, that they were not alone. . . . It was so typical of leftist cultural attitudes for *Cinéaste* to have this glaring omission in their "comprehensive" treatment of the issue of pornography. I think the feminist attitude to pornography is often quite different from the gay male one. That's something lesbians and gay men are usually aware of but avoid bringing up in the interest of unity.

With a few important exceptions, I think that gay men are almost always opposed to any form of censorship, because they remember what it was like in the closet, and they know that censorship will always be applied to their own legitimate cultural expression as soon as it's permitted anywhere. That's what's happening in New York right now: no sooner does the *New York Times* make its hypocritical, puritanical decision to refuse advertising for porno films than they take it upon themselves as well to decide what gay cultural manifestations are decent enough to be advertised in a family newspaper, refusing to run an ad for a gay theatrical piece called *Gulp* with no pornographic content whatsoever because somebody didn't like the title. It's the same with the Canadian government's decision to block the import of a gay sex manual while admitting a real flood of the comparable hetero manual, *The Joy of Sex*, or the U.S. prison system's refusal to allow gay prisoners to receive gay publications. The issue of censorship is far from closed.

CHUCK: Another aspect of the liberalism that I talked of before can manifest itself in straight men accepting gay men or gay film criticism but without learning what gay men have to say to them as men. I think straights can often be passive and smug about it. But they should become more active in learning about gay liberation. What do you think straight men should do, what should they read, to find out more, to become more active in coming to terms with their own sexism and fighting it?

TOM: Rather than telling straight men what they should or should not do, I think I'd rather say how important it is for gays within the left to come out and form a very visible and vocal presence within both the straight left and the unpoliticized gay movement. It's up to straight men to choose their own methods of self-criticism and activism.

Jump Cut, no. 16 (1977): 27–28. Reprinted in Peter Steven, ed., *Jump Cut: Hollywood, Politics, and Counter Cinema* (Toronto: Between the Lines, 1985), 281–285

Note

1 "The Left and Porno," Round table with Todd Gitlin, James Monaco, Susan Sherman, Lee Baxandall, Ernest Callenbach, and Julia Lesage, *Cinéaste* 7.4 (1977): 28–31, 53.

Rainer Werner Fassbinder

*   *   *   *   *

My first piece for the radical but populist Canadian gay mag The Body Politic *was quite a different story from writing for an American scholarly leftist journal: in short lots of pictures, write for the clone on the street, keep paragraphs short, and assume nothing—well almost nothing. Moralism about the Burden of Representation and my personal conflicts about promiscuity aside, I'm still proud of this early confrontation with someone I was right to call the seminal European filmmaker of the decade and a gay artist I consider on the same level as Wilde, Genet, and Pasolini and who was then just on the brink of the heady last phase of his career. The piece reflects the passion of my first year of teaching in which I'd had the unabashedly auteurist luxury of exposing a captive audience to my favorite directors, like the then trendy Douglas Sirk, but especially to the filmmakers I was beginning to take seriously as queer artists: not only Fassbinder but also Dorothy Arzner, F. W. Murnau, Andy Warhol, and Sergei Eisenstein. So what if this essay sounds like my course in film directors and ideology, diluted with a heady mix of role model therapy—I was inspired!*

So were the others in that first generation of post-Stonewall gay film critics, the best of whom happened mostly to be British, like Robin Wood, my friend Richard Dyer, and the late Andrew Britton and Jack Babuscio. And my engagement with them in the Fassbinder enigma makes me nostalgic for the days when we media watchdogs believed the world was on our shoulders.

And Fassbinder's romantic Ali is still one of my favorite films of all time.

*   *   *

The most important filmmaker in Europe right now, and possibly in the whole Western world, is a German, a radical, and gay (not necessarily in that order, or in any order at all): Rainer Werner Fassbinder.

Many gay activists apparently do not agree, judging from the lively debate that has appeared in the gay press about Fassbinder's 1975 "gay" film, *Fox and His Friends.* The debate has ranged in quality from intelligent analysis of the film's political and cultural context to emotional tirades of an astonishing ferocity.

I would like to explain why I think Fassbinder is so important.

Basically, it's a function of his potential rather than what he's actually accomplished, of his value as a model. Film scholars are learning more and more these days about how the movies have always supported the structures of domination with every image and sound. As a result, a whole new generation of radical filmmakers is searching for a revolutionary film language that will challenge and counteract this traditional complicity. Unfortunately, most of these filmmakers have revolutionized themselves right out of an audience.

Fassbinder is one of the very few of these radicals who have kept themselves in contact with a wide popular audience. And in fact, in recent years he has expanded that contact.

If Fassbinder cannot come up with a model of a radical cinema that is truly popular (or a popular cinema that is truly radical), then perhaps no one can. In any case, I think that a radical popular cinema is what the director of *Fox and His Friends* seems to be on the verge of finding.

The Lumpen and the Piss Elegant

By now, many readers of the gay press are familiar with the simple, almost one-dimensional parable that is the basis of the film. It is the story of a rather unattractive young carnival worker, Fox, whom we see in the first minutes of the film watching his lover get hauled off to jail, tricking with an elegant antique dealer with a Mercedes, and winning $200,000 in a lottery. The trick introduces him to a circle of pretentious middle-class gays, wherein he finds a lover, Eugen, and the love and attention he craves. But of course they love him for his money and butch proletarian image, not for himself. Fox doesn't care. He submits to exploitation and ultimate destruction at their hands with a combination of childish innocence and cynical masochism.

As far as losers go, Fox is not a particularly appealing one, and his victimizers are excessively vicious. All the same, Fassbinder orchestrates a pathos that is profound and direct. In fact, it is so direct that viewers expecting the so-called subtleties of bourgeois dramaturgy (as in *Sunday, Bloody Sunday*)

Fassbinder's *Fox and His Friends* (1975): refusal to be typecast. Museum of Modern Art Film Stills Library.

find it strangely repelling. The pathos is not a little enriched by the presence of Fassbinder himself in the role of Fox. His presence adds a personal dimension to this portrait of an archetypal victim and strengthens its passionate statement of despair.

Any film touching on the subject of homosexuality is bound to be controversial—we've been denied the right of self-expression and the right to see ourselves on the screen for so long that we expect every gay film that comes along to make up for it all. Which, of course, is impossible. No film can meet such expectations.

And Fassbinder's refusal to be a spokesperson for the gay movement is undeniably frustrating. It's disappointing that the first post-Stonewall gay artist of major international stature should refuse to be *our* artist as emphatically as his pre-Stonewall predecessors: Forster, Genet, Williams, Pasolini, Visconti, and the rest.

But Fassbinder's refusal to be typecast as The Gay Filmmaker is adamant. Only five or six of the twenty-five odd films he has made (an impressive achievement for a filmmaker whose thirtieth birthday was this year) touch on gay themes or include gay characters. And although most exhibit a discernible homoerotic or gay cultural sensibility, only two are set in a gay milieu.

This refusal must of course be respected. We must accept Fassbinder's lack of interest in those compact ideological statements we often demand of our artists but rarely get, just as we must accept, for example, the rights of gays who choose to work within a political framework outside of the gay movement proper.

Certainly one of the tenets of gay liberation must be the importance, indeed the urgency, of speaking out on all contemporary issues, not simply those that affect us directly. I would like to show Fassbinder is in agreement with this way of looking at gay liberation and has spoken out powerfully and passionately on the major issues confronting our society.

Fassbinder is not the first gay filmmaker who has seen the role of the individual in modern society in terms of victimization and humiliation—both Pasolini and Lindsay Anderson have seen things the same way—but Fassbinder's images of victims who have internalized the oppression of the outside world are especially sharp. The interminable final sequence of *Fox* provides perhaps the bleakest of those images—the body of the suicide lying like a piece of carrion in the gleamingly sterile setting of a Munich subway station, plundered by kids and hurriedly bypassed by two of his friends. Yes, it's one more gay suicide, but I think Fassbinder does it differently.

Fassbinder's most persuasive detractor from within the gay movement (Andrew Britton in the British journal, *Gay Left*, no. 3) has accused him of using the gay milieu in *Fox* as a metaphorical setting for his theme of exploitation within personal relationships and of using gay relationships as an image of oppression in general, thus confirming negative gay stereotypes and seriously insulting us to boot. Although Fassbinder is admittedly answerable for the effect of any one of his films, Britton's accusation must surely be qualified in the light of Fassbinder's many other films that deal with similar themes in other settings.

Fassbinder is certainly entitled to recreate in his work the gay world as he knows it—that curious border zone within the gay community where the lumpen runs into the piss elegant (a zone best explored by the Warhol/Morrissey duo a few years ago). I don't go along with those who would prohibit artists from washing the gay community's dirty linen in public. There's already enough censorship in the air. . . .

But to return to Fassbinder, no doubt some of the misunderstanding of his work is due to the vagaries of the distribution system. Fassbinder's North American distributors have seriously distorted our sense of this prolific artist by concentrating on those two of his films that are set within a highly stylized gay milieu, *Fox* and *The Bitter Tears of Petra Von Kant*, simply because their appeal to the gay community makes them highly saleable. *Fox* (not to mention *Petra*, which is particularly liable to be misinterpreted) should not be anyone's first Fassbinder.

In fact, films as distinctive and innovative as Fassbinder's need to be sampled and nibbled at slowly while a relationship between artist and spectator is built up gradually. Fassbinder doesn't fit in very well to a movie culture based on instant gratification. To be sure, Fassbinder is answerable for that too, but that's another issue.

Another frequent charge against *Fox* is that it doesn't reflect the reality of the oppressive, homophobic society in which the gay ghetto is situated. It is true that the only explicit sense of this context comes from a scene in which we are told that Fox and his lover have been kicked out of their apartment. And even here it is implied that there would be no problem if Fox were as respectable as his more finely feathered friends. But that implication is for me precisely the point that is being made.

Our society has certainly reached the stage where the privileged circles to which Fox is aspiring do not confront oppression in a palatable, recognizable form but in the more subtle ways that are brilliantly outlined in the film. For example, in the impeccable "liberal" tolerance of Eugen's parents (they try very conspicuously to behave like model in-laws and are offended only by Fox's table manners, not his gayness). Or in the exaggerated cultural pretensions and conspicuous consumption of the upper-class gay ghetto, an actuality we would be dishonest to deny. Here Fassbinder's observations are vivid and acute.

Andrew Britton angrily states that "there is no sense *whatever* that gayness and bourgeois ideology are in any way incompatible" because there is so little evidence of societal oppression of the gay community depicted in the film. Again I would say, that's precisely the point. Britton has no doubt discovered something I don't know about the incompatibility of gayness and bourgeois ideology, or perhaps he just doesn't read *The Advocate*. As far as I can see, the two seem to be getting along quite nicely, and Fassbinder is making this perception quite clear.

For gay liberationists to pretend that class loyalties within the gay community are not stronger than the mystical bounds of gay brotherhood is simply fatuous and irresponsible. (Goodstein and *The Advocate* have demonstrated this dramatically.) It is clear that the gay activist community must extend its solidarity to all oppressed groups within society; and surely Fassbinder's films, with their perspective of a whole range of society's outcasts, victims, and exploited classes, are an inspiring affirmation of this principle.

In any case, I find Fassbinder's criticism of the bourgeois gay milieu, his analysis of the dynamics of that milieu, to be extremely useful. As I've said, one of his targets is the ostentatious consumerism of Fox's new friends. The camera explores a range of settings, each one more crammed with the commodities and artifacts of bourgeois existence than the next. One particularly dense reviewer in *Fag Rag* wondered how on earth anyone could like the atrociously tasteless collection of antiques that Fox's lover gathers for their new apartment. Once more, that's exactly the point. Fassbinder overdoes it beautifully.

When the scene moves to the baths, the same observation is extended from furniture, clothes, and cars to the body and the genitals themselves. Fox meets his antique dealer friend in the mud bath (do they really do it in the mud in Munich?), against a backdrop of strolling naked young lovelies and carefully posed crotch shots—anonymous and almost disembodied. For me, the scene effects a stunning visualization of the ultimate degradation of the body, that objectification and consumerization of the body inherent in *The Advocate* lifestyle. The baths become one more environment packed with commodities, but here the commodities are youth, beauty, and genitals.

One more example, the scene where Fox gets himself picked up by the antique dealer at some roadside T-room, with blinking headlights and all (do they really use blinking headlights in Munich?), suggests another way we oppress one another. The almost ritualistic choreography of the cruise and the final moment of consent offers a deft analysis of the shifting role of power in such a transaction.

However, I would argue that Fassbinder's look at this particular gay milieu is not only a case of airing dirty linen. I think he has another goal in mind as well, and it's hard to tell how successful it is in its immediate cultural context of Fassbinder's straight German public. Regarding the use of the gay setting, Fassbinder says with his customary ambiguity:

> I think it's incidental that the story happens among gays. It could have worked just as well in another milieu. But I rather think that people look back at it more carefully precisely because of its setting, because if it had been a "normal love affair," then the melodramatic aspect would have loomed much larger. I think that a moment comes when people stop noticing that they're watching gays, but then they're going to ask themselves: "What have we just been watching? We've seen a story that took place among people whom we consider unnatural." And through such bewilderment, through a moment of positive shock, the whole story also looks different.

Elsewhere he explains further: "The idea that the film takes place among homosexuals is because the political aspects come out much clearer this way. When the social and political mechanisms are strong and working on an outsider group, then they work automatically on the so-called normal world."

In my opinion, the notion that a general audience will recognize those "social and political mechanisms" through a "moment of positive shock" is at least as plausible as the assumption that people will swallow the happy, wholesome, positive stereotypes we're supposed to want in the media. Certainly this is true of the relatively sophisticated urban audience that Fassbinder is likely to reach in the North American situation.

Anyway it's a notion that must be tested. If Fassbinder fails, the potential damage of a few extra negative stereotypes in a cultural environment already swamped with homophobia is inconsequential and well worth the experiment.

Roots: "Weepies" and "Film Noir"

"I am more convinced than ever that love is the best, most insidious, most effective instrument of social repression."

Fassbinder wrote this statement of a theme explored in *Fox* (and most of his other films) after seeing a 1957 Hollywood "weepie" called *Interlude. Interlude* is a story of a passing romance between June Allyson and a European orchestra conductor, played by Rossano Brazzi, from which Allyson emerges, as they say, sadder but wiser. *Interlude* was directed by Douglas Sirk, Universal Studios' master craftsman of "women's melodramas" or weepies during the fifties. Sirk is also a director who, as one of the more curious by-products of cultural imperialism, has had more influence on Fassbinder than anyone else.

The presence of this cultural cross-fertilization in *Fox and His Friends* may not at first seem terribly important. If you think you've seen that brutally direct manipulation of pathos before, it's because you *have*—on the late late show, where Sirk's kind of women's melodrama is regular fare.

It's generally agreed now that Sirk was better than anyone else at rehashing those same old dramatic formulas that caused Joan Crawford and Bette Davis so much suffering over the years. It's also agreed now that Sirk used the melodrama formula to give Eisenhower America some of the most probing interrogations it ever got. A sense of *Fox*'s roots in this tradition of the Hollywood weepie adds immeasurably to the effect of the film.

Most postwar European directors, Fassbinder included, have had their cultural contours shaped by Hollywood—the American domination of the European movie market made sure of that (especially in West Germany, where, with the help of U.S. occupation forces, the Hollywood monopolies were able to effectively stifle the birth of the West German cinema for an entire generation). After all, who could ever deal with Truffaut, Godard, or Chabrol without references to the Hollywood thrillers, gangster pictures, and, yes, weepies that the Nouvelle Vague grew up on?

In any case, Fassbinder's theme of the oppressive potential of love was first taught to him by good old Universal Studios. The rest of his Hollywood inheritance is just as important. For example, those scenes of unbearable pathos in which people's illusions evaporate before their eyes are a part of that inheritance. The scene in *Imitation of Life* (1959) in which Lana Turner listens incredulously while Sandra Dee tells her what a lousy mother she's been is resuscitated innumerable times by Fassbinder. For example, when his aging heroine in *Ali: Fear Eats the Soul* tells her grown-up children that she's going to marry Ali, a young Moroccan laborer, she gets to watch her

Douglas Sirk's *All That Heaven Allows* (1955): love, the most insidious instrument of oppression. Museum of Modern Art Film Stills Library.

son kick in her television screen and her daughter flounce out of "this pig-pen." Jane Wyman's monstrous children treat her exactly the same in Sirk's *All That Heaven Allows* when she makes a similar announcement about her gardener, Rock Hudson.

Hollywood also gave Fassbinder the archetype of the working-class hero(ine) who sleeps his or her way to the top because that's the only way to get there. There is also his baroque way of looking at things through railings and grills, or through foreground frames of bouquets and lamps and mirrors, and of using vertical elements of the set, bedposts or room dividers, to literally divide two quarreling figures from each other on the screen. It's right out of Sirk, naturally.

What it all means is that looking at *Fox* or *Ali* or *Petra* without reference to Sirk, and Hollywood in general, is a little like reading Eliot's *The Wasteland* without paying attention to the echoes of Dante, Wagner, and Shakespeare, or listening to Bach's *B Minor Mass* without picking up on the old German hymn tunes being reworked, or listening to Bob Dylan without reference to Woody Guthrie. It's possible, of course, but you're missing a lot.

Now, I'm not exactly a T. S. Eliot aficionado, and I would be the last person to endorse an artist who is content to address only that audience who knows Dante or Wagner—or Sirk for that matter—and I would be the first to assert the importance of the uninitiated response of the casual consumer in any art form. It is simply a question of recognizing that Fassbinder is building on a cultural heritage we all more or less have in common (thanks of course to the American monopoly on film distribution in Canada, etc.). And he's building a radical film practice on that heritage, reworking the old conventions to exploit their potential as analytical tools.

We've all been brought up, for example, on those marvelous old films in which Joan Crawford or whoever had to sleep, slave, or marry her way to the top (or murder in the film noir variations of the genre). If we're thinking of Sirk, substitute Barbara Stanwyck, Lana Turner, or Dorothy Malone. Her progress up the ladder would usually be reflected along the way by the gradual refinement of the material trappings of her existence, by a proliferation of the most gaudy and expressive outfits, furniture, and cars that Hollywood designers could come up with. But finally she would discover that love and happiness are seldom at the top, only a different kind of loneliness (suffering, poverty) than at the bottom. And if such movies implicitly, timidly, and obliquely analyzed American class structure and bourgeois values from within the bastion of capitalism itself, Fassbinder uses the same conventions to do the same, only far more directly. He refuses the gloss, the music, and the chronic last-minute happy ending with which Hollywood would hurriedly cover over the gaping void it had exposed.

So, instead of returning Fox to his previous lover and his contented proletarian existence, as Hollywood might have done, Fassbinder forces him to the logical conclusion of suicide; and where Hollywood might have discreetly and compassionately draped the corpse, cut to an epilogue, or even rescued him at the last minute, Fassbinder forces you to watch his body in that desolate setting, long past the excruciating point where you have had enough. And if such insistence makes you angry, fidgety, and alienated, it is because Fassbinder refuses you the relief that bourgeois dramaturgy usually offers in cathartic endings. At that point you are likely to think about what you've seen, about the way we let our social conditioning dominate our expectations in a relationship or the way we use our love to dominate or possess or exploit. At least Fassbinder is hoping that's how you'll react.

A number of feminists are discovering that the conventions of the women's melodrama are particularly useful in this direction. After all, most of the weepies ended up with the heroine making a sacrifice of some kind, of her love, her job, her children, her husband, etc. And so by using such conventions self-consciously, Fassbinder and these other filmmakers have found, the traditional oppressive stereotypes of women's roles can be exposed. In the *Merchant of Four Seasons*, when Fassbinder exaggerates and stylizes beyond all verisimilitude the suffering housewife stereotype (who puts up with being beaten and weeps perfect glycerine tears halfway down her right cheek), this, I'll wager, is what he is up to.

Problematics and Progress

I said that Fassbinder's perspective has included a whole range of social problematics. There is only enough space to sketch the contours of this accomplishment.

Often his work deals with specific social issues. At least three of his films, for example, deal with the situation of the *Gastarbeiter*—the "guest laborers" or temporary immigrants who provide most of the unskilled labor for the German economy. In many cases they fill jobs that Germans are unwilling to do. In *Katzelmacher* (1969) Fassbinder himself plays a Greek gastarbeiter, and as in his later masterpiece, *Ali*, a romance between the immigrant and a German woman serves to set off the many contradictions in the story's social environment.

The latter film contains a scene that articulates with stunning precision the way in which gastarbeiter are manipulated so as to divide the working class as a whole and keep wages down. The scene unfolds during the lunchbreak of a group of cleaning women, among them the aging heroine who has married Ali. The women are gathered together on a steep staircase for their sandwiches, together with a new coworker, Yolande, just arrived from Yugoslavia. The German women move away from Yolande to huddle on a landing just out of earshot to discuss their wages (higher than Yolande's of course) and the possibility of getting a raise—a raise that would not benefit Yolande, since "she's not in the same category anyway." Meanwhile the ostracized woman stares down at them in pain and confusion, her face framed by the prison-like bars of the railing (an old Sirkian trick, as I've

Fassbinder's *Gastarbeiter* melodrama, *Ali: Fear Eats the Soul* (1974): defeatist or didactic? Museum of Modern Art Film Stills Library.

said). This vivid, economical scene is as successful a piece of didactic drama as anything I've seen in Brecht. The whole relationship of racism to economics is revealed with matchless clarity.

Fassbinder touches on other such concrete situations—the cynical opportunism of the traditional leftist parties, the corruption of the police, the role of the unions in working-class life. . . . The list is virtually as long as his filmography.

However, his attention is most compellingly drawn to the general contradictions of our society: the oppression exerted by the institution of the family, alienation in work, the internalization of domination in alcoholism, fantasy, violence, masochism. . . . These contradictions are confronted with the unabashed directness that has become Fassbinder's trademark.

The landscape of contemporary Germany is continually evoked as an image of these contradictions, as cause and reflection of the psychological and material conditions of Fassbinder's characters. *Wildwechsel*, for example, an austerely told teenage love story made in 1972 (the title means "wildlife crossing"), is set in a drab provincial town whose major industry seems to be a poultry processing plant. Long lines of suspended, naked chickens form a backdrop to the tedious, mechanical work. Forceful Godardian tracking shots up and down the assembly line of chicken processors seem to posit a connection between the squalor of factory life and the inevitable violence that will destroy the hero's romantic dreams. It has to be this obvious on the screen because the dreams sometimes blur the connections in real life.

If we compare Fassbinder's work to that of the other current wunderkind of the international film festivals, Werner Herzog (*The Enigma of Kaspar Hauser* and *Aguirre, the Wrath of God*), the contrast is startling. Herzog's films are largely concerned with posing labored philosophical questions in heavily mythologized, historical, or exotic settings. Herzog himself expresses no interest in the domestic German audience and in fact is quite unashamed to admit that he is making films for hypothetical audiences, who alone will be able to appreciate his art. In the context of such, let us say, unseriousness, Fassbinder's stature as an artist of commanding relevance is indisputable.

I would not want my admiration for Fassbinder to pass as totally unqualified and uncritical. There are already enough Fassbinder freaks drooling over his Art in the cinemas of the Western world—thanks to the West German government, which actively pushes its new young filmmakers in the interests of German culture prestige.

I am simply suggesting that Fassbinder is saying a lot of things worth listening to. His films ought to continue to find an audience in the gay community, despite the widespread criticism he has met in the gay activist press.

Having said this, I would be dishonest not to articulate one or two questions I have about this remarkable filmmaker. For me his major liability is his susceptibility to misinterpretation by his foreign and nonspecialist audiences. There is an undeniable temptation to read his highly stylized, exaggerated use of melodramatic conventions as camp or parody, a sensibility that Fassbinder emphatically disavows. I occasionally find myself asking how a certain particularly outrageous gesture or detail of design is meant to be digested, if not with those distinctive squeals with which those of us who have a weakness for Divine, say, sometimes greet her presence in our more vulnerable moments. A very deliberate line is to be drawn between Fassbinder's sensibility and that of Divine's impresario, John Waters, or the presumptuous, execrable mockery of Fassbinder's Swiss contemporary Daniel Schmid, who confuses things by using some of Fassbinder's actors. Occasionally Fassbinder makes that line difficult to draw, and it is only the context of his whole career that makes it definitely possible.

Fassbinder can also be guilty of a vision so arcane that it cannot be penetrated. There are occasions when he revels in an ambiguity that is baffling rather than stimulating. In my opinion Fassbinder has hovered at times dangerously close to a kind of intellectualized formalism that has too often been the refuge of gay artists within the artistic avant-garde. (Curiously, the debate within *Gay Left* over *Fox* alludes at one point to four American gays, apparently disapprovingly, who have contributed to the American Underground cinema—Kenneth Anger, Constance Beeson, Jack Smith, and Gregory Markopoulos—all examples, as far as I'm concerned, of this lamentable elitist tendency among gays involved in High Art.)

Fassbinder himself speaks of his early films, many of which are rather baroque reworkings of American gangster-film formulas, as being "too elitist, and too private, just made for myself and a few friends. . . . You must respect your audience more than I did." In this respect it is certainly a credit to Fassbinder that, as his career develops, the moments of self-indulgence, the "onanistic" tendencies (as he puts it), become less and less important in his work, and more and more he communicates with his audience by means of his distinctive, socially engaged form of realism.

One final question stems from the almost overwhelming tone of despair, of defeatism, if you like, that dominates the majority of Fassbinder's films. As far as I can remember, there is only one happy ending in the ten or so Fassbinders that I've managed to see, and that one is qualified by a predictable toughness and ambivalence. I'm referring to the conclusion of *Ali*, the most romantic Fassbinder that I ever expect to see. The pressures of family and society have split up the heroine and her young Moroccan husband, but Fassbinder provides us with a self-indulgently sentimental moment of reconciliation, in the literally rose light of the dance floor where they first met. But Fassbinder cuts this short: Ali collapses from a mysterious internal injury that comes, a kindly doctor explains quite plausibly, from the stress of being an immigrant worker. So after these rapid turnabouts, the final scene finds the pair facing an uncertain future in Ali's hospital room, a future that only our Hollywood upbringing and the tenderness on the dance floor lead us to believe is possible.

Elsewhere, Fassbinder does not let us forget that the vicious circles and traps of our society and our lives offer no escape, and this insistence would seem inconsistent with his personal convictions. For example, he made these observations when an interviewer asked him about anarchists, the target of rather blunt satire in one of his most recent films: "I'm very interested in finding out how one can use the strength these people [anarchists] have. Now it's very important to me to make very positive films, and they are very clever people. They have great intellectual potential, but also an over-sensitive despair which I don't know how one could use constructively."

What is curious is that one is often tempted to describe Fassbinder's work itself in terms of "over-sensitive despair."

The issue is further complicated in that Fassbinder's series of five television films on working-class life (it was to be eight, but the government network got nervous) expressed an optimism, a faith in collective strength, that his films have seldom even hinted at. Again an interview shed some light on the question: the TV series *Eight Hours Don't Make a Day* departed in such a radical new direction for Fassbinder because

> all the plays and films I've written for were designed for an intellectual audience, and with the intellectuals one can easily allow oneself to be pessimistic and end without hope, because an intellectual is both prepared and inclined to reflect over it. But for the large audience which television offers, it would have been reactionary, nearly criminal, in fact, to represent the world as futile. Their world looks pretty futile to them in the first place, so one's just got to try and encourage them and say: "You've got possibilities anyway. You've got power to bear because your oppressors are dependent upon you." What is an employer without employees? Nothing. On the other hand, one can well imagine workers without employers. This attitude was the principal reason that for the first time I made something positive, hopeful. With an audience of 25 million ordinary people, you can't allow yourself anything else.

The appearance of three new Fassbinders every year, without any signs of abating, each one breaking new ground in some direction or other, is, however, undeniably something positive. And maybe one of them will turn out to be *our* film after all.

The Body Politic, no. 29 (December 1976–January 1977), "Our Image" supplement, 8–10

A Fag-Spotter's Guide to Eisenstein

*   *   *   *   *

More from the queer teacher popularizing film culture for the ghetto masses. The "movie still" essay format of this piece holds up twenty years later I think: I still agree with Brecht and Benjamin that captions are essential, the longer the better.

A nasty controversy ensued when a letter appeared in the next issue of TBP (Oct. 1977) accusing me of precisely the self-hating fag-spotting practice that I was trying ironically to appropriate. For reader Bruce Russell my "cultish jour-nalism" was an attempt to prove Eisenstein gay on the basis of my brief sentences on his women characters and an uncritical revival of the dubious pre-Kinsey "lists of famous gays" apologetics. I was quite the self-righteous queen in replying to this distortion of my work, with a hurt two-column retort, defending a text-based authorial analysis and effectively demolishing all criticism, of course. Fruit Machine readers can decide for themselves twenty years later, but that's water under the Nevski Bridge anyway: Bruce lives in Montreal, we're close friends, and I stand by every syllable. The controversy never went fully away, however, and two years later leading French Eisenstein expert Jacques Aumont would arrogantly and homophobically dismiss the queer biographical readings, with typical blindness to the history of underground homosexual cultures and networks in Europe.[1] With Aumont the Mexican cocksucking cartoons are not evidence, nor are seven more or less extant films, and denial is only a river in Egypt. And who gives a shit about heterosexual Parisian intellectuals paid to ar-gue with each other about Oedipus anyway?

My citations from pioneer queer critic Parker Tyler,[2] still alive in 1977, re-mind me today that even then there was a tradition we were building on, among other things a tradition of oral culture based on people who'd actually met Eisenstein. At the same time I'm proud that I was among the first of the baby boomers to reinterpret Eisenstein's legacy for the post-Stonewall audience,[3] per-haps paving the way modestly for later scholarly work by Harry Benshoff and Bill Nichols and artistic work by Derek Jarman and others.[4]

*   *   *

In *Introduction to Film History 200* they tell you Sergei Mikhailovich Eisenstein was the leading figure of the heroic first decades of Soviet cinema and one of the most influential filmmakers ever. They never tell you he was a homosexual.

He had to do a pretty good job of keeping in the closet during his life—whenever he entered a period of disfavor with the bureaucrats, the whispering always started. Straight art historians, who will tell you they think that an artist's sexuality has nothing to do with his or her art, have done an even better job of keeping him in the closet after his death.

An artist who was always very cerebral and impersonal in his approach to his films, Eisenstein is a particularly tantalizing subject for modern-day gay cultural historians, or fag-spotters (as a former roommate used to call me).

You really have to root around his films to find Eisenstein the homosexual. But he's undeniably there. The value of finding him is not simply in adding another feather in our cap but in adding to our knowledge of the history and the nature of our oppression, our sexuality, and our culture.

The stills I've assembled here are among the most useful from the few that are available, but as any survivor of *Intro 200* can attest, a still can do no more than suggest the definition and power of the moving image.

Our Old Friend St. Sebastian

You never have any doubt that there is a lot of erotic energy in Eisenstein's fascination with images of suffering, victimization, and martyrdom. It's not surprising that gay artists living within a homophobic society should often express themselves with such images, whether it's the gay Renaissance painters who continually overdid it with St. Sebastian at the stake or Mart Crowley reveling in the misery of his Greenwich Village faggots in *Boys in the Band*. With Eisenstein the martyrdom of his revolutionary heroes is always a pretext for an exaggerated, aestheticized indulgence in the ritual agony of the fallen.

During Eisenstein's stay in Mexico (1930–1932), the image of the martyr became a central preoccupation for the director, fired by the blinding sunlight, the death-obsessed Mexican Catholicism, and the poverty he saw all

Eisenstein: portrait on the queen's, er, czar's throne during the filming of *October* (ca. 1926). Museum of Modern Art Film Stills Library.

around him. At one point a fantasy of a martyr under the lash sparked a notebook meditation on the purely aesthetic properties of the image—but the jargon needn't fool anybody; it vibrates with sexual intensity:

> For me the delineation seems to stem from the image of the ropes con-
> straining the bodies of the martyrs, from the lashes of the whip on the

Eisenstein's *Que Viva Mexico!* (ca. 1930): erotic martyrdom. Museum of Modern Art Film Stills Library.

body's white expanse, from the swish of the sword before it makes contact with the condemned neck. Thus the naked line shatters the illusion of space, thus the line makes its way through color, thus the law of harmony splits open the varied chaos of form . . . the whips swish no more. The searing pain has given way to a state of warm numbness. The marks of the blows have lacerated the surface of the body, the wounds have opened up like so many poppies and the ruby blood has begun to flow.

The image reappears as a motif in the footage for the film that was never to be finished. Another variation of it was the ritual of the *corrida*, the bullfight: a whole cycle of his sketches intercut the image of the martyred bull with the image of our old friend St. Sebastian. But for the socialist, as for the Christian, the martyrdom of the hero is only a temporary setback, in fact, an advance in terms of the long struggle: Vakulinchuk's death in *The Battleship Potemkin* sets off a beautiful elegiac sequence of gliding ships and hushed processions of mourners, with a final outburst of revolutionary anger among the mourners, which culminates in victory.

Mexican Sojourn

Eisenstein was a timid but jovial intellectual who could never be a public homosexual in Soviet society the way his contemporaries, like Jean Cocteau or Gertrude Stein, could be, protected as they were by the polite tolerance of the artistic avant-garde. Even his biographers will deal with his gayness only in whispers and innuendos. One of them has reportedly suggested (off the record, of course) that it was Eisenstein's embarrassing sexual predisposition as much as his political intransigence that led to his periodic bouts of disfavor with the Stalinist bureaucrats. Even as a world-famous artist he didn't fare any better during his brief foray into the West at the end of the twenties.

After a few aborted projects in Hollywood, he attempted a Mexican film, backed by liberal American money and support. This was eventually withdrawn before the film was finished but not before the Mexican light, the Latin/Indian male beauty, and Eisenstein's perception of the Mexican struggle had inspired some of the most breathtaking unedited footage in existence.

It's also said that he brought back with him a trunkload of erotic footage, apparently shot in Mexican whorehouses, that so offended his sponsors that they let the American authorities destroy it. They were also very upset by his bundles of sketches, which one sponsor called "plain smut." One of them was apparently "a parody of Christian paintings showing Jesus and the two thieves hanging on crosses; the penis of Jesus is elongated into a hose, and one of the thieves has the end in his mouth."[5] All that is apparently left of the crucifix conceit and the delightful connotations it has (the identification of religious mysticism with sexual feeling?) is Eisenstein's filmed recreation of a Mexican Passion ritual included among the unedited material. Something the customs officials never did get their hands on is a wonderful snapshot of Eisenstein and a phallic cactus he mounted one day while strolling through the Mexican desert. . . .

Hero Worship

Parker Tyler states, in his treatment of Eisenstein in *Screening the Sexes*, that "hero worship is a natural part of the homosexual aesthetic myth" (316).

Eisenstein's *Que Viva Mexico!*: production still pertaining to footage of Mexican fishermen, apparently destroyed by American authorities or not used in latter-day reconstructions. Museum of Modern Art Film Stills Library.

Whether this can be accepted as a general principle or not, it's certainly clear that it was part of Eisenstein's own personal homosexual myth. All of his male characters are erotically idealized heroes of great immediacy and appeal—particularly the working-class figures that both history and personal conviction dictated as protagonists in his films.

Tyler describes Eisenstein as "having a great eye for human beauty, and more especially for male beauty" (317). One can only concur, looking at the knights from *Alexander Nevsky* (1938) or the sailors in *Battleship Potemkin* (1925). But it is more than a simple question of an eye for male beauty. The Marxist worldview that motivated his films provided a natural channel of expression for this sexual aesthetic. The physical beauty of the male proletarian hero arose from a unique confluence of erotic sensibility and political belief.

Her in Hymn

Only one of Eisenstein's seven films shows any interest in or talent for female characterization. This aspect of his work sets him clearly apart from
his straight contemporaries Pudovkin, Vertov, and Dovzhenko, all famous
for their stirring and complex portraits of women caught up in the process
of revolutionary change. Eisenstein's women are usually the barest of shadows, stereotypes, and walk-ons in a predominantly male universe. In *Ivan
the Terrible* the two significant women are crudely one-dimensional carica-
tures, a blond madonna and a repulsive ogre. The exception to all of this is
Marfa Lapkina, the real-life peasant whom Eisenstein starred in his 1929
hymn to collectivization and rural progress, *The General Line (Old and
New)*.

Marfa is presented as an impishly androgynous and childlike woman,
vividly detailed in flesh-and-blood terms. Posed grinning behind the wheel
of the collective farm's new tractor, she has none of the softer feminine
touches that the straight Soviet filmmakers give to even their women
machine-gunners.

Drag Finale

Ivan the Terrible (1944–1948) was Eisenstein's great last film, a three-part
epic interrupted by his death. It is rightly regarded by Tyler as the richest resource for the fag-spotter. There may be more of Eisenstein's gay/hero worship in his stylized portrait of the powerful tyrant Ivan, usually seen as a Stalin prototype. But there are a lot of other things going on too. The pretty,
blond, effeminate Vladimir, a cretin set up by Ivan's rivals as pretender to
the throne, clearly comes across as a negative stereotype (dressed up in a
czar's trappings so that a waiting assassin will kill him instead of Ivan). As
Tyler says, Vladimir is as pretty as a Hollywood starlet and is portrayed by
Eisenstein as a witless mama's boy, constantly pursing his lips and batting
his eyelashes.

Gay artists have often been able to express an explicit interest in homosexuality only within the safe limits of the dominant stereotype of gayness
as evil and decadent—look at Visconti, with his gayness-as-fascism trip in

The General Line (1929): Eisenstein's peasant androgyne Marfa. Museum of Modern Art Film Stills Library.

The Damned and his gayness-as-plague trip in *Death in Venice*. Stalinist Russia was no exception, and the character of Vladimir constitutes the only direct reference to homosexuality in Eisenstein's entire career.

Ivan's handsome bodyguard, Fyodor, is also of great interest. His is a more traditional kind of butch beauty than Ivan's stern, angular good looks. At the peak of his power Ivan has surrounded himself with a troop of gorgeous young soldiers. (In actuality they were played by an elite group from the Red Army chosen by Eisenstein for the film. Their presence on the set sent nervous ripples through officialdom.) Part II of *Ivan* bursts from black and white into a garish color climax centering on this troop, the Oprichniki, and their leader, Fyodor. Tyler describes it well: "What happens in the lively revel held by Ivan as a rather paganish prelude to midnight mass is that among all the male dancers we see a single ornate female figure wearing a mask and breastplates from which strings of beads pour. She is very much

The pretty, blond, effeminate Vladimir (center) in *Ivan the Terrible* (1944–1948) clearly comes across as a gay stereotype—constantly pursing his lips and batting his eyelashes. Vladimir constitutes the only direct reference to male homosexuality in Eisenstein's entire filmic portfolio. Left is the handsome bodyguard Fyodor and right the Stalin figure Ivan. Museum of Modern Art Film Stills Library.

the center of attention from the male dancers as Ivan looks on with a subtle but fascinated smile. Then there is a climax to this jumping and whirling; all stand transfixed in pose. At this, the peasant girl is seen to remove her mask. The person revealed is the handsome, virile young leader of the Oprichniki" (319). Fyodor, of course. The most beautiful of all removes the mask of femininity, throws off his drag for his czar. We could be forgiven for seeing this fantasy as an appropriate climax to a career in which Eisenstein the homosexual had to hide behind Eisenstein the intellectual, the aesthete, the politician, and the survivor.

The Body Politic, no. 35 (July–August 1977), "Our Image" supplement, 15–17

Notes

1   Jacques Aumont, *Montage Eisenstein*, translated by Lee Hildreth, Constance Penley, and Andrew Ross (London and Bloomington: BFI/Indiana University Press, 1987).

2   Parker Tyler, *Screening the Sexes: Homosexuality in the Movies* (1973; New York: Da Capo Press, 1993).

3   Andrew Britton's series on Eisenstein for *Framework* was due to begin in a few months, "Sexuality and Power or the Two Others," *Framework* 6 (autumn 1977): 7–11, 39; and "Sexuality and Power," *Framework* 7/8 (spring 1978): 5–11. Britton would focus mostly on *October* and *Ivan*, based on seventies phallus'n'castration *Screen*speak.

4   Harry Benshoff, "Homoerotic Iconography and Anti-Catholic Marxism: Proto-Feminist Discourse in Sergei M. Eisenstein's *Que Viva Mexico!*" *Spectator, The University of Southern California Journal of Film and Television Criticism* 2.1 (1990): 6–17; Bill Nichols, "Eisenstein's *Strike* and the Genealogy of Documentary," in *Blurred Boundaries: Questions of Meaning in Contemporary Culture* (Bloomington: Indiana University Press, 1994), 107–116, especially 112, 172 (n. 14). Jarman's *Caravaggio* is among his many intertextual treatments of Eisenstein, in this case the homoerotics of mourning from *Battleship Potemkin*. See *Hard to Imagine* (124–125, 132–137) for my nineties update on Eisenstein and the phallic cactus photo.

5   Yon Barna, *Eisenstein: The Growth of a Cinematic Genius* (Boston: Little, Brown, 1973), 182.

Derek Jarman's *Sebastiane*

*　　*　　*　　*　　*

Of all the pieces in The Fruit Machine, *this is perhaps the one I am most ashamed of, the one where I was most wrong, wrong, wrong. Why did I respond so fiercely to* Sebastiane? *Perhaps I was unable to distance my critical response from my own troubled arousal by all those nude Roman soldiers playing frisbee, my own indifference to* s/m, *and my own missionary moralism about liberation politics. I vividly recall that night in the beautiful Outremont cinema (not yet ravaged by mallism) but can hardly believe it was that much of a novelty to be in a crowd of 700 gay men those days in Montreal. We take a lot for granted in the nineties. The first San Francisco gay and lesbian film festival had begun the previous year, and embryonic queer film events were stirring here as well. The decade of cinematic famine was coming to an end, and the delirious energy of the eighties, of which Jarman was the* central *figure, was prophetically evident in that film I didn't get. . . . I'm sorry, Derek.*

*　　*　　*

The premiere of *Sebastiane*, a new British gay film, was preceded by an active word-of-mouth campaign and a highly effective promotional photo showing a young man having his buns whipped by a Roman centurion.

The theater was packed the night I attended. I had never seen so many gay men together in one place in Montreal before. The crowd that night was high simply from the exhilaration, I would judge, of being together for the first time with all the lights on.

Ninety minutes later the same crowd shuffled out into the night transformed. This time there was a collective feeling of humiliation, of being insulted and exploited.

It's hard to believe that a director could be so utterly wrong, so entirely misguided in his estimation of his audience.

Sebastiane was apparently conceived as an erotic fantasy on the legend of St. Sebastian, the young Christian soldier traditionally depicted as a human

Sebastiane (1976): I'm sorry, Derek. Museum of Modern Art Film Stills Library.

dartboard gazing heavenward in the ecstasy of his martyrdom. For some reason this image has had a special meaning for male homosexuals as far back as the Italian Renaissance, but Derek Jarman, the writer-director of the film, has failed to come anywhere near what that meaning may be for contemporary gays. The film comes across as a second-rate skin flick all dressed up in a costume that doesn't fit.

In fact, the only thing that distinguishes *Sebastiane* from the realm of soft core is the honesty of the latter. The film is so clumsy and unpersuasive in its pretensions to seriousness that it would probably work as camp were it not so tedious.

Having removed the religious content of the myth, the director has failed to find anything else of substance to inject into this empty pageant of pretty men in loincloths and armor running around a pretty Mediterranean landscape. The film critic for *Gay Left* has credited Jarman, a former set director for Ken Russell, with the intention of making a statement about sexual repression and violence, but this assessment of a tawdry jumble of s/M formulas seems rather generous to me.

The film, as everyone knows by now, is done entirely in Latin. This has been interpreted in many ways—as an attempt to mask the inanity of the script, as a gesture toward historical authenticity, as an appeal toward the liturgical inclinations of the presumed audience, and as a clever gimmick. It is successful only as the last of these. Likewise, the use of a cloyingly pompous stylization in the mise-en-scène does little to divert attention from the film's visual and dramatic vacuum.

Sebastiane seems to have put one over on some observers however: one British critic I used to respect sees a "pattern of voyeurism central to the film's main thrust" and interprets the film's interminable slow-motion love scene in the surf (by two men who apparently don't have genitals) as a "pastiche" of this staple of the straight porno genre. I know it is important to encourage gay artists, but this willful confusion of alleged intention and verifiable effect does more harm than good.

It's not the first time that Canadian distributors have picked up a low-quality foreign gay film to exploit on the growing local market. This may be the first time that they have used the trappings of "art" and respectability to stir up their trade. They seem to think that gay men swallow any film as long as there's enough skin in it. Maybe this time, for once, they could be proven wrong.

The Body Politic, no. 41 (March 1978): 19

Medical Thrills: *Born a Man . . . Let Me Die a Woman*

* * * * *

Talk about marginal—am I the only person in the world to have seen this film? As moralistic as this piece sounds today, at least I hit on a film that turned out to be prophetic of a certain wave of anatomical-identity documentary of the nineties. I remember I was so taken by the marquee and posters that I persuaded a photographer I had a crush on to come down with me and take a picture to illustrate the review (both pic and photographer are now lost). I'm still fascinated that sex-med documentary was kicking around the soft-core porn circuit in the late seventies, decades after its prime. But I'm no longer the only one, for exploitation film has become a hot research topic.

* * *

Montrealers had a chance this fall to see heterosexist ideology take its baldest and most brutal form in a sexploitation documentary about transsexuals called *Born a Man . . . Let Me Die a Woman* (A Hygiene Film!). The film, apparently American in origin, packed them in for seven weeks at a soft-core house in the most respectable stretch of St. Catherine Street, just across from Simpsons.

The whole sordid thing is narrated by a Dr. Leo Wollman, who reminds us several times of his M.D. and Ph.D. while showing in explicit detail how medicine can correct Nature's "monstrous biological joke" of "imprisoning" a woman in a man's body (or vice-versa). In addition to gory close-up examination of surgical nip-and-tuck and of newly fashioned genitals, both male and female, the good doctor also treats us to dramatized episodes depicting the suicide or self-castration of transsexuals who can't deal with it. We meet the predictable, a half-completed woman who engages in prostitution to save up for the rest of her operation (followed, of course, by a shower in order to show her shriveled-up penis).

Dr. Wollman also provides us with the opportunity to meet some of his victims, occasionally poking their silicone-taut breasts to show off his craftsmanship. A few tell their own stories. One, a young Puerto Rican woman in nail polish and negligee, apparently quite a success for the doctor, tells an engaging story of growing up in biological "prison" within a large, poor family and a macho culture. But an offhand remark that if she had any children she wouldn't want them to be gay suddenly explodes a mass of contradictions that the film is trying to avoid.

I always thought the pseudoscientific sexploitation flick had gone out with the fifties, that *Sex Kittens at College* had edged *Damaged Lives* (an early and extremely profitable treatment of venereal disease) off the market. Not so. *Born a Man* points toward a whole new horizon for this venerable film genre.

The narrator claims at one point that once upon a time "anatomy was destiny," but now, thanks to the advance of modern medicine, etc., etc. In fact, what he and his despicable freak show demonstrate is a whole new way of enforcing the tyranny of anatomy, a tyranny now made respectable by the aura of science. The issues raised by sex-change surgery are still not entirely clear. But in the meantime, someone is making a lot of money off people who have listened to its promises.

The Body Politic, no. 49 (December 1978–January 1979): 41–42

Murnau: The Films Behind the Man

*   *   *   *   *

This next piece continued my pedagogical mission with The Body Politic*: I clearly loved and no doubt envied (from the vantage point of hedonistic Montreal) the platform given to me by these Toronto gay-lib zealots who were about to embark on the last beleaguered decade of a major episode in Canadian alternative publishing and resistance to state-imposed censorship.*

This may be the least inspired of the queer ancestor series I published in TBP. *The reason is, I confess, that I actually don't respond personally to Murnau's films. Intellectually I respect their artistry, and personally I find it hard to resist empathizing with the filmmaker as an isolated homo, but they just don't do it for me (though I can't deny my guilty pleasure in the exquisitely sensuous orientalist beefcake of* Tabu, *which has now been rediscovered, thanks to its circulation on video, by a new generation who will never see* Sunrise*).*

Again I owed a debt in this piece to a tradition of queer hermeneutics, which I saw myself adapting to a nonspecialized public, namely to fellow Canadian Robin Wood, whose brave "Responsibilities of a Gay Film Critic" had just come out,[1] and the pioneer European archivist, Lotte Eisner. To the latter I would now be much more generous than I was as a thirty-year-old "positive image" upstart in 1978: today I'm amazed by how on-target and ahead of us all that grand old lady was all along.

*   *   *

Friedrich Wilhelm Murnau (1888–1931) is one of the perennial superstars of film history and one of the most influential directors of the silent cinema.

Murnau made more than twenty films, first in Berlin and later in Hollywood, before his sudden death at the age of forty-two in a California highway accident. Many of these films are now lost.

Murnau is chiefly remembered for only six of them: *Nosferatu* (1921), *The Last Laugh* (1924), *Faust* (1926), *Sunrise* (1927), *City Girl* (1929), *Tabu*

(1931). To a general film public, some of the titles may be well known, although most of the films themselves are rarely seen. They are probably inaccessible to all but hard-nosed movie buffs because of their layers of melodramatic silent film conventions.

Beyond the legendary reputation of the films, Murnau himself is also remembered for being a homosexual. The details of his life, often sensationalized, qualify him perfectly for two intersecting romantic stereotypes—the Myth of the Great Artist and its subsidiary Myth of the Tormented Homosexual Artist. His flight from Hollywood in search of Beauty in the South Seas, his early violent death, the sensitive, suffering exile—these generalized romantic images have all worked to prevent us from understanding either the man or his art.

Reading about Murnau, one is swamped by that clumsy vocabulary by which academic art criticism exalts what it prefers not to understand: *genius, greatness, classic, visionary.* There are also those perennial ten-best-films-of-all-time lists on which at least one Murnau film is always obligatory (*Sunrise* having edged out *The Last Laugh* in the last generation but now receiving competition from *City Girl*). And one can always expect the trolley ride sequence in *Sunrise* to be described as "one of the most lyrical passages in the world cinema."

The other part of the Murnau myth is built on a slightly different vocabulary: *tortured restlessness, perfect taste, tenderness, shyness, slender fingers, European sensitivity brutalized by Hollywood compromise.* Lotte Eisner, the acknowledged authority on Murnau's life, elaborates: "His shy nature, burdened with a weighty heritage of typical German sentimentality and morbid timidity, led him to admire in others the muscular strength and vitality he himself lacked. There was something godlike about him personally—tall, slim and straight, with his clear cut features, keen eyes and beautiful golden hair."[2]

Even when the matter is approached head-on, and some of this obscuring verbiage is swept away, it is still seen as a question of "homosexual sensitivity" or "homosexual sensuality."

Eisner, fortunately, is one of those few who attempt to deal directly and sympathetically with Murnau's gayness. "Murnau had homosexual tendencies," she writes.

In his attempt to escape from himself, he did not express himself with an artistic continuity which [is easy to analyze]. But all his films bear the impress of his inner complexity, of the struggle he waged within himself against a world in which he remained despairingly alien. Only in his last film, *Tabu*, did he seem to have found peace and a little happiness in surroundings which abolish the guilt-feelings inherent in European morality. . . . Murnau, born in 1888, lived under the ominous shadow which the inhuman Paragraph 175 of the pre-1918 German Penal Code, lending itself to the horrors of blackmail, cast over him and those like him.[3]

When it comes to a coherent study of Murnau's gayness, however, Eisner is somewhat at a loss. For example, she quite rightly alludes to the most unabashed eroticism in any of the films, Murnau's exquisite celebration of undraped male bodies in *Tabu*: "Murnau offers us an apotheosis of the flesh: the feats and canoe races are only pretexts for showing those godlike bodies. He was intoxicated by them. A sail unfurls like a sheet of shining silk, and suddenly the dark bodies of natives are seen among the rigging like ripe clusters on a grape-vine."[4] But elsewhere, she focuses on examples that are trivial or isolated—a "sleek and effete" male character in one film, an "androgynous" one in another, unconventional female characters in yet another, vague connections made with "certain vagaries of sensibility" and with "the subtlety of his art."[5] Clearly, a reliable analysis does not emerge through these details.

Eisner's sentimental absorption in Murnau's alienation, in his longing for Beauty, Exile, and Death, ultimately implies that those qualities are aspects of some universal homosexual sensibility rather than functions of a specific personality dominated by a specific historical context.

Other critics have commented on Murnau's artistic flight from political struggle. It is not lack of interest but an active suppression of—and a long uneven grappling with—politics that shapes Murnau's work. By *politics* I do not here mean the usual collective, societal scope of the word. We may find echoes of the upheavals of the twenties in the works of Murnau's gay contemporaries, writer André Gide or filmmaker S. M. Eisenstein, but it would be pointless to search for such echoes in Murnau's work. In fact, Murnau's preference for the devices of allegory and abstraction, for studio artifice, constitutes as total a rejection of this kind of politics as do the esoteric literary visions of Jean Cocteau or Gertrude Stein. The political struggle I am speaking of is situated on the personal level, which is often prior to and necessary for the grander level of collective politics. Murnau's work should be seen as the terrain of a long, uphill struggle with his own socially condemned sexuality and with his need to express that sexuality in his work.

He could never do so explicitly, of course—the commercial dream factories of Berlin and Hollywood saw to that. A popular filmmaker could never be allowed the latitude by which an André Gide or a Jean Genet was able to express his sexuality on the printed page. But all the same, the marks of Murnau's struggle are indelibly etched in poetic form on celluloid.

There is no need to make a gay role model of a "rediscovered" Murnau. The details of his life do not support what would amount to distortion and myth making of another kind. Tracing the patterns of contradiction and repression that shape Murnau's films, however, helps us to understand more fully the work of one of the most significant figures of film history. Perhaps more important, it enlightens our own history: we become aware of how Murnau's art was shaped by his place in the heterosexist society of the day. "History is not part of art," said Eric Bentley, "but art is part of history."

Robin Wood is the critic who has come closest to exposing vivid patterns of struggle visible in Murnau's films. Wood, an openly gay teacher at York University in Toronto, observes that all of Murnau's major films (with the possible exception of *The Last Laugh*) are built on an identical narrative pattern—a united heterosexual couple whose union is put in jeopardy by a third figure who is sinister, ambiguous, and male (again, there is an exception: the archetypal twenties "vamp" in *Sunrise*). This pattern is resolved tragically in *Nosferatu, Faust*, and *Tabu* by the Christian-like self-sacrifice of the heroine. In *Sunrise* and *City Girl* (significantly, the two Hollywood films among the six), the pattern is resolved with the "happy end" convention of popular melodrama.

Whether tragic or happy-ended, each film is a moving and convincing "affirmation of the potential wholeness and redemptive power of heterosexual marriage." The paradox of a homosexual being forced to devote his or her career to the exaltation of heterosexual love is hardly an unfamiliar one. What is striking, though, is the utter intensity and authenticity of Murnau's affirmation, the heartrending earnestness of his concern "with the couple, with the sense of the marriage relationship as having prime and central significance in human life." It is Murnau's seriousness, overstated and even heavy-handed, that in retrospect gives his work and life such a tragic hue.

Yet there is something askew about his ideal heterosexual couples, and the most erotic elements of the early films paradoxically are not attached to them but to the villains, the sinister third figures that he always introduces to pose a threat to these couples. The vampire of *Nosferatu*, Mephistopheles in *Faust*, the vamp in *Sunrise*—all have a kind of dark and magnetic sensuality about them. In each case Murnau seems to be equating this sexuality with evil, both dramatically and iconographically.

Wood sees the pattern thus far as an unequivocal record of Murnau's self-oppression, a way of negating his own homosexual feelings by equating sexuality with evil. "There remains a sense," Wood says, "that the affirmation of homosexual love is the product of intense personal need, and that it represents, in its whole universalizing/idealizing bent, a wish-fulfillment bought at a great cost. . . . Beautiful as the film's idealized image of marriage is, one cannot escape the feeling that in relegating the City Woman (and Nosferatu before her) to the night and the marshes, Murnau was degrading his own sexual energies, under the overwhelming weight of the dominant sexual ideology."[6]

Things change after *Sunrise*. With *City Girl* and *Tabu*, Murnau's struggle comes closer to being resolved. Instead of degrading his own sexual energies, it seems that Murnau has learned to accept and affirm those energies, although still within the bounds of the heterosexual formulas of popular melodrama. He has learned to understand and decry the forces in society that had led him—and many of his contemporaries—to deny their feelings with repression and shame.

It may seem ironic that a final affirmation should only be possible in exile and that this affirmation should be expressed in as tragic a film as *Tabu*. But the forces of social control must necessarily win out in the end. The doomed lovers are reunited only in the ideal otherworldly realm of the rising sun (an image that concludes several of Murnau's earlier films as well). We should not be very surprised by this resolution of the theme. Murnau, a homosexual artist within heterosexist society, was unable to escape this contradiction even in the midst of the paradise he thought he had found in the South

Seas. But in *Tabu*, at least, he achieves a resilient vision of the beauty of sexual love that for the first time seems to reinforce his sense of self-worth as an artist.

Heterosexual Ideals—Inside Out

In Murnau's films there is an idealization of heterosexual love that must be seen as a "wish-fulfillment bought at great cost." Jean Cocteau has captured in *The White Book* the essence of this tendency: "It was, then, in order to follow the others, that I began to falsify my nature. As they hastened toward their own truth, they dragged me toward falsehood. I pretended to share their enthusiasms while having to overcome my feelings of shame."

But Murnau's celebration of heterosexual love is hardly ever expressed in believable physical terms. Heterosexual love is always seen as a transcendent spiritual force and the ideal couple more a spiritual unit than a fleshly one. Murnau had a reputation among producers for not being a "sexy" director. His lovers habitually relate to each other in stilted theatrical poses. His heroines are "unsensual," dour plaster-cast madonnas as in *Faust* or *Sunrise*. Even the most fully realized of Murnau's heroines, the tough-but-gentle waitress Kate, of *City Girl*, has a brunette "prettiness" that Eisner calls "harsh" and that seems overshadowed by the soft "sweetness" of her farmboy husband, Lem. Other male leads have this same presexual sweetness about them. They are usually blond, fluffy haired, and wide eyed, with movements and expressions that are innocent and childlike, occasionally effeminate.

On closer examination, the stereotyped patterns of heterosexual love are everywhere slightly off center or inside out.

Angst: The "Homosexual Artist" Myth

It's possible to decode a slow struggle toward an affirmation of sexuality in Murnau's films. But is there a parallel with his actual life?

Biographer Lotte Eisner lets slip a few hints through her annoyingly discreet chronology, but these hints stop short of fully supporting a pattern of gradual self-acceptance. Her book contains only unconnected references to

F. W. Murnau: studio portrait, date unknown. Museum of Modern Art Film Stills Library.

Murnau's gayness: an acknowledgment that his brother tried to suppress information about Murnau's sexuality after his death; the same brother's recollection that young Wilhelm had not been interested in girls like the other boys (he "was not attracted by the pretty girls; he was attracted rather by those who were sensitive or a bit odd, especially if they were witty too"[7]); the mention from time to time of well-known gay figures in Berlin and Hollywood with whom Murnau associated; the evidence that Murnau related sexually to young male Asian employees—a "very handsome" Malayan servant in Berlin, the Filipino chauffeur who drove his limousine the day of the fatal crash.

Obviously, a full-scale biography, no holds barred, is necessary before we can begin to understand how the vivid record of struggle in Murnau's films corresponds to patterns in his life. In the meantime, a violent death provides great raw material for myth making.

"Homosexuality, real or supposed, was a favorite topic of Hollywood gossips during the Thirties," observes gossip Kenneth Anger in *Hollywood Babylon*.

> Few around the Fox lot had not heard that director F. W. Murnau favored gays when it came to casting. Murnau's death in 1931 inspired a floodtide of speculation. Murnau had hired as a valet a handsome fourteen-year-old Filipino boy named Garcia Stevenson. The boy was at the wheel of the Packard when the fatal accident occurred. The wicked tongues of Hollywood reported that Murnau was going down on Garcia when the car leaped off the road. Only eleven brave souls (Garbo was there) showed up for the funeral. Garbo commissioned a death mask of Murnau and the solitary Swede kept this memento of the German genius on her desk during all of her years in Hollywood.[8]

Eisner's tone is more elevated: "The ancient Greeks represented death as a handsome young man, with the sombre and enigmatic beauty which the young Filipino who drove Murnau to his death no doubt possessed.... Murnau's natural predispositions were as decisive a factor in the subtlety of his art as in his premature death.... All that remains is his work. That is still young. Eternal."[9]

The Myth of the Homosexual Artist is catered to by many examples of gay artists who have died prematurely, tragically, and (preferably) violently. Arthur Rimbaud, Marcel Proust, Hart Crane, Garcia Lorca, James Dean, Montgomery Clift, Yukio Mishima, Pier Paolo Pasolini—all have had their lives molded to fit this self-fulfilling stereotype by their biographers. Murnau is no exception. The myth inevitably capitalizes on the alienation and self-destructiveness of their lives, on their narcissistic obsession with ideal Beauty and Death (or Violence and Escape).

(clockwise from upper left) Murnau's *Faust* (1926), *Sunrise* (1927), and *City Girl* (1929). Museum of Modern Art Film Stills Library.

It also refers, often by implication, to their inability to procreate except in the "realm of Art" and even, as most recently in the case of Pasolini, to the "he-was-asking-for-it" quality of their deaths. All of these are seen to come from the essence of the homosexual imagination—fueled by the obsessive, irrational nature of the homosexual personality.

Villains: Seducers to Patriarchs

All of Murnau's ideal heterosexual couples are threatened by disruptive forces personified by evil third characters. But these characters are evil in a compellingly sensual way. Take, for example, the irresistible vampire count of *Nosferatu*. In one scene the hero, waiting for Nosferatu, sits up in bed all night quivering in fear (or anticipation?).

In *Faust*, Mephistopheles towers over the passive hero; in a similar setup in *Sunrise*, the vampish city woman overwhelms the peasant hero with her magnetic sexual power. But with the next film, *City Girl*, this pattern starts to change. A familiar, menacing sexual villain—the leering brawny-shouldered farmhand Mac—almost overcomes the resistance of the heroine, Kate, but the more powerfully threatening force in *City Girl* comes from the brutal Bible-thumping patriarch, who is intent on breaking up his son's marriage (see accompanying illustrations). The visual echoes between the vampire Nosferatu and this patriarchal figure are striking, but the sensuality of the former has evaporated. For the first time Murnau's disruptive force represents not forbidden sexuality but social and familial restrictions on sexuality. Repression has replaced desire as the source of evil in Murnau's universe. In *Tabu*, Murnau's last film, the force of evil is also represented by a figure of social control, Hitu, the wizened old priest who succeeds in separating the two lovers. He is, according to Robin Wood, "the externally imposed 'Thou-Shalt-Not' of society."

Tabu: Sensual Affirmation

The new thematic pattern appears fully defined in *Tabu*, Murnau's last film. It is a tragic love story of a pearl diver and a sacred virgin who attempt unsuccessfully to escape the taboo imposed on the virgin by tribal law. In this film sexuality is no longer equated with evil and death but with innocence and life. "Pure love" is no longer separated from eroticism; instead, there is a "perfect harmony between the sensuous and the spiritual."

The world Murnau found in Tahiti touched some essential part of him, and he recorded his reactions on paper as well as on celluloid. While filming *Tabu*, Murnau wrote to his mother:

> There is no work and no worries, where the shining days go by in games and dancing, bathing and fishing, and the night innocently brings all lovers together. When I think I have to leave all this I already suffer all the agony of going. I am bewitched by this place. I have been here a year and I don't want to be anywhere else. The thought of cities and all those people are repulsive to me. I want to be alone, or with a few rare people. When I sit outside my bungalow in the evening and look at the sea, towards Morea, and see the waves break one by one and thunder on the reef, then I feel terribly small, and sometimes I wish I

Murnau's *Tabu* (1931): production still or figure study of extra. Museum of Modern Art Film Stills Library.

were at home. But I am never "at home" anywhere—I feel this more and more the older I get—not in any country nor in any house nor with anybody.[10]

Of a handsome Polynesian candidate for the lead male role in *Tabu*, Murnau wrote:

His smile was like a ray of bright sunshine; you only had to clap your hands for his whole body to sway in a dance of delight. It was a dance for the arms and body more than for the feet. The hips are rolled sideways and forwards, faster and faster, more and more voluptuously, perfectly freely. Mebao had more grace, a finer figure, greater passion than any of the rest. He was an orphan from early childhood and grew up freely and independently, like an animal in the jungle. The marvellous harmony of figure makes him look like a Greek god, a model for the Olympic games, a delight of nature.[11]

The Body Politic, no. 51 (March–April 1979): 31–34

Notes

1 Robin Wood, "Responsibilities of a Gay Film Critic," *Film Comment* 14.1 (January–February 1978): 12–17.
2 Lotte H. Eisner, *Murnau* (Berkeley: University of California Press, 1973), 214.
3 Lotte H. Eisner, *The Haunted Screen* (Berkeley: University of California Press, 1973), 98.
4 Eisner, *Murnau*, 202–203.
5 Ibid., 222.
6 Robin Wood, "F. W. Murnau: On *Sunrise*," *Film Comment* 12.3 (May–June 1976): 18.
7 Eisner, *Murnau*, 16.
8 Kenneth Anger, *Hollywood Babylon* (New York: Dell, 1975), 172.
9 Eisner, *Murnau*, 222–226.
10 Ibid., 213.
11 Ibid., 211–212.

An Unromantic Fiction: *I'm Not from Here*

by Harvey Marks

*   *   *   *

Harvey is still a friend of mine after all these years and still a filmmaker, though he's now gone on to "development" in Hollywood with a gay feature Swallows *released in 1999. I remember a passionate fling, years before he made this film, in the cluttered Lower East Side York building once inhabited by Auden and Trotsky (not together) that he shared with his gentle country songwriter lover Ralph, who would die of* AIDS. *Harvey also introduced me to* Straight to Hell *and the genre of artisanal raunch porno, which got me thinking seriously about eroticism. A breach in ethics to rave a film by a friend? I don't know, we had to stick together back then. . . .*

*   *   *

Though it seems gay people will never be able to let up on their aggressively self-defensive posture against the dominant media, it's nice to know there's an increasing amount of affirmative action happening on the image-making front. I'm referring to the growing number of short, noncommercial films available that are positive, authentic, and useful.

One such film, *I'm Not from Here*, recently had a promising debut at the Museum of Modern Art in New York and is slated for its Montreal premiere in March at *Naches*, the Gay Jewish group. The filmmaker, Harvey Marks, is a New Yorker who has, until now, preferred experimental films. He has miraculously financed them through odd jobs and by cutting corners. Now he's branching out into fictional filmmaking and may just succeed in becoming an artist speaking to and for all of us.

I'm Not From Here is the story of a nineteen-year-old young man stumbling through the same awkwardly beautiful experience of coming out that scarcely any of us escapes. The experience of coming out has rarely been filmed from the inside. The only time I can recall a gay sexual initiation having been filmed without sensationalism, stereotype, or sentimentality is the unforgettable gymnasium scene from Lindsay Anderson's *If.* In it, the pubescent schoolboy looks on in awe as his older friend flexes his body on the high bar.

Ryan, the hero of Marks's forty-five-minute story, is torn by the conflicting signals given off by his body and by his social environment. Obedient to his conditioning, he bravely but vainly tries to repair his foundering relationship with his "girlfriend." Following a quarrel, he borrows Daddy's car and, after exchanging a few glances through his windshield, picks up a hitchhiker. Ryan may have done it before, but this time it turns into a pivotal experience—a blanket, some woods, and a "trick" with enough grace not to cater to Ryan's instinct to get it over with fast, silent, and guilty.

What follows is a slightly melodramatic twist that Marks based on a real-life incident. Though this twist does jar with the low-key, unsentimental approach, it also serves as a device to force Ryan to come to terms with the contradictions of his various feelings and to begin to affirm his identity. The last scene shows Ryan, calmer, buoyed by the memory of his hitchhiker, stalking another encounter.

Joe Bacino, the amateur actor who plays Ryan, will never be an Al Pacino, but his unglamorous ordinariness is a strong point of the film. By avoiding the trap of romanticism, Marks succeeds in getting very close to the interior experience of this young man.

As with all first films, there are minor technical and dramatic problems, but *I'm Not from Here* is an important addition to the cultural resources of the gay community and a stirring document of our reality.

The Body Politic, no. 51 (March–April 1979): 38

The Gay Nineties, the Gay Seventies:

Samperi's *Ernesto* and von Praunheim's

Army of Lovers or Revolt of the Perverts

*   *   *   *   *

Two European films, Ernesto *and* Army of Lovers or Revolt of the Perverts, *both now available on video in specialized queer circuits, caught my eye that year in the local film festival. Thus began my regular series of mainstream festival reports over the next decade. It was a frustrating experience, for the most part, talking about films that would mostly never find commercial distribution and circulating in the cynical and brainless festival environment where potluck was the order of the day. My hyperbolic enthusiasm for* Ernesto, *a minor though admittedly breakthrough film, suggests not only the continuing scarcity of product but also that I had not yet caught the cynicism in the air. Or maybe it means I was going through a thing about butch Italian workers with big mustaches. Samperi went on to obscurity, but von Praunheim was to consolidate his place as one of the key queer filmmakers of the next two decades, a visionary with an uncompromising conscience. Guess which lines they blurbed for the dust jacket of the published* Army of Lovers *script.*

*   *   *

Judging by the recent World Film Festival of Montreal, lesbians and gays are more visible than ever. The presence of a homosexual has by now become a virtual formula in many film genres, but the formula usually isn't very appealing: the gays assembled on the festival screen were given, for the most part, the choice of being repressed, psychopathic, homicidal, suicidal, victimized, or just plain miserable. Often they ended up dead as well.

All the more refreshing then were the three or four films that escaped this formula and presented our lives in an original and revolutionary light. The two films that did so for gay men, *Ernesto* and *Army of Lovers or Revolt of the Perverts*, were by no means flawless, but greatly encouraging nonetheless.

Ernesto is a young high school graduate strutting about his first job as a warehouse clerk in turn-of-the-century Italy, dressed to kill in bowler hat and watch chain. One day his life changes: the most handsome and dreamy-eyed of the laborers in his charge stares intently at him. Ernesto stares back and offers a cigar. The laborer asks, "Do you know what it is like to be the friend of a guy like me?" Ernesto seems to know and plays hard to get for a moment, and then, as the audience gasps, scarcely ten minutes into the film, the two men embark on one of the most stunning series of love scenes in the history of the movies.

No doubt a complete lack of expectations and a feeling of discovery regarding this first film by an unknown Italian director, Salvatore Samperi, have been partly responsible for my unaccustomed hyperbole, as well as the fact that such a subject has never before been broached in a film. Here, finally, is the rare combination of realism and romance that *A Very Natural Thing* and other films of the last decade have aimed for but fallen short of. As a sketch of the dynamics of a cross-generational and interclass relationship and of the rites of gay initiation, *Ernesto* is masterful. It is also, if you look, a profound analysis of the politics of family and social control, and within the relationship, of the politics of role playing, bum fucking, and power. As if that were not enough, Samperi has provided a suggestive speculation on what the gay subculture must have been like in Mediterranean society eighty years ago. With the wealth of sunlit detail that Italian directors can bring to period fictions like no others, we learn, for example, of the crucial role of cocoa butter suppositories! Now that gay historians are beginning to uncover our past, fiction like this will be vital to our mythical reclamation of that past. Finally, and some will find this most important of all, this tender but unsentimental story of an awakening adolescent is more erotic than the entire last decade of hard core.

Unfortunately, when the first hour of a movie is such a watershed in the evolution of our image, it's hard to settle for an ending that's anything less. At the same time as Ernesto learns more about society's sanctions against homosexuality, he begins to tire of his lover's idealism, learns to use his class privilege to manipulate him, and finally, inexplicably, as if out of sheer boredom, humiliates and abandons him. By this point the movie—like Ernesto—has imperceptibly lost its innocence. The early romanticism has soured into the world of cynicism of Ernesto's middle-class social milieu.

A period of bisexual dalliance follows, culminating in an economically advantageous betrothal engineered by Ernesto's family and accepted by him with a shrug in the film's last freeze-frame image. The shrug is not so much tragic as it is complacent.

Ernesto is based on an autobiographical novel by the Italian poet Umberto Saba (1883–1957). I am told also that the novel ends abruptly at the end of Ernesto's gay initiation and that his bisexual phase and betrothal are inventions of the script. This is plausible—exactly at that point this sensitive and earnest tale suddenly switches mood and direction (not to mention sexual orientation) and degenerates into just another modishly cynical comedy of growing up. I even wonder if we're intended to view the homosexual episode as simply a customary digression on the part of a "normal" heterosexual adult.

It is difficult to swallow whole this portrait of one of our forefathers who turns into a nasty and duplicitous young man. But the film is so close to a breakthrough on so many levels that even the staunchest of media watchdogs will want to see it again.

If *Ernesto* had the advantage of complete surprise, Rosa von Praunheim's *Army of Lovers or Revolt of the Perverts* was anticipated by its audience with tense nervousness. The German filmmaker's 1970 film, *It Is Not the Homosexual Who Is Perverse but the Situation in Which He Lives*, a series of agit-prop skits denouncing the commercialism and political lethargy of the gay male ghetto, is as notorious as its title long. Von Praunheim not implausibly argues that the film played a pioneering role in the German gay movement because of discussion it provoked, but not all viewers are convinced. Just last year a Boston reviewer (*Gay Community News*) managed to find a place in his description for all these labels: destructive, hostile, moralizingly aggressive, amateurish, aurally abrasive and disjoined, visually banal, roughly edited, stagy, contemptuous, uncompassionate, negative, offensive, and politically inopportune.

The nervousness was unnecessary. This time the filmmaker had the largely gay festival audience almost entirely on his side. For one thing, von Praunheim has switched to a more conventional and more polished documentary format. *Army of Lovers* is basically a perceptive record of many developments in the American gay movement during the seventies. Not only the parades and celebrations are revisited but also the political tests that have shaped our struggle, from Stonewall itself to the Briggs Initiative and Boston-Boise. Von Praunheim also goes back beyond Stonewall and evokes our prehistory—the medieval persecution of witches, the German gay movement under Magnus Hirschfeld squelched by the Nazis, the growth of the semiunderground gay organizations in the United States in the postwar period. In some of the film's best moments, the original founders of the Mattachine Society and the Daughters of Bilitis provide the camera with their own reminiscences of those years.

This is by no means an "objective" journalistic survey. Although the early radical groups appear in an aura of nostalgia, the old Gay Activists' Alliance Firehouse glowing like a shrine, the narrator minces no words when it comes to the "conservative, elitist" Gay Task Force and deftly satirizes gay religion, civil rights organizing, and the commercialism of ghetto culture.

One merit of von Praunheim's perspective is its breadth. Everyone has a say from Third World gays to Parents of Gays and Over-Forties—well, almost everyone. Von Praunheim's view is unabashedly that of a gay man, phallocentric some will say: there is none of the scrupulous balance between women and men that was the strength of *Word Is Out*. This is indefensible, yet von Praunheim is completely up-front about this shortcoming. I found his self-criticism in this regard sincere and perhaps more provocative than a ritual formulation of the correct line might have been. There is something to be said for his assumption that he cannot be a spokesperson for lesbians. All the same, the lesbian input, where it occurs, is very effective. I am thinking, for example, of the hard-hitting response by an angry, articulate lesbian to Grace Jones's objectifying performance at a Gay Pride Rally and her gay male audience's combined mockery and adulation at the time. Another victim of invisibility is the gay Left. This is curious because von Praunheim shares much of the radical perspective of the ghetto and the need for us to struggle alongside "all oppressed people." This becomes more than annoying when you consider the lengthy attention to some preposterous Hitler clone claiming to represent large numbers of gay Nazis. Von Praunheim clearly cannot resist the attraction of sensation and spectacle, even when this undercuts his commitment to a responsible analysis. The same question arises from the long concluding parts of the film, which serve as a platform for the idiocies of pornographer Fred Halsted and the philosophizing of John Rechy, whose voice is worth hearing to be sure but somewhat less oracular than von Praunheim thinks.

Although I've emphasized the documentary aspect of *Army of Lovers*, a strong theatrical element is still present in the film. Intercut with the actual footage is a series of agitprop skits of varying effectiveness. The skits sometimes fill in with boisterous vitality the unfilled parts of our history (Hirschfeld, for example, and even Stonewall). At other times the skits, delivered head-on with Brechtian directness, enlarge the documentary material with incisive commentary. In the best of these the performers camp about in front of a macho meat rack, primping and prancing as they mimic the tough posturing of the Mandate Men behind them and thereby succeed in exploding the dubious by-products of the gay civil rights movement ("700 leatherbars and the right to serve in the army").

The skits, like the film itself, are fiercely unapologetic. There is still much of the 1970 von Praunheim in this utter refusal of sentimentality, respectability, and romanticism. But now he is more in step with his audience: surely we're beyond the need for films we can show our parents. *Word Is Out* answered this and other needs: it was stirring in its intimacy, its sense of the flowering of individual lives. *Army of Lovers* answers other needs. It's a noisy and rambunctious epic of our collectivity, a perceptive essay on (gay male) sexuality, a brainstorming of questions to take us into the eighties. Unlike *Word Is Out, Army of Lovers* will likely never be televised or even shown commercially, as much because of its repudiation of slickness and respectability, I'm sure, as because of one or two suck scenes. Hopefully, it will be available nonetheless for groups and special screenings. That might be for the best: the way to see this buoyant film-celebration of the Stonewall decade is not alone in front of the tube or in a crowd of strangers but surrounded by other lovers and perverts.

The Body Politic, no. 58 (November 1979): 37–39

Montgomery Clift Biographies: Stars and Sex

*   *   *   *   *

Why was I doing all these reviews when I was supposed to be accumulating schol-
arly publications for my tenure file? Well this Montgomery Clift piece was pen-
ance to the Cinéaste *editors who were so hurt that I'd (justifiably) trashed their*
homophobia in the rival mag Jump Cut. *I'm actually quite proud of this rare en-*
try in the book review genre—a chance to quote that great gay musical West
Side Story! *My colleague Carole, who is an expert on method acting and parsi-*
monious with her strokes, actually complimented me on the piece.

*   *   *

Monty: A Biography of Montgomery Clift, by Robert LaGuardia, and *Mont-*
gomery Clift, by Patricia Bosworth.

Two crucial changes Hollywood movies underwent in the fifties involved
their style of acting and their mythology of male sexuality. In fact, the
change in acting style was a vehicle for a broader change, the revolution in
Hollywood's conception of what it meant to be a man. Three stars were at the
center of both changes, and of these three, Marlon Brando and James Dean
have cult followings that pursued them into the seventies. The third, Montgomery Clift, is the least adulated by posterity, but he actually preceded and
paved the way for the entry of the other two into the American mythos.

Last year two widely read biographies of Clift appeared and now seem to
be reviving a cult that in its day was every bit as idolatrous as those for
Brando and Dean. More important, the two books bring into focus basic
questions about Clift's place in film history and the history of screen performance, as well as his place in the evolution of American sexual ideology.

In the fifties, the stone-faced jock and the unflappable seducer were suddenly replaced by a man capable of wincing in anxiety, weeping, or even
showing affection. This new man testified to the decline of the Cooper-
Wayne-Gable model that had provided the crippling norm for generations of
moviegoers. The new man accomplished in Hollywood what Salinger was

doing in his fiction and Tennessee Williams was doing in the theater—shattering the constricting ideology of the family and ripping off the mask of stoic machismo, "all muscle and no brains," as Holden Caulfield put it.

It was no coincidence that Clift and Brando were both associated with Williams's roles on the stage and screen. It was no coincidence that Clift and Dean were predominantly homosexual (Williams's homosexuality and Brando's occasional flirtations with a bisexual image are well known) or that the screen personas of all three stars had unambiguously gay elements. Never before had Hollywood exploited gay resonances, consciously or unconsciously, as part of a male star's image (Valentino is an arguable exception). They called Clift "sensuous," "sensitive," "vulnerable," "offbeat," "complex," "a loner," and spoke of "the nuances of feeling that the scriptwriter dare not let him speak." The new biographers speak more forthrightly of "sexual ambiguity," "eroticism," "androgyny," even "femininity."

It could not be argued, of course, that Hollywood turned its back on male chauvinism or heterosexism—far from it. What occurred was a broadening of the behavioral and social range within which it was permissible to be a man. Hardly any straight-macho icons made it through that decade. America was spellbound by the spectacle of the three stars grappling onscreen and offscreen with the lot of social alienation and sexual nonconformity, and Hollywood capitalized on this spell to revitalize a product—masculinity—that wasn't selling anymore.

By now a critical consensus has found *Montgomery Clift* by Patricia Bosworth to be superior in every way to Robert LaGuardia's *Monty*, which had nonetheless beat its rival to the presses, the Book-of-the Month Club, and the best-seller lists. Bosworth's book is considerably more thorough and relies on a wider array of sources, including Clift's correspondence, scanty but rich (e.g., "Is it stewing in this pissmire having no idea what the next blab of the telephone will bring"). Bosworth also writes much more cleanly and clearly than the competition, keeping the editorial melodrama to a minimum (though even she succumbs to the "Tortured Life" temptation far too often). Her history is also much less gossipy than LaGuardia's (though who is not secretly glad to know that Jennifer Jones stuffed a mink jacket down the toilet when she discovered her costar preferred men?). To her credit,

when Bosworth throws out a comparable morsel—Clift's ranking on the peter meter, for example—it is always directly relevant to her theme.

On the whole I have great admiration for the evenhandedness and control with which Bosworth follows Clift's trajectory: from his protected childhood to his first prominence on Broadway as a juvenile prodigy and later as
a clean-cut leading man, and, finally, his ascent into the Hollywood firma-
ment in the late forties with the ensuing, unremittent struggle that led up to
his classic booze-and-pills, star-as-victim death in 1966 at the age of forty-
five.

I would, however, like to point to one conspicuous gap in Bosworth's research that is all too significant. Her preface lists all of the Clift associates interviewed—agents, costars, family, friends, lawyers, even barber. Missing,
obviously, are Clift's lovers. The seriousness of this gap becomes apparent
when it turns out that the author located one of the lovers after all, a man she
calls Josh. Josh shows us a Monty who is otherwise totally absent from the
book. Instead of the anguished artist, we see for a moment a tender, sensitive lover squirming under the restrictions of a homophobic society:

> "Our affair was for me the most beautiful experience in my life, I'll
> never forget it. We were still sexually rather pure and innocent. We
> laughed a great deal, and played together. . . . When we were alone it
> was like Monty and I were shut away from reality for a couple of hours.
> It was a disorienting experience. Alone we could be emotional and
> passionate but outside we had to hide our feelings. . . . One of the
> things that was starting to torture Monty back in 1940 was the fact
> that he had to hide his sexual feelings. He despised deception, pre-
> tense, and he felt the intolerable strain of living a lie."

From the remaining four or five men with whom Clift shared his life in
enduring relationships, we hear virtually nothing. Of Clift's sexual life there
is little other than the outside views of straight friends and relatives who are,
at best, politely disapproving and protective and, at worst, openly hostile,
some even providing antigay slurs for Bosworth to quote (without comment). Toward the end of the book Bosworth unavoidably introduces a distant and negative account of Clift's last major relationship, with a French-
man she calls "Giles" (LaGuardia calls him "Jean"—both writers use

pseudonyms for Clift's male lovers but real names for the female lovers he occasionally courted in his attempts to live up to society's expectations; this infuriating practice has the ostensible intent of preventing the men "social embarrassment," according to LaGuardia, but comes across as anachronistically and patronizingly coy). Bosworth conceives of this, and one or two other relationships mentioned in passing, in terms of "keeping," "exploitation," and pathological mutual destructiveness. One wonders what "Giles" 's perspective might be.

"Rick," one of the lovers tracked down and interviewed by LaGuardia, a major figure in Clift's life not mentioned by Bosworth, was a very important find indeed. "Rick" provides a moving view of their relationship during the early fifties that would be unrecognizable within Bosworth's narrative, a fine set of photo-portraits of his lover sunbathing dreamingly, and an anecdote that conveys a vivid sense of the pressures within the closets of Hollywood during those years: he recalls how after the shooting of Clift's second film, *The Search* (1948), Fred Zinneman's story of a GI's friendship with a refugee boy after the war, the star agonizingly arrived at the decision to delete an improvised line in which he had called the boy "dear."

Yet LaGuardia's up-frontness and resourcefulness in the face of Clift's sexual life is canceled out by his tendency toward dime-novel psychologizing of the tackiest sort: "Libby Holman (an older woman friend of Clift) was attracted to young men whose homosexuality was bound up with weak ego structures. Her instincts were those of a domineering mother; for these tortured young men, close association with her was rather like the promise of new life, new sexual security, a return to the womb."

Even Bosworth cannot resist an occasional descent to this level. The biographical data are all so familiar—dominant mother, absent father, older women friends—who could resist serving up the most available, ready-made stereotypes?

Clift's death also fits the stereotypical pattern a little too snugly. Neither biographer comes close to the real significance of his miserable end. Neither recognizes to what extent Clift's tragedy and death were the inevitable consequence, without exaggeration, of the homophobia around him. Deprived of his work during the last years of his life, separated from his lover by family machinations, deserted by friends, Clift was hounded by a pack of homophobes like Frank Sinatra, Clark Gable, and John Huston (to name a few names for once, courtesy of the two books' anecdotes), and by all the cruel contradictions of being brilliant and a fag in the Hollywood of the Eisenhower era.

The radical new performance style by which Clift and his contemporaries expressed the new masculinity has also become a myth, the myth known as the Method. Deriving indirectly from Stanislavsky, this naturalistic acting style gained currency on Broadway in the late 40s and grew to dominate the Hollywood dramatic genres in the 50s. In retrospect it has become the most telling mannerism of the period, a style that looked so realistic then having now become another of the many realisms of film history that have followed one another in succession. It was the perfect idiom not only for the rejection of the machismo of the prewar era but also for a decade of ideological retrenchment, of scoundrel time, as they say, in which individualism was the ruling dogma and psychology was the privileged discipline, both behaviorist and pop-Freudian at the same time. It was the age of Paul Newman's Billy the Kid in *The Left-Handed Gun*, Dean's Jim Stark in *Rebel without a Cause*, and Clift's Matthew Garth in *Red River*, all of whom rebel out of oedipal frustration because of fathers distant, absent, cold, or wearing an apron—depraved on account of being deprived of a normal home, as the Jets say in another 50s artifact, *West Side Story*. Dreiser's *American Tragedy*, a condemnation of a political system, becomes George Stevens's *A Place in the Sun*, an idealized love story built around the interplay of personality types. Clift played the murderer-hero, of course, in a role that was in many ways emblematic of the decade—not as Dreiser's pawn of social forces but as a psychological specimen, in his own words, as a "kind of guy who has some charm, but basically he conceals and dissembles about everything. . . . He's tacky [!] and not that bright, but he's overwhelmingly ambitious" and (in Bosworth's paraphrase of Clift) a "quintessential mama's boy."

Clift's place in this revolution in acting style known as the Method is thus a major one. His pioneering experiments with the behavioral authenticity, the intense intimacy, and the repressed neuroticism of the Method performance at its best have resisted the passing of time in a way unlike Brando's mumblings.

Bosworth makes it clear, however, that as much as Clift was a prototype of the Method actor, he had not swallowed the Method whole. He was less involved with the Actor's Studio than many of his contemporaries and skep-

Montgomery Clift: studio portrait in *Red River* costume (1948).

tical about some of the Method's canons, particularly sense-memory. Clift's more eclectic approach also included the classical training he had assimilated from Alfred Lunt in his Broadway days. It was as cerebral as it was visceral and always involved enormous amounts of research and study. Relying heavily, almost expressionistically, on the precise gesture as a signal of the personality and on his talent for mime, he prepared each movement and line painstakingly, endlessly, usually relying less than his contemporaries on improvisation.

Perhaps the reason Clift was able to exploit the Method so successfully was because of all the emotional and behavioral resources his sexual nonconformity made available to him. Bosworth is quite perceptive in this regard. She calls it "making use of his femininity" in his projection of the fragile sensitivity that was his trademark. She also speaks frankly but all too briefly about the notion of androgyny, remarking on Clift's "cruising sexual swagger" that set off sparks in millions of swooning women. Rather than the narcissism it connotes for her, however, I read Clift's style as one of sexual availability and openness, with nuances of passivity even, so marked in its contrast to the repressed, closed-off indifference of previous male images.

Clift was also an innovator in terms of his economic position in Hollywood. One of the first truly independent stars, he chose scripts on the basis of personal interest and was never bound by studio fiat. Clift was very much a prototype of the modern performer-auteur, both in the classical sense of the star-icon à la Dietrich or Cagney, in which a star's continuous personality dominates a film vehicle regardless of script or director, and also in the new Hollywood sense of a performer making contributions to many phases of a production—conception, production, script, characterization—à la Beatty, Nicholson, or Jane Fonda. *The Search* was just one of the films for which Clift contributed extensively to the script and production as a whole, through a close creative relationship with the director, major involvement in the writing, and improvisation on the set.

Clift must also be seen as central to Hollywood's attempts in the fifties to compete with the threat from the European art cinema. Always classified as an intellectual and associated with prestige products with "artistic" aspirations, Clift was one of the few major stars of the period to work consistently with scripts by writers like Zavattini, Williams, Arthur Miller, and Jean-Paul Sartre and with classy directors like Elia Kazan, John Huston, and Fred Zinneman.

Yet as a transitional figure straddling two eras of Hollywood history, Clift was also rooted in the traditional star system. A massive publicity apparatus at his disposal, he was mobbed by fans everywhere he went, covered by *Life*, discussed endlessly by the fanzines in terms of his upcoming marriage to Liz Taylor, and all the rest. His disfiguring car crash in 1956 and eventually his death simply provided more grist for the mill. Even his conscientious preparations for his roles—boxing and bugle playing for *From Here to Eternity*, for example—were manipulated as publicity copy, as signals of huge budgets and Oscar merit. Obviously, his pioneering kind of masculinity was no less marketable.

As with the traditional stars, the subtleties of Clift's acting and the laborious applications of his craft often became secondary on the screen to the impact of his presence. Both biographers are drawn irresistibly, like the swooners of the past, to his charisma, his hypnotic visual power. They revert inevitably to the awestruck terms of reference reserved only for stars of the magnitude of Garbo. Not all Broadway actors who migrated westward had the good fortune of Clift, Brando, and Dean to possess an almost magical interaction with the camera, the gift to speak directly and mythically to an era. In this sense every one of Clift's seventeen film roles was the same, an inscription of the same continuous personality, with only the costumes and scripts different. This dichotomy of intellectual and idol, these contradictions within this transitional figure, which are perhaps largely responsible themselves for the power of the myth, need rigorous analysis. Bosworth and LaGuardia, neither of them film historians, have stopped short of providing the required analysis of the myth, of Clift's place in the history of film performance, the American star system, and the film industry.

Surely a biography that cannot step back to the analytic distance and contribute to our understanding of a star's career is perpetuating a cult rather than demystifying it. The least we must demand of the current crop of star biographies, of which Bosworth's is admittedly one of the best, is the probing of the contradictions that all myths express and smooth over. In Clift's case, by bolstering the myth of the tormented artist-martyr "maddened by his homosexuality" (as Bosworth's dust jacket phrases it), to what extent is heterosexist society continuing to view suffering, self-destruction, and artistic talent as inherent in the lot of the homosexual in order to absolve itself of its perpetration of that suffering? To what extent does the myth of the isolation and romantic agony of the artist serve to prop up the political and cultural structures of a society that packages creativity, merchandises culture, and isolates art as irrelevant to the quality of life as a whole?

Cinéaste 10.1 (winter 1979–80): 58–59

Gay Cinema, Slick vs. Real:

Chant d'amour, Army of Lovers, We Were One Man

* * * * *

With this piece I entered the era of the queer film festival, then called gay, a bit later "lesbian and gay," and even later "queer." It is incredible that, as I write, my prophetic last sentence has come true with Bent *finally (and anticlimactically) hitting the theaters eighteen years later! My self-righteousness about lesbian invisibility in the 1980 Montreal festival would spark a nasty rejoinder to* TBP, *with the festival organizers comparing me to a venomous snake. My principal crime was offering criticism rather than support to alternative community institutions, and for allowing this reading I belatedly apologize now two decades later. In my defense I made a declaration that encapsules much of the flavor of gay-lesbian community politics at the end of the seventies:*

> *It's surely a basic principle of our movement that gay male institutions (economic, cultural, social) should share their superior resources and power with the lesbian community. In explicitly rejecting this principle, Sortir allies itself with the Rush and Honcho hawkers and the Mafia discos. Cultural products, our images of ourselves, are not commodities like liquid incense. At a time of growing attacks against us by the media, the police and the judges, and growing attempts to divide us, an exclusively 'male-oriented' cultural event of the scope, outlay and influence of the Semaine is inexcusable and unacceptable.*

Although the clash may be as indicative of the English-French divide as any other, there remains to this day in Montreal a lesbian-gay cultural and political split unmatched by any other major North American city. Go figure.

I went on to organize my own lesbian and gay film festival in 1982 called "Sans popcorn," with lots of gender parity and perhaps less real community consultation than I would have liked (midnight screenings of Ulrike Ottinger for women only!!!). I'm still proud of that accomplishment, but the burnout meant

I would never do it again. . . . Montreal now has one of the most successful queer film and video festivals on the continent, "Image & Nation," having celebrated its tenth anniversary in 1997.

* * *

It is always a major event to be able to see twenty-five gay films at once, half of them features. This was the menu offered by Montreal's *Semaine du cinéma gai* last June. But it is a major *political* event in the year that brought us *Cruising, Windows,* and forty-five sauna arrests in fast succession, and saw *La Cage aux folles* enter its second year doing for gays what blackface minstrel shows and Stepin Fetchit did for blacks.

This unprecedented chance to see how far we've gotten on the screen was somewhat soured, however, by a serious gap, namely the exclusion of lesbians from the planning and from the screen. The group of gay businessmen who organized the festival, *Sortir, Inc.*, apparently did not invite lesbian input nor even consult the gay community at large in advance.

The one film that did reflect lesbian input, *Word Is Out* (English version), was canceled halfway through its scheduled screenings, leaving high and dry the few nonboycotting women who arrived to see it later on. The only remaining film "about lesbians," Fassbinder's *The Bitter Tears of Petra von Kant,* is generally considered by lesbian critics to belong to the "freak show genre" of men's films about lesbians. The phallocentric nature of the entire week should not have been a surprise to anyone who saw the image used on posters and programs: a Soviet-style sculpture showing two very square-shouldered male harvesters looking butchly into each other's eyes.

Apart from this gigantic step backwards for the Quebec gay community, there's also good news: the movie lineup was indeed a feast. The *Sortir* organizers' major coup was to import four major new French films—Phillippe Vallois's *Johan* and *Nous étions un seul homme,* Jean-François Garsi's *Milan bleu,* and Lionel Soukaz's *Race d'Ep,* a compendium of a century of "images of homosexuality." Quebec lesbians and gay men have always been short-changed in terms of French-language versions of gay films, so these premieres were met with great excitement.

One important result may be that the situation will improve now that a gay public is clearly visible. The smaller screening rooms are beginning to wake up—the Cinéma parallèle couldn't believe the huge lineups they got for Jean Genet's *Chant d'Amour* and for German filmmaker Werner Schroeter's camp operatic epics during the spring and are certain to follow these successes up.

Genet's classic was also shown during the week and was without a doubt the hit of the whole affair. *Chant d'amour* (Song of Love) seemed to compress into its silent twenty minutes everything a gay male cinema can or should be. The images are somewhat cloudy because of thirty years of underground reproduction. But the famous prisoners-in-heat glow through the blur like a cave painting that suddenly reveals through layers of smoke a whole new era of human history.

I say that *Chant d'amour* is a prototype for the gay cinema, not in spite of its marginal, shoestring mode of production but perhaps *because* of it. Like many of the best films in the festival, *Chant* is rough and cheap, but its painful tenderness and energy are all the more compelling for this reason. Such films may lack the technical slickness, the stars, and the narrative roundness of the mainstream films, but they make up for it in their closeness to the roots of our experience, their emotional and artistic authenticity, and their political astuteness. Genet, a veteran of countless orphanages and prisons, is like our best filmmakers in having to look no further for a subject than his own experience. But the film is not only about physical and sexual confinement; it also shows characters resisting their confinement, struggling against it to establish the most tenuous of human and erotic contact among themselves—contraband flowers swung through window bars, cigarette smoke blown through a chink from one solitary cell to another. The prisoners also resist through autoerotic rituals and fantasies that are childlike in their simplicity and lyricism. One even ends up feeling pity for the voyeuristic guard who cannot himself break through his own prison of sadism, guilt, and repression.

As I've said, the best films of the week were marginal or independent, like Genet's—notably *A Bigger Splash*, Jack Hazan's dramatization of painter David Hockney's life and loves; or Kenneth Anger's underground classics *Fireworks* and *Scorpio Rising;* and the French films *Race d'Ep, Milan bleu,* and *Johan.* Yet many of the most promising gay independent films were passed over, in my view—films I would describe as belonging to a more militant political current than the above "artistic," "avant-garde," and "life-

Jean Genet's *Chant d'amour* (1950): everything a gay male cinema can or should be. Frame enlargement.

style" films. The closest the week got to the militant current was Rosa von Praunheim's feature documentary, *Army of Lovers or Revolt of the Perverts*, a film whose overall bent is more journalistic than subversive.

Not surprisingly, much of the independent cinema of the week ran into some audience resistance, in some cases boos and walkouts. Both film programmers and filmmakers would have been better off to meet audiences' Hollywood-trained moviegoing habits and expectations at least halfway—by programming all shorts with features, for example, or by making films that exploit existing film conventions rather than acting as if they didn't exist. One filmmaker who successfully gets away with the latter strategy is American lesbian Jan Oxenberg, the festival's most conspicuous noninvitee, who wittily and deftly overturns traditional iconography of lesbians and sexual roles. As for the best (and only?) example of Quebec militant filmmaking, Harry Sutherland's *Truxx*, the English version was not invited, and the

French version, according to reports, is still in hock at the lab because the filmmakers are broke. Any gay businessmen around who like movies?

Compared to these omissions, other snags were only what could have been expected in a first attempt at such an event. Organizers learned that weekday-afternoon screenings don't draw crowds, that straight filmgoers care little for gay cinema, and that the straight press would give only token coverage.

Although many filmgoers found the $3.50 price too steep, reports have it that the investors lost money. Five thousand paid admissions, however, indicate a market. Future festivals should consider a modest scale, as well as the use of state-subsidized cinematheques or parallel screening rooms, all of which seem open to gay programming.

The other advantage to a noncommercial agreement would be a greater tendency for spectators to be supportive of filmmakers still struggling only half successfully to find the language and images that have always been denied us. For $3.50 the temptation is always to expect Dolby stereo and John Travolta, and the week's most conclusive insight is that significant gay filmmakers will not be working with either of these ingredients for some time.

The telephoto image of a Paris pissoir, black and white, grainy and blurred, revealing beneath its blank partition a whole procession of male feet, shuffling and hesitating, grouping together in fours and sixes. A pair of pant cuffs bounces up and down in an unmistakable rhythm, a pair of jeans suddenly drops to ankle level, a pair of legs sprawls out from beneath the partition in a moment of sublime double-jointed recklessness when nothing else matters. . . .

Another image is sunny, sharp, and Eastmancolor. A bare-chested soldier named Rolf, a cross between Marlene Dietrich and Gary Cooper, wrestles in a bright forest clearing with another man, Guy, lithe and dark. It is the ritual of macho combat that functions as a kind of surrogate fuck or preseduction warm-up for straight and not-so-straight men.

These very different images are from two recent French features, *Johan* (1976) and *Nous étions un seul homme* (We Were One Man, 1979), respectively. Their director, a 32-year-old gay man, Phillippe Vallois, was a star attraction, with his films, at Montreal's *Semaine du cinéma gai* in June. The two films seem to epitomize, if the offerings of the week were any guide, two of the main directions the gay cinema is taking as it moves into the eighties.

Johan, like the pissoir scene, is the recreation of lived experience in an authentic setting, rambunctious and fresh, loose and low budget.

The film is not really about Johan, a gay man whom we never see because he's in jail. Instead, it's about a group of filmmakers and their friends who are making a film portrait of Johan in his absence, piecing together evidence and fantasies of the absent figure. Is Johan the narcissistic youth caressing his pectorals in the sauna, rejecting suitor after suitor with the explanation that he only makes love with his twin brother? Or is Johan the charmingly voluble sadist with the earring, or the spacey drag queen who can't keep her ballet slippers stiff, or perhaps the director himself, obsessed with his need for self-expression?

It doesn't really matter, since it's all a pretext for a head-over-heels series of sketches and vignettes from the lively ghetto subculture it focuses on— brief but perceptive glimpses of terrains and personalities, moments of absurdity, alienation, and community. Curiously, it was one of three or four films in the week that show the latter—it is a film full of the laughter and the conversation of gay people being together.

We never really learn why Johan is in prison. The gap is maybe significant. If he's there because he's gay, it would be the only hint in the film of the institutionalized homophobia surrounding this milieu. Vallois and too many of the directors in the week avoid this subject far too much. The characters in *Johan, Saturday Night at the Baths, Milan bleu*, the contemporary episodes of *Race d'Ep*, and even the two Fassbinder films move about within their ghetto stamping-grounds, preoccupied with their lusts and anxieties, completely oblivious to the hostile political environment around them. You would never know from the French films, for example, of the particular set of circumstances that allowed fascist thugs to send another guest at the festival, director Lionel Soukaz (*Race d'Ep*), to the hospital for a few months during the Paris gay film festival several years ago. There is no sense that *Johan*'s chic young men are in any way threatened by violence or by housing discrimination, or that coming out exists for them as a real political problem. As for oppression on the job, there's not even the suggestion that any of them have or need jobs and even less acknowledgment that most lesbians and gay men can't stay up all night because they have to work the next morning. This is a far cry from the social sharp-sightedness and responsibility of other gay films we've had, like *Nighthawks*, *Fox and His Friends*, *The Naked Civil Servant*, and even *Word Is Out*, in which characters' sexual identities are always situated in relation to economic and political survival.

All the same, *Johan* is a fine model of the kind of personal, low-budget filmmaking outside of the industry that lesbians and gays would do well to explore further.

Vallois, however, was not content to stay marginal after *Johan*. After his succeeding feature likewise failed to find a distributor, the director stepped clearly beyond the limited audience of a film like *Johan* and into the mainstream with *Nous étions un seul homme*. As the sunny wrestling scene suggests, this most recent film aims for traditional star power and a commercial discourse of romance and myth (disguised as psychological "realism" of course), and strong audience identification.

Though the film is set in the very concrete historical reality of occupied France in 1943, what you take away with you are those misty moments when the two characters fight and make up, pout and pant, kiss and die. Assuming gay people at large are going to keep demanding their myths as much as any public, I'll take Guy and Rolf over Luke Skywalker and Princess Leia any day.

There are also the tedious entanglements by which Vallois thickens the plot and delays the gratification of the final fuck—namely two standard triangles, one involving a dog the German takes a liking to, the other involving Janine, a young village woman whom Guy has sex with now and again. Janine functions largely as a plot mechanism: as a foil for the two lovers, as a voyeur, and finally as an unwitting trigger of disaster when she leads in the Gestapo. . . . It's not really very much of a novelty for a straight woman to find herself on the outside corner of a movie triangle like this, though it's usually the lesbian or gay man who gets that role (*Fame*, *The Rose*, *Happy Birthday Gemini*). Whenever a straight woman does end up as the excluded one, the misogynous overtones of the pattern always disturb me (*Heartbeat*, *Dog Day Afternoon*, *Lonesome Cowboys*, *Saturday Night at the Baths*, *A Very Natural Thing*, *Scarecrow*, *Montreal Main*). The woman always seems to be a sounding board for the male to develop his sexuality on—to discover he's gay or to prove he's straight to himself or to the audience—or the source of barriers to the course of true love. She is seldom developed as a character in her own right. Vallois cannot extricate himself from this trap.

The Occupation backdrop is another element of the film that is potentially very suggestive: Jean Genet made unforgettable use of this backdrop in *Funeral Rites*, his novel of the forbidden play of eroticism and power between victor and vanquished. Vallois, however, doesn't really go beyond using the political backdrop as a distant malign destiny, which we know will finally close in and destroy the lovers in their idyllic forest hideout after ninety minutes. In *Nous étions un seul homme*, there is too much of the arbitrariness of the old "dead-queer" formula ending for the final disaster to be fully satisfying.

But it's a good try. Vallois's film is encouraging in that it is close enough to the ideal of a film that deals authentically with gay love and at the same time that can survive in the marketplace. If Vallois and the other filmmakers in the festival with the same goal persist (and listen to their gay public), we may just end up with a cinema that is genuinely popular and gay at the same time. Perhaps the film versions of *Bent* and *Rubyfruit Jungle* will be the first big breakthroughs (if they can ever raise the money).

The Body Politic, no. 66 (September 1980): 30–31

Nighthawks, by Ron Peck and Paul Hallam

*   *   *   *   *

I still remember Nighthawks *very fondly, no doubt because of my own teaching and the many classroom melodramas I've also lived. The aftertaste of Anita Bryant was still in the air in 1980, so the issue of gay teachers was not an abstract one. But beyond its topicality* Nighthawks *is still one of the great unrecognized teacher films—right up there with* To Sir With Love, Mädchen in Uniform, Taxi zum Klo. . . . *This review in our short-lived local French-language magazine is one of many that have an autobiographical edge: it reminds me of the peer pressure one faced around tricking, of the discussion group of queer veterans of the Left I belonged to, the "Triangle du collectif rose," who were trying to integrate class into sex/gender analysis and did great demos and fabulous desserts along the way. Translated from the French.*

*   *   *

Quebec lesbians and gays had a chance over the summer to see one of the two or three best films that the decade after Stonewall has brought us. *Les cités de la nuit,* the subtitled version of *Nighthawks,* by British directors Ron Peck and Paul Hallam, was a special treat, especially after a Gay Cinema Week that offered few revelations.

Nighthawks is the simple story of Jim, a young teacher who by night likes cruising in London discos and by day conscientiously teaches geography to ungrateful teenagers. As the credits suggest, the film is virtually a collective achievement by the London gay community.

At the start it was going to be a documentary on gay life, from demos to discos, for which Peck and Hallam had already gotten ready hundreds of interviews and a pilot videotape. But their project was refused by the public arts funders (a phenomenon we're quite familiar with here). So the filmmakers had to work for two years to finance the film through small donations from London gays. Finally, a West German TV network offered the funding necessary for completion. (Is it a coincidence that *Word Is Out* and

Revolt of the Perverts were also made thanks to TV investments?) Meanwhile, the concept had changed—the film had become a fiction feature on one gay man's experience. On its release, *Nighthawks* became a box office sensation in England, a hit at Cannes last year, and an American critical success.

It's clear that the long gestation of the film and the marshaling of multiple resources from many collaborators are at the root of its impressive authenticity and political astuteness. But I don't mean that it's only agitprop: on the contrary, Jim is far from a political role model. As a geographer he's much more worried about the urban environment in which his pupils are living than about his gay sisters' and brothers' oppression. Just like everyone else, Jim has moments of obsession and despair, as well as of lucidity. In general, he's an ordinary guy, well adjusted, happy and hardly disturbed by the schism between his classroom days and his dance-floor nights. He likes his autonomy and values his one-night stands, which, he claims, often turn into friendships (although we see very little of them in the film, as several gay critics have noticed).

Ken Robertson's performance as Jim is admirably nuanced and controlled; he's very convincing in the naturalist tradition in which the English excel (*Nighthawks* recalls the work of Peter Watkins [*Edvard Munch*], Ken Loach [*Family Life*] or Jack Hazan [*A Bigger Splash*]). In the disco Robertson is wonderful when he parades about, drink and cigarette in hand, pecs pumped up, in front of the other nighthawks; wonderful also when his voice trembles as he has to defend himself to his principal. Other actors, clearly amateurs, are no less convincing in the supporting roles.

The great virtue of the film is the way it engages as much with Jim's professional life as with his sexual and social life. (How many Burt Reynolds films totally neglect the characters' work, their entire economic life?) This is important because the workplace is one of the fiercest sites of oppression for homosexuals. The special moments of *Nighthawks* happen in his professional milieu. In fact, there are two moments when Jim comes out: once voluntarily to Judy, a straight colleague who becomes slowly and with difficulty his friend, and, the other time, when he is ambushed by his pupils who are much less discreet and tolerant. This latter sequence, clearly improvised on location in a real school, is the highlight of the film: his students accuse him, maliciously, of being a faggot, a queer, a drag queen, and so on, and also of coming on to the boys in the class. Jim keeps calm despite everything and patiently tries to undermine his pupils' primitive prejudices, but in vain. Then a ray of encouragement lights up when one of the girls comes to the rescue of this man she admires as a teacher and not as a sexual being. Outwardly, Jim seems cool during his two different comings out, but we feel his closeness to panic each time. It goes without saying that the choice of a teacher as hero is strategic.

Jim's social life in the bars is much less tumultuous. We see him meet several more or less nice young men, and we begin to recognize them in his company. The camera succeeds in bringing the spectator into his adventures: we cruise at his side. During long takes on the dance floor, we help him choose a target and then zoom in on the prey. It's a very subtle game the camera is playing, inviting us as matchmaker to root for the handsome young worker with the rosy cheeks and then to feel let down when our hero drops him. For the next morning, Jim drives him to the Underground, instead of to his workplace as he does for more promising candidates.

We immediately become suspicious of a cute and hairy Fine Arts student who flirts shamelessly with both Jim and the camera, while he dances with someone else. Jim, less observant than we are, pursues in vain the hairy one, despite our better judgment. Some spectators have found these experiments on perspective too long, but those who don't require a Hitchcock pacing in their movies will discern an eloquent statement of the importance of rituals of looking and being looked at within our ghetto culture.

Jim seems quite aware of his attraction to younger, less privileged men than he, those who don't have the luxury of his car, who can't live alone like him, who don't have his job security. The film is very sensitive to the subtleties of these interclass encounters both outside and inside the gay ghetto. Jim can express himself in his job and live more or less openly and freely. On the other hand, the worker that he meets cannot afford his own apartment or live his sexuality in front of his straight roommates; another encounter, unemployed, is sentenced to look unenthusiastically for any kind of dehumanizing job.

The stress put by the filmmakers on the repetitive ghetto rituals is brilliant and evocative: the rituals of chatting superficially with a stranger in a bar, then making love with the same stranger, then the gestures of waking up beside the now slightly less unknown individual, the verbal choreography of the inevitable decision to follow up on a trick or not. But there are also

Nighthawks (1979): rituals of looking and being looked at. Museum of Modern Art Film Stills Library.

moments of tenderness, of humor, of powerful eroticism. Among the mechanical gestures of these meetings, there are always instants of that miraculous understanding between two strangers, of those little discoveries that often become adventures even if one already knows they are fleeting.

Does *Nighthawks* express a moralistic point of view on ghetto culture? Probably yes. In fact, why did the directors choose to close on one of the hero's moments of obsession (he can't go home without dropping by a club) rather than on a moment of awareness or growth? But their judgments, if any, are ambiguous enough to stay open. Although a friend of mine found the film too didactic, it's rather a film that asks questions without answers and sympathetically provokes spectators without preaching.

It's also true that there are urgent issues that the film doesn't deal with—our relations with lesbians and other oppressed groups, for example; the politics of gender fares slightly better, accented through Judy's struggle to survive in a tense and constrictive marriage, which is perhaps an oppression related to Jim's.

In any case no film can be the *Das Kapital* of the gay movement, as the filmmakers have explained: "The film shows only a part of the gay milieu, and only certain aspects of the main character's life. The film doesn't 'cover' everything, as some people would like, but such a desire only reflects the seriousness of the situation: there are so few films with or about gay characters. We need hundreds of gay films, not only five or six." Nevertheless, it's gay critics who have been among the most sparing with their praise. *The Body Politic* was the most severe: in their view, it's just another pity-the-poor-homosexual film. It's perhaps inevitable that controversy will greet such an honest, authentic, and perceptive movie, the "bravest film of the year," according to an American critic. It's not a propaganda film for straights or for parents of gays. It's a film for us, from us, about us, gay men, a film that refuses to let us leave the theater indifferent. And as such it's a film we can be very proud of.

See it as soon as it comes back to the screen, even if you've already seen it (it's better the second time). We know that the sequel to *La Cage aux folles* has already been shot and will come out at the start of 1981—*Nighthawks* will act as a preventive antidote.

Le Berdache, no. 13 (September 1980): 43–44, 46

A Saturday Night Surprise:

Burin des Roziers's *Blue Jeans*

*   *   *   *   *

Hard to believe the era of the potluck B-movie double feature existed in Montreal as recently as the late seventies. Needless to say the director of this lovely little film, discovered by some fluke, would never be heard from since—nor would the film. Blue Jeans *was another teacher film that touched me profoundly, though, unlike* Nighthawks, *it depicts the student side. Interestingly, the synopsis I then disliked now strikes me as amazingly neutral (aside from the ring of "exploited"). I recognize this professionalism could never be expected from an English-language reviewer in North America; it reminds me of the curious cultural tolerance I was increasingly appreciating in Montreal, the cosmopolitan paradise where I had lived for less than four years. Translated from the French.*

*   *   *

Blue Jeans, a 1977 French feature written and directed by Hugues Burin des Roziers. French teenagers come to England for the summer to learn English. Among them is a boy who, rather than being interested in girls, forms a friendship with an older boy instead. That seems suspect to his classmates, who make fun of him, and persecute him. The poor boy ends up being exploited by a homosexual instructor.

Such was the hardly promising synopsis in the weekend *La Presse*. And the publicity captions were even worse: "Youth, blue jeans, kisses and summer . . . the time for pleasure!" That kind of synopsis hooks me every time. I don't trust straight journalists' impressions of films with gay themes, but there's something definitely masochistic in my compulsion to subject myself to the worst big-screen homophobia, and that's what *Blue Jeans* seemed to guarantee.

Imagine my astonishment at not finding some kind of French *Cruising* but a little film that treats subtly and sensitively the delicate subject of gay love among young people and between different generations.

Blue Jeans is the history of the first love (one more time) of a boy about thirteen years old, scarcely entered into puberty, who finds himself madly in love with a slightly older and more experienced teenager who is already smooth with the girls and decorated with a hint of mustache. The teenager is at first flattered by the boy's crush but rejects him as soon as his peers start teasing him. Our hero doesn't know how to deal with this first rejection or with his "normal" classmates' horrible brutality. He cries a bit too much and seeks consolation and advice from his teacher, a slightly lugubrious young man (who reminded me of the young Charles Laughton). The teacher is very sympathetic and knows how to give good advice and, by the time the boy turns up for the third time, starts feeling courted himself. In fact the scriptwriter gives him the role of introducing his young charge to the world of adult sexuality. . . .

The hero cries some more.

It's a very discreet sequence but perhaps not enough so: it prompts the straight spectator to give the mechanical *La Presse* response, that is to say the automatic label of exploitation. And it confirms the stereotype of the predator teacher that gets straights so upset and in consequence becomes a real threat to all of us.

Taking refuge in the forests of the Auvergne with his aristocratic family, the hero of course meets a second young man whose sexual orientation we don't know and with whom his friendship doesn't get sexual for the time being. The latter listens attentively to the boy's story and asks him to show him how to catch crayfish, all alone in the woods. . . .

At the end of the film it is clear that the hero has learned much more than English during his summer vacation, that he has few regrets, and that he is going to grow some more.

As I was saying there are some regrettable moments in the film. But otherwise I recommend it strongly for the excellent performances by the young actors and for the marvelous authenticity of a story that I wager is autobiographical. Burin des Roziers, of whom I know nothing at all, knew how to capture gently the pressures that kids feel, both social and biological pressures, having to do with conformity, roles, and sexuality. He's surely a filmmaker whose next film we must watch for.

At the St. Denis the film was twinned with an execrable Italian gangster film; one more proof, if we needed one, that Quebec film distribution is deaf and blind. (Fortunately, the censor is too: *Blue Jeans* would be classified as PG or R in the States or Ontario—or more likely banned outright—but here receives the much deserved label "Pour tous." Bravo!)

Blue Jeans will probably not become a classic in the cinematic evolution of young gay love, on the order of *Mädchen in Uniform* (we urgently need a revival of this German lesbian masterpiece), *Les Amitiés particulières*, and *If.* . . . After all, we're no longer in 1932, 1964, or even 1968. Nevertheless, the three gay men who spent a Saturday evening at this surprising show (among a mob of young hetero couples waiting for another Italian gangster film, perplexedly eating their popcorn) recommend it to you without hesitation.

Le Berdache, no. 15 (November 1980): 56–57

Caligula

*   *   *   *   *

This review reflects my canon-subversive conviction that trash, especially quix-
otic and dismissable trash like this, deserves thoughtful analysis. But did I really
see this film in both New York and Montreal to compare the two versions? Did
I really compare it to The Blue Lagoon, *another piece of dismissable trash that*
remains for me one of my guiltiest pleasures? I was clearly on my feminist kick
but not yet able to reconcile feminist convictions with a cultural recognition of
porno. The reference to Ronald Reagan's recent election makes me realize that
this review of a mad emperor movie inaugurated the eighties for me, not so inap-
propriate in fact. . . .

*   *   *

Caligula, the self-styled erotic epic of Roman decadence, made $55,000 dur-
ing its first weekend in Montreal. The theater was packed, thanks to the *Ga-*
zette's free publicity (never hesitating to suck up to U.S. industrial cinema
while systematically ignoring gay cinema). It's a real event.

The version of *Caligula* offered to the Quebec audience is more or less
equivalent to what's been playing in New York for more than a year, with a
few exceptions. There are fewer hard-core close-ups (although the erotic sequences are still franker than those permitted to date by Quebec censors,
who are already the least neurotic in Canada). And they won't let us have a
few homoerotic frissons that are in the American version either: for example, a long "come shot" in which a grand Roman lady has beautiful young
men ejaculate all over her in order to use the sperm as lotion. Caligula asks
her if that also encourages hair growth, a line that makes no sense without
the preceding shots.

Caligula has the same format as the American soft-core skin magazine
Penthouse: the sandwich format that surrounds a porno centerfold with layers of so-called serious journalism (though it's ultimately much less serious
than the centerfold). No surprise then that the film's producer is Bob Gucci-

Caligula (1980): gay actor Sir
John Gielgud (left) and Mal-
colm McDowell on the set.
Museum of Modern Art Film
Stills Library.

one, godfather of the *Penthouse* empire. The layers of celluloid sandwich are
blatant: on the outside, the historical epic, shot expensively in Rome, with
British stars like Malcolm McDowell, Sir John Gielgud, and Peter O'Toole; a
prestigious scriptwriter, Gore Vidal; and a score by Prokofiev. There's even
a biblical epigraph: "What shall it profit a man if he gain the whole world and
lose his own soul?" (Did Guccione actually read that?)

What's the sandwich filling? Several porno sequences, of a style and content that completely contradict the rest of the film, have been inserted by the
heavy hand that *Penthouse* readers will recognize all too well. In them, *Penthouse* "Pets" make love with each other, hairdos Roman-style naturally,
thighs painfully parted for the voyeuristic lens.

How does the filling contradict the sandwich? The historical film tries to
demonstrate the relationship between sexuality and social domination; the

porno insert sequences incarnate themselves that relationship—the "Pets" are in front of the camera, Guccione and his customers behind it.

We might ask why the Gucciones and their straight men need to mix lesbian eroticism with their porno soothers. The establishment cinema offers us two kinds of lesbians: villains and "Pets." But the most explicit image of lesbianism in our society has been left to porno, where the lesbian loses her villainous quality and becomes arousing, a "Pet." Straights maintain their control over women by creating the fantasies of women that they need. Pornography controls and exploits lesbianism by defining it as purely genital sexuality—in close-up, thighs parted. Any old theater on the Main offers the same lesbian formula. Even the first Quebec skinflick, *Valérie* (1969), had its own lesbian, a topless dancer whose caresses are spurned by Valérie (she naturally has to preserve her charms, although already unveiled for the spectator, for her eventual savior, the straight Québécois male).

Why was Guccione so unsatisfied with *Caligula* that he had to insert genital close-ups? First, as the *Gazette* headline shouted, "*Caligula* is full of sex and violence!" But this violence is all directed against men, except one scene where a woman is raped, of course. This is the straight male porno formula turned upside down: we all know that straight men who watch porn prefer to watch women being massacred than men being castrated and disemboweled. Second, as I've suggested, the original film aspires to analyze the links between sexuality and fascism. It's a fairly conventional theme already attempted by Pasolini (*Salo*), Visconti (*The Damned*), and Cavani (*The Night Porter*). But this is not necessarily a theme that pleases fascists or Gucciones. How does the emperor Caligula exploit sexuality as a vehicle of his own domination? Among other things, he diverts the senatorial elite with an extravagant brothel while he usurps their power. *Caligula* is thus somewhat self-destructing as a film: porno that arouses and deflates at the same time.

The sex-fascism theme can be dangerous for lesbians and gays. How many times have we been informed by the media that the Nazis were repressed homosexuals? It's an old song and dance: homosexuality causes the decadence of our society, and sexual liberation will bring on the collapse of our civilization as it did for the Roman Empire. *Caligula*, at least its original conception as directed by the Italian filmmaker Tinto Brass before his dismissal and Guccione's intervention, seems to be the Italian straight Left's version of this perilous myth that gay historians are now beginning to explode. John Boswell, for example, demonstrates in *Christianity, Social Tolerance, and Homosexuality: Gay People in Western Europe from the Beginning of the Christian Era to the 14th Century* that the last centuries of the Roman Empire were much more conservative than the centuries of its peak. Is it possible that *Caligula* is the first porno film to please the Moral Majority that has just elected Ronald Reagan?

It's not the first time that Tinto Brass pushes this myth of decadence. His previous film, *Salon Kitty*, looked at the Nazi empire through the same erotophobic glasses. But *Salon Kitty* still explains more clearly than *Caligula* how the state uses eroticism as an instrument of control and how the state controls sexuality, all the while offering the same metaphor of the state as brothel.

There's another reason for Brass's dismissal: he's actually a rather talented filmmaker. Traces of this talent are actually visible on the screen in *Caligula*. For him, epic spectacle is a powerful and eloquent medium. Swarming, labyrinthine sets evoke street theater, the circus even, all expressing his astute vision of Roman society. It's a vision considerably less foggy than that of *Fellini Satyricon*, the genre's prototype. Brass's images are cold, symmetrical, frontal, and imperial. If in *Salon Kitty* Brass got his inspiration from an unexpected source—Eisenstein's quasi-Stalinist epic *Ivan the Terrible*—here his inspiration is as painterly (he borrows from Jacques Louis David, the favorite painter of another emperor . . . Napoleon) as filmic (is it Griffith's *Intolerance* that Brass is evoking to suggest a fourth empire, the American Babylon?).

I don't know how to evaluate Vidal's contribution to all this. Vidal has written considerable historical fiction on the ancient period that I am not familiar with, unfortunately, but I respect enormously his iconoclastic essays and his contemporary fiction (*Myra Breckinridge* [1969] and *The City and the Pillar* [1948] are both decisive points in the evolution of American gay fiction). I think, in any case, that I recognize in *Caligula* certain moments of *Myra*'s wit that Guccione wasn't able to extract after Vidal refused to stay in the credits. The basic conception of the character of Caligula is also surely his: his only refuge in his illicit relationship with his sister, his profound innocence and his vulnerability, and the terrible cruelty that inhabits this innocence at the summit of absolute power, a power without any social con-

The Blue Lagoon (1980): guilty pleasure. Museum of Modern Art Film Stills Library.

straint whatsoever. This sympathetic portrait reminds me of Billy the Kid in another film written by Vidal, *The Left-Handed Gun* (Arthur Penn, 1958), where violence expresses psychic wounds also. Caligula cries that he is all men and no man at the same time. This essentially sadean and pessimistic vision is completely opposite to that transmitted by another current American hit, *The Blue Lagoon.* This other speculation on sexuality without social constraint proposes an eroticism that is soft, modest, boring, and heterosexual! That's much more pornographic than *Caligula* and much less true.

Le Berdache, no. 19 (April 1981): 57–59

Taxis and Toilets: Ripploh and His Brothers

* * * * *

Another teacher film? Another film festival report? I was already feeling the trap of reporting on festivals yet continued to publish them regularly. Here I was bolstering the assumption that festivals rather than everyday fare were where it was at, especially the international Montreal festival that was beginning its slow slide into mediocrity. Hindsight allows two further glosses: first, this was the year a strange new cancer was first reported and would within a couple of years make Taxi, *with its lighthearted romp through hepatitis,* STDs, *and unprotected behaviors, an all but unwatchable swan song of the Stonewall era. As for Ripploh, I was certainly part of a consensus about the merits of his film, but he would scarcely be heard of again. Second, I sensed that we were on the cusp of technological paradigm shifts, but was I ever wrong in hinting that Super 8 (film that is) had anything to do with it!*

* * *

We've had gay movies before that have been funny or sexy or tender or politically intelligent. Now we have a film from Germany, *Taxi zum Klo* (Taxi to the Toilet), that manages to be all of these things at once.

Because these qualities were in low supply at last month's Montreal World Film Festival, a reflection on the worldwide movie slump, *Taxi* automatically became one of the most talked-about Festival entries.

Frank Ripploh is both the star of this highly autobiographical work and its director. In it he replays his life as a fairly effective teacher and an insatiable toilet queen. Frank is remarkably un-hungup about the contradictions of classroom and cubicle and has even evolved a system for marking homework during lulls in the glory-hole beat. Sex is a part of the continuum of Frank's life, along with his Chilean Solidarity meetings and his faculty bowling nights. The fucking is all there on the screen, fragmented by neither the censor's cuts nor those of the self-censor, nor by the pornographer's alienating close-ups. The sensuous mingling of bodies is so unencumbered

Taxi zum Klo (1980): homemaker Bernd (left) and prowler Frank in the film's finale. Museum of Modern Art Film Stills Library.

by the baggage of repression that I was reminded of Pasolini's fantasies of medieval pansexuality in *The Decameron, The Canterbury Tales,* and *Arabian Nights.* But the fragile balance of Frank's loyalties cannot go on forever, and Frank finally explodes it (literally) by showing up for class in pink belly-dancer drag (the real-life Frank was fired for coming out in less cinematic circumstances via a magazine profile).

Meanwhile, Frank has been setting up house with a lover, Bernd, whose idea of a good time is cooking dinner for two. The old monogamy/adultery premise that has been a mainstay of bourgeois drama for centuries thus resurfaces, but Ripploh plays with the tension without the moralist posturing, the sentimentality, and the easy compromises that we're used to. Ripploh doesn't force Bernd into the shrill homebody stereotype and is aided by the sympathy and wit of his real-life ex-lover's characterization. Both sides have their legitimacy. The ending is left unresolved.

This familiar couple angle is what attracts and holds the film's large straight audience, I would guess, but the complacency engendered by this attraction never lasts very long. The hetero couple beside me kept getting hooked on a reassuring scene of domestic melodrama only to get jolted out of their seats by the next golden shower interlude.

Gay audiences are much more absorbed, I think, in Ripploh's encyclopedic forays in every other direction (are there any gay features that haven't felt the compulsion to cover the whole spectrum of our lives?). Frank's relations with the outside straight world are sketched with admirable conciseness and insight, from the classroom full of adoring pupils to the medical establishment where he gets his anal warts probed. Ripploh also confronts the major issues within our community, from our relations with straight women (lesbians are absent from the film, as they were for the entire festival) to transgenerational sex; he does so with full respect for these issues' complexities, avoiding the extremes of both agitprop and defeatism that often cloud our images of ourselves. His vision is founded on the self-affirmation that is our political necessity, and it's good to know that this is possible within the gloomy culture that brought us *Fox and His Friends, The Consequence*, and Rosa von Praunheim (Ripploh used to be called Peggy von Schnottgenberg).

Now that *Taxi* is slated to appear in the New York Film Festival (under the Americanized title of *Taxi to the John*) and has reportedly been sold to a Canadian distributor, it may reach the North American audience it deserves. But don't hold your breath, Toronto—we know what the Ontarian censors think about good healthy sex.

Taxi was part of an abundant series of recent German features shown at Montreal that underline, in case anyone was still doubting, that the German cinema is the liveliest in the world. The lionized superstars like Fassbinder and Herzog are only the tip of the iceberg. In their shadow (undeservedly?) is a diversified output that seems to provide ample space to feminist, radical, and gay filmmakers, in apparent contradiction to the stepped-up political repression in West Germany (PR is surely one reason why the state subsidizes the new cinema and promotes it so energetically abroad). . . .

Other festival finds included *Salo or the 120 Days of Sodom*. At long last a Canadian showing of the Pasolini update of de Sade, one of the truly great films of the seventies. The castle of libertine enslavement is overturned and historicized, transposed to fascist Italy. Definitely a subject for future discussion, but in the meantime cross off Ontario once again. The good news is that *Salo* has been under active consideration by the Quebec Censor Board and has not yet been refused. . . .

The Kiss. On the surface, this baffling Brazilian film by Bruno Baretto (*Dona Flor and Her Two Husbands*) is a black parable of homophobia: a man falsely denounced as gay for having impulsively kissed a male accident victim is ostracized by society and family. No gay spectator will remain unmoved by the sight of "faggot" daubed over the hero's car and home, or by his escalating paranoia. But the undeniable punch of this idea is softened by drawn-out questioning of whether the hero might really be gay (as if homophobia is valid when directed against real homosexuals). What is more, a real homosexual turns up in an apparently tongue-in-cheek denouement that confirms the stereotypes of depravity and obsession, to all-round audience laughter. The film is ultimately unintelligible: who knows what sense Latin American audiences are making of it, if any? . . .

Tous les garçons (All the Boys). This year's new Super 8 section of the festival suggests the importance of this cheap, flexible medium for gay and other minority cultures. *Tous les garçons*, a simple coming-out story made in 1979 by a 19-year-old Trois-Rivières student, Yves Laberge, has already been shown as an official Canadian entry at Cannes. A young man is shown poised at the point of self-acceptance, remembering childhood gender conflicts and experiments with drag. As the director himself puts it, "The film doesn't present any problems or solutions. Its only message, if it has one, is that sexual orientation is not a matter of choice but a reality that people adapt to." An encouraging sign of activity on the Quebec gay film scene.

The Body Politic, no. 77 (October 1981): 33

Bright Lights in the Night:

Pasolini, Schroeter, and Others

*   *   *   *   *

This piece may represent the ultimate pit of pessimism in The Fruit Machine: *it was a bad year. Perhaps my grouchiness reflected my exasperation with the petty rivalries of Canadian festivals and with our bread-and-circus pathology. I wonder if I should relook at Lambert's films on the chance that this pan is another mistake on the order of my* Sebastiane *boo-boo? No, I was on much steadier critical legs in 1981 than in 1978. But at the same time I was going to absolutely hate* Matador, *my first film by an unknown Spaniard named Almodovar a few years later. . . . Positive image aesthetics die hard, and I only sense how far behind me I've left them when I hear my students in 1998 echoing my own certainties of two decades earlier. Lambert, for all I know, has disappeared into the abyss of film history as fully as Mary Stephen has (both beneficiaries of nondiscriminating state funding and nondiscriminating cokehead pomo programmers), but Schroeter remains one dynamite European filmmaker who has undeservedly never caught on in the English-speaking world. In any case, there are a couple of things worth remembering in this piece, all overshadowed by any chance to write about my idol* PPP.

*   *   *

Hardly anyone still expects that Hollywood will deliver a decent gay movie during the present century. It stands to reason that we should look to independent filmmakers for images that are positive and true, right?

Wrong, according to the independent films that recently swamped Montreal moviegoers during the International Festival of New Cinema, the annual October antidote to the more commercial August festival.

The most depressing aspect of the surly films outlined below is that gays and women have contributed to all of them, either as filmmakers or players. The films reflect our increasing visibility, to be sure, but show no inkling of the political precipice on which that visibility has placed us. I'm not demanding agitprop from independents (they hardly reach enough people anyway), just a little accountability to the women and gays in the audience.

Independents used to be the only filmmakers who dared to show our faces in the days before Stonewall—artists like Kenneth Anger, Jack Smith, Robert Frank—with brave disregard for the ostracism and prosecutions that inevitably followed. Now the tables are turned: independent films, like those of the Berlin artist/critic Lothar Lambert, chief guest of the festival, are an excellent place to look for vivid images of misogyny, homophobia, and, worst of all, gay self-hatred.

Lambert's 1 Berlin-Harlem is a sympathetic portrait of an American black man facing alienation and racism within German society. Women and gay men just happen to be the hero's worst tormentors, the former depicted as castrators, cockteasers, and ogresses, the latter as sniveling serpentine parasites. The film ends with the hero politely turning down a gay come-on by means of fatal strangulation, a means fully legitimized by the film. We are even relieved when the hero gets off scot-free. In short, here is a crummy "dead queer" movie that makes *Cruising* look like *Word Is Out*. I was not surprised that sexual violence against women turned out to be a major ingredient of Lambert's other films, but I was somewhat mind-boggled by his cheerful acknowledgment of his gayness in the warmly approving postscreening discussion.

Justocoeur, an independent feature by Mary Stephen, a Canadian working in Paris, left me with similar feelings. Made partly with Canadian subsidies (doesn't anyone among the grant givers know how to read?), this artsy melodrama drove most of the audience staggering out before the end. The central character is a woman dancer whose relationship with two gay men fulfills all of the misogynist corners of the "fag hag" stereotype: she is a spoiled, childish, neurotic, narcissistic, jealous, manipulative clotheshorse. The men are no more appealing, and all three characters look, act, and talk as if they have stepped out of the pages of *Vogue*. The only consolation is that they don't get slash murdered in the end, a conclusion spectators who stayed to the end may have been hoping for.

Do American independents show any more solidarity than these European counterparts? Two recent "New Wave" features coming out of New York get just as much mileage out of gay and feminine imagery, once again with full participation of their subjects, with no less offensive results. Lesbians have often complained about male avant-gardists using fraudulent depictions of lesbian eroticism to hold audience interest during aesthetic experiments. Eric Mitchell's *Underground USA* and Amos Poe's *Subway Riders*, two much-touted New Wave specimens, do exactly the same thing. Both sustain their pretty webs of Day-Glo/neon aestheticism and genre posturing with gay imagery—tough hustlers and fluttery queens in the former and lesbian lovemaking in the latter. If these two empty works are any indication, it's time the gay community reevaluated its careless alliance with punk culture.

For me the only moments of encouragement in the festival came from Werner Schroeter, another German independent, famous for his love of kitsch, opera, melodrama, drag, and theatricality and various campy blends thereof. Schroeter's *Weisse Reise* (White Journey) is a spirited, colorful fantasy of two beautiful young sailor-lovers who travel around the world together, loving and languishing against dreamily exotic backdrops. It's bright, sexy, and joyous, but Schroeter's reliance on backgrounds of simpering, silly women, the feminine cliché as aesthetic surface, left me a bit uneasy.

Schroeter's other new feature, *La Répétition générale* (Dress Rehearsal) avoids this liability. Because of its documentary foundation, this report on a world theater festival in France is full of women who are livelier, deeper, stronger, and more serious than the frivolous shadows of Schroeter's other films. An assembly of mimes, clowns, singers, and assorted freaks lets the filmmaker indulge in his obsessions with performance and spectacle to the fullest. At the same time, paradoxically, this exercise in "nonfiction" is his most personal film, among other things an essay on gay love and a declaration of passion for a festival participant of whose dark open face the camera never tires.

But the good feelings generated by Schroeter's rapidly evolving career, still largely unappreciated in North America, were torpedoed by a final insult on the part of the festival organizers. What was the infamous CBS report on the gay menace in San Francisco, *Gay Power, Gay Politics*—the ultimate document of the Moral Majority antigay backlash—doing in a festival of "new" "independent" films? This monumental goof is a chilling reminder about the reliability of our sometime allies in the "arts community."

Salo (1975): Pasolini's analysis of fascism at porno-chic prices. Museum of Modern Art Film Stills Library.

The festival season is finally over, and we can turn back for solace to the Hollywood monopolies. At least with Famous Players we know who our real enemies are.

More than five years after its European release, Pier Paolo Pasolini's *Salo* finally opened in Montreal on October 9 for its first Canadian theatrical run. The Quebec *Bureau de surveillance du cinéma* okayed the film a month after its sellout appearances at the Montreal film festival, but with a hitch. The film is restricted to a single art house known to be frequented by "cinephiles," in order not to "assault" the general public. This is the first time the Quebec board has distinguished between general and specialist audiences in its censorship policies, a move paralleling a recent "liberalization" by the Ontario censor board that also discriminates in favor of the elite film audiences at museums and art galleries.

Salo's distributors were quick to take advantage of their product's forbidden aura and are raking in an unprecedented $7 per ticket. Thus far only the *Penthouse* production of *Caligula* had dared to ask this porno-chic price. The publicist, not far behind, announced the day after *Salo*'s opening that a print of the film had been "stolen" on its way from the border and assured the media that "you can't get more explicit than this film," a statement whose blatant untruth can be immediately verified in any Quebec porno house. The murdered gay filmmaker's adaptation of the Marquis de Sade's *120 Days of Sodom* is notable for the transposition of Sade's fantasies of torture, simulated with exaggerated artificiality throughout, into the context of an analysis of fascism. One of Pasolini's innovations, unique in world cinema, was thought to be the real stumbling block for the Quebec censors (who routinely approve for the masses the sleaziest celebration of rape and torture). A bibliography inserted at the start of the film recommended further reading by such dangerous and obscene writers as Simone de Beauvoir and Roland Barthes.

The Body Politic, no. 79 (December 1981): 32–33

Patty Duke and Tasteful Dykes

*   *   *   *   *

We seem to have had an early lesbian chic phase back in 1982, what with Mariel Hemingway's Personal Best *and these three early Canadian entries from some of the darkest days of Canadian film history (known as the Capital Cost Allowance years). My perception of lesbian representation had admittedly a crusader quality to it, and I didn't pay much attention to "appropriation of voice" discourses that had occasionally come up around the groundbreaking appearance of the lesbian special issue of* Jump Cut *the previous year: if no one else was going to write about these films, I was. In any case, this piece anticipates one trend that would continue: TV movies as a site of positive image solidarity, whether in Canada, the United States, or the United Kingdom (Channel 4 was launched that same year and the rest is queer-film history!). Sara Botsford, by the way, went on to become a major Canadian TV star, but was Patty Duke ever heard from again? This turned out to be Claude Jutra's penultimate film: one wonders if Alzheimer's was already being felt on the set. In rereading this do I detect myself moving away from seventies judgmentalism?*

*   *   *

It's basically a light funny love story about a couple who want to have a baby and have a severe handicap because they are both women. . . . It's tastefully done. The only sexual scenes are heterosexual. . . . I'm basically playing any woman you might see on the street. There are no outright signs of homosexuality. We're just two very decent people who happen to be homosexual.—*Patty Duke Astin, on the Vancouver set of* By Design

It was in a sense a political film because it had two strong women protagonists. And even though they were lesbian, I think the acceptance of sexual choices is something which women are entitled to. If we can get people to care about two lesbians, that is making a stride foreword [sic]. . . . When we went out to sell it, you can't imagine the trouble we had. People looked at the script and said that's not funny. . . . One thing I

By Design (1981): Patty Duke (left) and Sara Botsford as tasteful dykes. Museum of Modern Art Film Stills Library.

want to do is make films without women as victims or sexpots. . . . On the other hand, I'm the one who insisted that we had all the sex in *By Design.—Beryl Fox, producer of* By Design

It never rains but it pours. Three new Canadian/Québécois movies about lesbian couples have just surfaced in Montreal, and at press time Mariel Hemingway is still nowhere in sight.

All three were well-intentioned, positive films with major input by women; only one of the six partners ends up dead; and, most incredibly, no one ends up, like Mariel Hemingway, with a man.

By Design is an expensive new comedy (budget $3 million) by feminist producer Fox and transplanted Quebec director Claude Jutra. Astin and a fine new six-foot Canadian actress named Sara Botsford play lovers, both fashion designers who decide they want to have a baby. They eventually persuade a harmless male chauvinist in their employ to help out. It takes. Both become pregnant through an unlikely twist, one has a miscarriage, and a happy girl-child ends up with two proud mothers.

By coincidence, *Désiré . . .* , a short by young director Francine Langlois (in French), uses an almost identical story (minus the miscarriage) and only a fraction of the budget. Here the setting isn't so classy, with flannel shirts replacing the *haute couture* velvet.

Last and least is *Arioso*, a slick TV movie from Radio Canada scripted by novelist Louise Maheu-Forcier. A writer tearfully remembers her lover killed in a car crash caused by a rejected male suitor. Now paralyzed because of the accident, the writer relives the idyllic memories of their relationship, finally resolving to preserve her memories and her love in her writing.

The six lesbian characterizations, for all their strengths, are compromised, to say the least. There are the blunders you expect whenever lesbians and gays are conceived by outsiders. Wait till you see the lesbians dance by rocking stiff-jointedly back and forth, holding their partners out at arms length!

The usual ideological messiness is also beneath the surface. I'm not speaking of the role-playing stereotypes, though the trappings of wealth and elegance in the two features are suspect, and the miscarriage and freak crash certainly add to our grisly necrology of dead queers in the movies (the crash was "the negation of our right to exist and love," lesbian activist Jeanne d'Arc Jutras wrote to *Le Devoir*). More serious is the question of straight prurience about lesbianism that has made fraudulent lesbian fucking a staple of pornography. Of the three films, *Arioso* is most guilty of this (despite its prime-time family audience), with its whole misty pastel ambience borrowed from *Emmanuelle* by way of David Hamilton. For me, however, this voyeurism was only a bit more troubling than the other two films' opposite tendency, their eagerness to be chaste, "tasteful" (to borrow Astin's word). These films, *By Design* especially, desexualize and thus dehumanize the lesbian relationship. Even the word *lesbian* is conspicuously suppressed in both *By Design* and *Arioso*. To her credit, Langlois is much more open to nonprurient, spontaneous kissing and touching between her lovers than is Jutra.

All the same, I won't go along with a blanket condemnation of this recent batch of films. I've been complaining too long about media neglect for that. Stirrings of insight and future hopes exist in all three of these films, even in *Arioso*. For one thing, the insemination films suggest that comedy is a good place to look for future breakthroughs. After all, aren't our own best films about ourselves comedies, from *Comedy in Six Unnatural Acts* to *Taxi zum Klo*? *Désiré* . . . in particular succeeds in building a "light, funny" tone on a refusal of tired moralizations and sentimentalizations, and an awareness of the subversive possibilities of our lives. Langlois and Jutra both show their heroines wandering about sizing up potential studs and come up with surprisingly fresh and funny views of the presumptions of the straight male animal. All three films perceive the humor, as well as the oppression and comfort, of the closet, and all are more or less skilled in imaging the behavioral nuances of lovers who trust and support each other.

Even *Arioso*, for all its suds, surprised me with dialogue like this exchange between the writer and her suitor, who is taunting her for her lesbianism without ever saying the word: "Do you know what you are?" "Yes, I know. So say the word then, if you enjoy it. Say it. Men love that word. They use it against you when you resist them. Say it."

Some small ground exists, then, for encouragement. Contributors to all three films should be kept in sight, and Forcier has been writing positively about lesbians since before Stonewall. Mightn't *Arioso* be yet another woman's script betrayed by a male director and crew—it wasn't she who put all the guck on the lens, the pastels in the decor, and plenty of both on the actresses' eyelids. As for Jutra, it must be remembered how he came out himself, solitary, courageous, in his first feature, the autobiographical *A tout prendre*, almost twenty years ago. If *By Design* takes off, will he return to the subject that he has had to suppress ever since? Fox, for her part, has struggled doggedly to produce commercially viable women's features in the Canadian context for almost a decade, mortgaging and remortgaging her home again and again. Despite such past failures as Joyce Wieland's *The Far Shore* and Jutra's film of Margaret Atwood's *Surfacing*, Fox is still bursting with ideas about bringing women into the film industry and deserves another chance at least. These films are precedents that the film and TV industries may well follow up on, not to mention independents like Langlois. I am told that Radio Canada is already delighted with the seven-to-one ratio of positive calls to negative after *Arioso*.

No, the nonsexist utopia has not yet arrived in movieland. But there are reasons for cautious optimism.

The Body Politic, no. 82 (April 1982): 38

Two Strong Entries, One Dramatic Exit:

Luc ou la part des choses, Another Way, and *Querelle*

*   *   *   *   *

Nineteen eighty-two was the year of Making Love, *Hollywood's disastrous attempt to cash in on the latest of the periodic queer cycles that have turned up regularly throughout its history (yes, even during the Hays period). This time it was* La Cage aux Folles, Victor Victoria, Personal Best, *then the* Making Love *flop, and then the predictable decade of silence until* Philadelphia. *Needless to say, as a critic on the political margins, I studiously ignored the brave but pathetic spectacle of Harry Hamlin and Michael Ontkean pretending they were gay and instead as usual found myself in the trap of focusing on the foreign festival fare. Although I was right that Michel Audy undeservedly would never catch on, even in Quebec,* Another Way *has become a modest classic, whereas* Querelle *remains in the firmaments—especially if you don't have to see it more than once every five years or so. Students don't really respond to it these days, especially if they're shown the original English-language version: I haven't changed my mind about the downbeat alienation stuff and the shock of dirty talk in an art movie going over much better in a foreign language. This review was my passionate farewell to Fassbinder, a queer artist I responded to personally more than any other— even though (especially since?) he'd been so vicious to me when I'd interviewed him the previous year with idolatry and labels in my eyes. How was he to know I wasn't just another know-it-all gay-lib academic?*

*   *   *

Limousines and Lana Turner retrospectives don't keep starving Quebec filmmakers happy, but the Montreal World Film Festival usually keeps gay moviegoers at least occupied. This year was a real high. Not only did we get the first ever gay (or rather lesbian) film from Eastern Europe, the miraculous Hungarian *Another Way*, and the first gay feature out of Quebec in al-

Another Way (1982): a Hungarian film telling it like it is. Museum of Modern Art Film Stills Library.

most a decade, *Luc ou la part des choses*, but we were also treated to a sneak preview of Fassbinder's last film, *Querelle*, a dramatic exit if I ever saw one.

The Hungarians always did have the gayest of all the Soviet-bloc national cinemas, from the sensuous socialist-feminism of Marta Meszaros to the long-legged peasant-butch chorus lines of Miklos Jansco. Enough of ambiguity. *Another Way* is up-front. Set in the tense political atmosphere of the late fifties, it shows the love relationship between two women journalists. One of the women, Livia, is married. The other, Eva, has been around and so makes the first move—stealing Livia's panties. Wonderfully portrayed by Jadwiga Jankowska-Cieslak (she got the Cannes best actress prize), Eva refuses to compromise either her lesbian identity or her political integrity. The two refusals seem one and the same: it is no accident that a bureaucrat, enraged at her insistently truthful reporting about peasant collectivization, calls her a "lesbian bitch." At one point the lovers are arrested for necking in the park and are told by the cop that they're not in America. This is far truer than he knows: when was the last time you saw a film from the West in which the lesbian set a moral or political standard by which all others were judged and found wanting?

Luc ou la part des choses (1982): a small-town teenager's crisis of self-discovery. Museum of Modern Art Film Stills Library.

Of course, it all ends tragically. But, as in *Bent*, quite similar in its images of underground survival and resistance, the dead queer is a martyr of history, not a victim of artistic bigotry.

Luc ou la part des choses (Luc or His Share of Things) is an engaging low-budget feature about a 20-year-old mechanic's crisis of self-discovery. Can you believe that this tender and positive film was coproduced by the Quebec Ministry of Education for the training of psychologists and social workers? It turned out so well that it will be opening soon theatrically.

It's a steamy summer in Trois-Rivières. Luc and his friend François, resisting familial pressure to get married, are spending a lot of time lazing around with their girlfriends and even more time with each other. Stripped down to their jogging shorts, they work on a boat that is to take them out on a two-week escape. Or else they lie around on the roof drinking beer—Trois-Rivières comes across as a town of lyrical, hazy roofscapes, the kind of pretty little place gay people can't wait to get away from, though director Michel Audy views it with great affection. Louis, the obnoxious town faggot who keeps showing up when the two couples or the two buddies want to be alone, strikes the only note of discordance.

One day Luc goes for a cycle ride with a blue-eyed, dark-bearded stranger and lets himself get carried away on the banks of a river where they've gone skinny-dipping. Word gets out, and things suddenly change. Luc is queer-bashed by two drunken coworkers and impulsively swallows a handful of pills. He spends the last half of the film listening to François's endless professions of support and tolerance. He also gradually opens himself up to Louis, who doesn't seem so obnoxious anymore and understands things that François cannot. Starting to rebuild his identity, Luc finally heads for Montreal, where the rooftops may not be so lovely but where there may be space to grow.

In a sense *Luc* is a kind of working-class *Making Love*, without the glossiness and softheadedness and with more willingness to leave the ending open.

I was afraid *Querelle* was going to be a mess. Neither Jeanne Moreau nor Brad Davis had had experience with Fassbinder's style of filmmaking. Furthermore, shooting this German adaptation of a French classic in English was asking for trouble. But I should have known: we couldn't have asked Fassbinder for a more magnificent testament.

Querelle is a faithful reworking of Jean Genet's 1953 novel of the existential sailor who murders, loves, and double-crosses. It is also a highly original work, Fassbinder's gayest and most passionate film and in some ways his most experimental one.

Fassbinder retains most of Genet's sexual iconography but adds a few contemporary touches, from the cop's Folsom Street leather getup to Davis/Querelle's Nautilized biceps. And although Fassbinder drops Genet's head scenes to concentrate wholly on fucking doggy style, he retains Genet's deliriously religious vision of sexual submission, transforming close-up sweat and spit into sacraments. Fassbinder has always distrusted sexual passion, but here, in keeping with his source, he lets out all the stops. A final kissing scene escalates from the earlier fuck scenes, with Davis/Querelle unable to fuse completely with, or pry himself away from, the lips of the fellow murderer he suddenly loves so much that he must betray him.

Querelle (1982): Fassbinder's dramatic exit—Saint Brad (right) and the man who will fuck him. Museum of Modern Art Film Stills Library.

This electric combination of star presence and outlaw ecstasy is a milestone worthy of the decade, light-years beyond the nice characters and chaste, awkward embraces of *Making Love*. I repent all the contempt I've ever felt toward Brad Davis for his closety roles in *Midnight Express* and *A Small Circle of Friends*. Now, with this courageous and committed performance, Davis can serve as our very own celluloid saint.

It's a film you will either love or hate, perhaps both. The sets are too gorgeous, stylized in the extreme, even for Fassbinder, with cock-shaped towers on the Brest seawall and orange Day-Glo skies. The slow-motion combat ballets and Marguerite Duras pacing are uncompromising to say the least. And of course there are the problems with casting and voices that I expected. Jeanne Moreau looks very unhappy, and it's hard not to snicker as she tells Davis/Querelle in her deadpan voice, "I've dreamt a lot about your prick. You have a solid, heavy, massive prick, not elegant but strong." The lugubrious male narrator is no less distracting when discussing similar affairs in Genet's literary slang: "Querelle, having always been fucked, didn't know how to fuck a guy." But Fassbinder's power has always lain in his nearness to the ridiculous. *Querelle* is no exception.

My excitement about these three important films is tempered by the question of their distribution. *Querelle* will certainly get released—you're never hotter than when you're just dead—but will it last? I predict that the straight critical establishment just won't be able to deal with it: *Variety* is already warning exhibitors against the film's "tedium," its "pretension," and its "specialized chances." *Luc*, I'm afraid, is also doomed to a short commercial run. Critics have started pooh-poohing its "didacticism," and I have my doubts whether the producers will push for the subtitling necessary for exposure outside Quebec. Its most important career will probably be in the educational and alternative ghetto. As for *Another Way*, I haven't heard a thing, though its chances may not be too bad with its Cannes prize and its slot in the upcoming New York festival. But don't hold your breath. If *Personal Best* can't break even despite its *Playboy* publicity, is there any hope for a Hungarian film that tells it like it is?

The Body Politic, no. 88 (November 1982): 41–42

Hollywood's Change of Heart?

(*Porky's* and *The Road Warrior*)

*   *   *   *   *

A time capsule of a long hot summer of 1982. I'm glad someone kept a record of these images of banality and hate. Most of these minor films I saw in the small university town of Bloomington, Indiana, where I spent what would turn out to be a very historic summer: during the long empty evenings Hollywood was force-feeding me, thanks to its monopoly on the U.S. hinterland, but during the day I was researching in the archives of the Kinsey Institute. From here would emerge fourteen years later my life's work, Hard to Imagine. *Quelle divided sensibility!*

Randal Kleiser and Colin Higgins, hmmm. I did have at least some kind of an agenda in my filmgoing, a purely scholarly curiosity about the presence of gays within the industry and their stamp on the assembly-line product in which queers seemed to be more and more visible and less and less nice (I forget how I knew Kleiser and Higgins were gay, other than the usual gaydar). Thirteen years later Kleiser came out and made one of Hollywood's more underrated AIDS *melodramas,* It's My Party. *Meanwhile, the talented comic Higgins was long since dead, one of the early Hollywood casualties to the embryonic epidemic that I was only vaguely aware of that intense summer in Indiana.*

There was a third film-related activity in Bloomington that summer: biking out to the crystal blue quarry immortalized in Breaking Away *and indulging my obsession with country swimming au naturel. But alas the natives stayed trussed up in Speedos, and Dennis Quaid never showed up to dive off the rocks with me. No wonder I kept going to the movies.*

*   *   *

It's the hottest movie summer ever for the box office. Now that Hollywood's gay "wave" of last spring has been absorbed in the summer swamp, you may wonder if the movie industry's change of heart has registered in the year's other films. Not a chance. Though virtually every commercial and art film

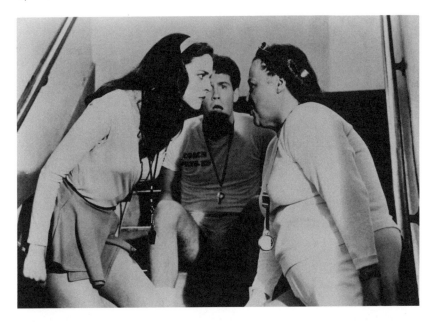

Porky's (1982): obese, castrating, lesbian gym teacher in boy-meets-girl flick. Museum of Modern Art Film Stills Library.

these days has some kind of lesbian or gay reference, the same old roster of stereotypes and formulas seems hardly ruffled at all. Some samples from the current crop:

Queer Villains. Bubblegum sex is one of the big moneymakers of the year and a lot of the boy-meets-girl flicks have gay nasties hovering in the background. *Porky's*, the most profitable Canadian feature ever, is the most odious of them all and features as a heavy an obese, castrating (literally) lesbian (implied) gym teacher. *Private Lessons*, another fantasy of heterosexual initiation, has a gay blackmailer with a toupee as its villain. *Summer Lovers* sets the bubblegum formula in the Greek isles. The pretty American hero gets a lot of sun and sex and is occasionally harassed by a creepy Greek transvestite. Though there's no hint of lesbian intrigue between the hero's two topless girlfriends, the worldly French one asks him if he's ever made it with a man. When he replies that he's come close (move ahead one square), his uptight American girlfriend tells him not to, since things are already complicated enough (go back two). Very true, but the most obvious thing about *Lovers*, in case no one has noticed, is director Randal Kleiser's (*Grease, The Blue Lagoon*) sure eye for beefcake, or rather calfcake. If only he directed as well as he leers and makes money. Incidentally, more beefcake from the Hollywood closet is in the jock-strap locker-room production number from Colin Higgins's *The Best Little Whorehouse in Texas*, a bubblegummer for over-thirties. But I digress. Other trends in gay villainy continue in the action picture. The het-rapist heavies of the fascist vigilante epic *Death Wish II* are given eyeliner, earrings, nonmissionary rape positions, and buddy-buddy rape scenes for an extra frisson of repulsiveness before Charles Bronson blows them to smithereens. And of course there is *The Road Warrior*, a huge hit, in which bland macho hero is pursued by snarling war-painted gay villain avenging his boyfriend. So what if it's all lots of fun—it's still scary when audiences cheer a gay character getting creamed.

Queer Jokes. In *Night Shift*, the comedy sleeper of the summer, poor pimp Henry Winkler finds himself in jail and says things couldn't be worse. Gay cellmate winks and blows him a kiss. Winkler says he was wrong. Very funny. In the same vein, *The Pirate Movie*, another bubblegummer, offers a few mincing pirates whenever the complete dearth of ideas becomes too evident. Who said Australian movies were tasteful? Last year's *On Golden Pond* has been playing around all summer because of the Oscar. If lesbian jokes come from Saint Henry Fonda, they must be all right. Is it a coincidence that such jokes surface in a film with Hollywood's two toughest actresses?

Sad and Lonely Department. The main qualifier here this season is Roberta Muldoon, the six-foot transsexual ex-football player in *The World According to Garp*. She's so dignified and noble despite her depressing loveless life. The pubescent jerks I saw the film with, however, insisted that she was the funniest freak they'd ever seen and drowned out all the dialogue for twenty minutes after each of her appearances (so much so that they missed the antifeminist theme). The only other Sad and Lonely I've seen recently (now that *Fame, 10, Partners,* and *Victor Victoria* have come and gone) is James Caan's suicidal twerp in Claude Lelouch's *Les uns et les autres*, finally released in English as *Bolero* after an endless Montreal run in French. Are there no more liberals out there?

Dead Queer Movies are a bit less popular now that low farce has taken over from slash thrillers as *the gay* genre. But just for the record, the opening audience-grabber of the British gangster flick *The Long Good Friday* is not one but three gay corpses, one stabbed in colorful detail during a shower encounter at a public pool.

Lesbian Freaks. A huge moneymaker in Quebec this year has been *Scandale,* a boring jerkoff rip-off masked as political satire. Watch for a hip fuck scene where two s/m/punk lesbians run scissors over each other's genitals. An English-Canadian version is imminent.

To make a long story short, the movies aren't exactly discouraging the queer-bashers among the mass market of fifteen-year-old white straight males that movies are made for. Furthermore, now that the lackluster financial performance of the gay "breakthrough" films has contradicted the *Cage aux folles* gold rush, we might as well settle in for another decade of the negative bit parts and fag jokes.

Is it time to show some more *Cruising*-style muscle? Black groups in the States have launched a boycott of a long "white list" of films made without black input, targeting dozens of films, including E.T. The same tactic could not work for us. More effective pressure could aim at single projects, as happened with *Cruising.* I've heard that Hollywood's most notorious homophobe, Paul Schrader (*American Gigolo*), is developing a script on the life of the gay Japanese writer Yukio Mishima. Let's tell Paul to mind his own business, and make him listen.

Unpublished, 1982

Dreams, Cruises, and Cuddles in Tel Aviv:

Amos Gutmann's *Nagua*

* * * * *

Another talented young filmmaker who would die of AIDS*! What a morbid job this re-editing has turned out to be—and the worst is yet to come. Gutmann's second film to make the rounds,* Amazing Grace *(1992, the year before his death), also turned out to be a fine one and this time received the recognition it deserved at home.*

* * *

Not being a fan of the heterosexual Israeli cinema, I had certain trepidations before my first exposure to the gay Israeli cinema last month at the Montreal World Film Festival. Especially since it was to be a film about a gay Israeli filmmaker making a film.

Nagua, then, was a refreshing surprise. In fact it was by far the most pleasant and positive gay movie in a festival cluttered with a half dozen or so "gay" movies so morbid and morose that they made last year's revelation *Querelle* seem like *The Dick Van Dyke Show*.

Robi, *Nagua*'s hero, works in his grandmother's grocery store, cruises the Tel Aviv parks, and cuddles with his married buddy while dreaming of their future appearance on the Academy Awards presentations show, all the while waiting somewhat unrealistically for a windfall from a rich film producer. His mother lives in Europe and keeps sending him letters, hoping that his next film won't be about "that subject" again; his grandmother complains good-naturedly about being left to look after a pederast and screams "terroristi" whenever she sees an Arab. Robi is also lining up his cast, maybe someone from among his tricks or his friends, but wonders at the same time whether he wants to make movies just to be able to push people around.

He's no angel of course: he can be a little arrogant, gets crushes that are

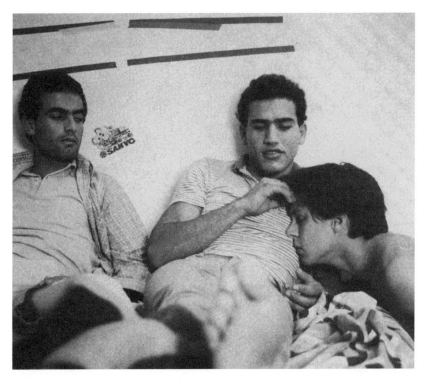

Amos Gutmann's *Nagua* (1983): Robi (right) and his Arab boyfriends. Publicity still.

as dumb as any of yours or mine, and tends to be a bit cruel to people that come on to him. In short he's no more fucked up than the rest of us. But he's enormously likable, and this presumably autobiographical portrait works because it's so unpretentious and sincere, managing to combine self-criticism with a healthy self-esteem. Not to mention a finely tuned sense of humor and an understanding of and respect for lust. I don't know anything about the director and cowriter, Amos Gutmann, except that he's in his twenties, is Hungarian-born, is a graduate of the Tel Aviv School of Television and Film, and has to be very brave, very persistent, and very talented to have made this film. Let's hope Gutmann will not turn out to be one of those flash-in-the-pan filmmakers who have managed to unload their whole soul on celluloid and then never get a chance for a sequel.

Robi's story is vividly textured by a sense of the Israeli society around him—its Americanized youth culture, its laid-back Mediterranean aura continuously intruded on by references to the permanent war footing, its pervasive homophobia, and its "multi-cultural" composition. With regard to the last of these, the film is relatively up-front. At one point Robi harbors an Arab neighbor who has been "hurt in an explosion" and ends up getting him to fuck him, seemingly out of a vaguely rebellious whim that I'd rather not analyze. There's no sense in the film of the Israeli gay movement though, which I understand to be having a fairly hard time, but a very colorful sense of the gay *community* (despite a rather unfortunate impression that everyone is under thirty, male, and gorgeous).

At the beginning of the film Robi tells us head-on that Israeli society won't accept his film because it's not about war heroes or social workers and that the gay community won't either because it isn't positive or ego enforcing. He's right about the first one: I hear that the government has caused trouble all the way from the financing (they blocked a grant) to its accreditation for foreign festivals (a film showing an Arab fucking a male Jew as Zionist propaganda?). I'm not surprised. But as for the gay response to *Nagua*, Robi may be wrong. *Nagua* is by no means perfect, but we haven't had such a tough, sensitive, self-aware, funny little film about ordinary gay people from anywhere in ages, and I hope it catches on.

The Body Politic, no. 98 (November 1983): 40–41

Hauling an Old Corpse Out of Hitchcock's Trunk: *Rope*

*   *   *   *   *

A lot of water has flowed under the bridge since 1983, and much has now been written about Hitchcock's homophobia, which rather than "too obvious to get in a tizzy over" has turned out to be rather complex[1] (not to mention other aspects of his sexual ideology). And we've also had Tom Kalin's disturbing remake of the Leopold and Loeb case, Swoon (1992), one of the revelations of the New Queer Cinema. And, oh yes, Rope *scriptwriter Arthur Laurents eventually made it official. This all probably makes* Rope *look a lot more interesting now than it did in 1983, but I still stand by my aversion to the Hitchcock industry all the same.*

*   *   *

A lot of hoopla has surrounded the release of five rare Hitchcock films made in Hollywood between 1948 and 1958. The first of them, *Rope* (1948), which premiered recently at the Montreal Film Festival, has been eagerly awaited by gays because of its reputation as the only Hollywood movie made before 1960 with explicitly gay protagonists.

I had never met anyone who had seen *Rope*. But I knew like every other film buff that it involved a gay male couple who murder a classmate to test pop-Nietzschean philosophy about moral superiority or something and then serve cocktails to the victim's family and fiancée on a trunk containing the corpse. Vito Russo describes the script's 1948 run-in with the censors, who removed all the "homosexual dialogue" like "my dear boy."

As it turns out, the film is an archival curiosity of interest only to specialists in Hitchcock and camera movements, embarrassing dabblings in the margins of the career of an Important Artist. What is more, the film as it now exists confirms Russo's account and is so bowdlerized that most spectators wouldn't even have picked up on the two murderer's gayness without the helpful program notes. I caught only one explicit reference: at the end they are accused of having killed a man who lived and loved as they never could. Nevertheless, there's no doubt that they're supposed to be gay: 1983 spectators aren't used to the devious codes used thirty-five years ago to maneuver gay and lesbian characters around the censors. This happened especially, as Richard Dyer has noted, in "film noir," the brooding thriller genre that provided most of the rare gay characters during the dark ages of Hollywood's self-censoring Production Code (the men were usually fastidious, luxury-loving villains of a Nazi or other similarly warped persuasion).

This may or may not prove what a horrid homophobe Hitchcock was, a thesis that *Christopher Street* recently promoted in an unaccountably angry and shocked cover story. I don't disagree with the argument, but Hitchcock's homophobia, to my mind a slightly obsessive version of the usual run-of-the-mill forties variety, has always seemed to me only slightly more interesting than, say, Picasso's sexism or T. S. Eliot's Anglicanism—that is, crucial to an understanding of their work but too obvious to get in a tizzy over. In any case, of the five new releases, *Rear Window* (1954) and *Vertigo* (1958) are indisputably more worthy of revival than *Rope*, since they are about the voyeurism and obsession inherent in (hetero)sexuality, a subject that the late great straight Sir Alfred was presumably more knowledgeable about.

What was most interesting for me in *Rope*, curiously, was two footnotes. The first is the identity of the scriptwriter, Arthur Laurents. Laurents is known also as the writer for *West Side Story* (which assembled more famous closet cases as collaborators than any other musical in world history), as the scriptwriter for the 1977 ballet-film turkey *The Turning Point* (which emerged stripped of Laurents's gay subplots to present an unrecognizable, strictly hetero New York dance scene), and most recently as the director for the hit Broadway version of *La Cage aux Folles*. A very "interesting" career. Why would gay writers have written homophobic scripts way back when? Quite obviously, the only way to express your sexual difference directly, at least in Hollywood, was within established homophobic conventions, and the most appropriate convention was the film noir. So what if your gay characters were cold-blooded killers—at least they had wit and style, which is a lot more than costar Jimmy Stewart had.

The other footnote is actor Farley Granger, who plays the tremblingly timorous partner who doesn't have the stomach to calmly eat appetizers on a corpse. He's my favorite of the small group of "sensitive" stars who became associated with "unmasculine" roles at this time. Hitchcock, it goes

Rope (1948): "sensitive" star Farley Granger quivers at right. Museum of Modern Art Film Stills Library.

without saying, didn't appreciate Granger's exquisite loveliness (at least not as much as Luchino Visconti did, squeezing him into tight white uniform breeches for his epic *Senso* [1954]), but Granger is a fine presence in *Rope* all the same. I kept hoping that he would stop all that tedious quivering that Hitchcock was putting him through, beat the rap, and escape with his lover far away from all those boring straights on the set, perhaps to live happily ever after in Morocco. Maybe Laurents can provide a sequel when he's done with *La Cage*.

The Body Politic, no. 99 (December 1983): 40

Note

1 See an excellent dossier of six articles in Corey K. Creekmur and Alexander Doty, eds., *Out in Culture: Gay, Lesbian, and Queer Essays on Popular Culture* (Durham: Duke University Press, 1995), 183–281.

Sex beyond Neon: Third World Gay Films?

*　*　*　*　*

The overthrow of the Marcos regime was still a few years away, but at least the Argentine junta had just met its comeuppance. And things seemed hopping in general throughout the South during this peak of the Rambo/Reagan era. Once again a Hollywood production, this time an unusually good one about Third World politics, acted as my foil for the modest films I was trying to rescue from oblivion: Kiss of the Spider Woman. *This time they're not all exclusively "gay" films, and that may be why this is one of my better festival reports.* Camila *is the only one of these films that I've seen since, and I love it now much more than I seemed to then, not only because of the furry-chested Spanish heartthrob who plays the weak but gorgeous priest, nor because it retroactively became a "gay film" when director Luisa Bemberg later came out, but also, well, because I'm older now, as she was when she made the film, and am sorry I called it "pretty," and because outside of the cloudy festival context, it is a great film.*

Meanwhile, history was galloping fast: the same issue of The Body Politic *had the first farewell to the late Rock Hudson.*

*　*　*

Statistically at least, the ninth annual Montreal World Film Festival was the most successful ever. So big and indiscriminate that one's benumbed senses can scarcely distinguish real patterns and revelations from hype and noise. Nevertheless, profiting from the chaos, one could lose oneself in a few selected corners and find interesting things going on that seemed totally unrelated to the (boring) Official Competition and Official Hoopla.

This is exactly what I did, and I was happily surprised to discover that the Third World films buried all over the festival were astir with fascinating imagery of sexual ferment and even a glimpse or two of gay liberation. Surprised, because my experience of films from the developing world, with the possible exception of Brazil, has been of rigidly straightlaced images of the family and traditional sexual roles as a refuge from a chronic economic and

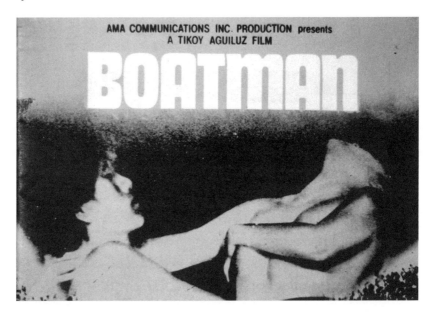

Boatman (Philippines, 1985): sex scenes and anguished politics. Publicity still.

political crisis. Now there are hints everywhere that sexuality may be connected to the political realm after all. It was those hints, both bold and tentative, that made the Third World entries infinitely more appealing than the jaded neon silliness of the Isabelle Adjani vehicles clogging the rest of the festival.

A case in point was *Boatman*, a violently incoherent first feature by Philippine Tikoy Aguiluz. A tragedy of a country boy trapped as a porno star in the Manila sex industry, *Boatman* exposes the permeation of sexual alienation and consumerism throughout Philippine society along with walkmans and U.S. military bases. Sexual diversity is also visible, with some harsh background images of Western gays exploiting native teenagers, and a relatively sympathetic foreground portrait of a fluttery queen who befriends the (unassailably straight) hero. Included along the way is an acerbic satire of Hollywood companies using Philippines landscape for their *Rambo*-style Vietnam shoot-em-ups. But Aguiluz plays the sex game and the *Rambo* game both ways, aiming for and apparently getting a big box office hit: every ten minutes there is the requisite sex scene, complete with misty close-ups and elevator music, and the final explosion of violence at the end would do Hollywood proud (the hero is beaten to a pulp and then vividly castrated). Does the castration somehow expiate the director's guilty success, does it function as a puritanical punishment for the hero-victim's sexual corruption, or is it a symbolic statement of the victimization of Philippine society by imperialism? Probably all three, but in the meantime sexuality is incontestably established as the anguished terrain of politics.

Such anguish is nowhere apparent in Désiré Ecaré's *Visages de femmes,* a seductively light essay-fiction from the Ivory Coast on changing women's roles. For once, such a discourse focuses not only on economic and political struggles but on sexual ones as well. Ecaré matches traditional women's choruses about the joy of cheating on their husbands with a funny narrative about a young village woman who is doing just that, centered not on guilt and treachery but on pleasure and sensuality. Until recently positive erotic images were all too rare in African films. Ecaré's centerpiece is the heroine's long romp with her hunky boyfriend by the village pond. After hours of basic aquatic fucking and jungle gamboling, the heroine still wants more from her limp, exhausted paramour and, leaning back, points imperiously at her still unsatisfied cunt.

Things will never be so simple in Latin America, where open and joyous expression of any sexuality, let alone the nonpatriarchal variety, has as often as not been linked to death or to the spectacle of tropicalismo marginality. But the edifice of Catholic guilt is beginning to shake. The genre of women realizing taboo desires is going strong, for example. It's incest in Venezuelan Fina Torres's lovely *Oriane* (one of the festival's slew of first features by women) and in Cuban Humberto Solas's *Amada,* and it's kinky adulterous slumming in the Brazilian *Alem da Paixao,* by Bruno Barreto (who may have inaugurated the genre with *Dona Flor and Her Two Husbands* in 1976).

The Argentine version of the genre is *Camila,* a well-publicized romance based by Maria Luisa Bemberg on an actual incident involving an heiress and a priest under a nineteenth-century dictatorship. The parallel with repression under a more recent junta is all but explicit, and it's easy to see why this pretty film about doomed sexual passion has been seen as the official cinematic celebration of that country's return to liberalized civilian rule.

I preferred three other Argentine celebrations of liberation, however, perhaps because they deal with recent history directly rather than through the oblique coding of romantic legend. *Los Chicos de la Guerra,* a probing of the victimization of Argentines of all classes by the Falklands war, is notable in my mind for the decidedly nonmacho image of its vulnerable protagonists. *La Historia Oficial* is a kind of Jane Fonda melodrama in which a middle-class, middle-aged woman, exulting belatedly in the joys of motherhood after adopting a child during the junta, slowly awakens to the fascism and machismo of official history: her adopted child was stolen from "disappeared" parents, and her husband, whom she must now defy, has been instrumental in the oppression around her. As befits the Jane Fonda genre, her prim hairdo slowly loosens and tumbles down around her shoulders as she begins to revolt against her enforced ignorance. Norma Aleandro's performance as the doughty heroine won her the Best Actress prize at Cannes and I'm sure had no small part in securing the Public's Prize for *Historia Oficial* at the Toronto festival.

The fourth Argentine film, *Adios Roberto*, I've saved for last because it was among the festival's most unexpected pleasures. This comedy about a placid man who leaves his wife and child and suddenly finds himself with a male lover with whom he is very surprised to be very happy seems to me to be, in its own modest and somewhat timid way, among the first filmic statements of gay liberation from the Third World (Hector Babenco's *Pixote* was another such milestone). The references to the immediate political past may be fewer than those punctuating every other Argentine film I saw (only a few jokes about such things as police harassment and death squads), but *Adios Roberto* must still be considered another expression of the new breath of fresh air in the country and its cinema. Even the clichés—the lover is a bit too fussy; a lesbian character is a bit too severely madeup; the triangle of emergent homosexual, abandoned wife, and lover is a bit too stacked—seem resuscitated by the new faces and new context.

To North American eyes *Adios Roberto*'s timidity may seem disappointing. Socially, the gay couple is situated within a respectable urban middle-class universe that is light-years from *Pixote*'s lumpen denizens and all the other Brazilian drag queens of the *cinema novo* and after (*Alem da Paixao* has two of them, a real one, an aging plump cabaret performer right out of *Cage aux folles* who also has a small part in *Kiss of the Spider Woman*, and a phoney one who strips off his wig to become a macho stud to help the heroine discover her sexuality). Equally timidly, Roberto's fine romance has no kissing and no sex, unless you consider sex to be a gentle pat on the stomach and the drunken arms-over-the-shoulder prelude to the film's momentous seduction. ("Stay with me." "You're drunk." "Not as drunk as I'm letting on." Cut to the morning after.)

Perhaps it's understandable that director Enrique Dawi didn't want to rush things. After all gays and lesbians were targeted by the fascists along with leftists, unionists, and other subversives, and the great gay Argentine novel *Kiss of the Spider Woman* could only be made in Brazil with Hollywood stars and money. *Adios Roberto* is a film about freedom, not homosexuality, was the standard old lie Dawi had ready for the Montreal audience. But it's only a white lie because *Adios Roberto* is obviously about both.

The Body Politic, no. 120 (November 1985): 31–32

Fassbinder Fiction: A New Biography

*   *   *   *   *

One of the last pieces I wrote for The Body Politic *before the historic experiment was dissolved by its heroic collective. The exemplary community political newspaper, aptly named, succumbed not to the hate campaign of the Tory government and the Toronto police but to burnout and the forces of the marketplace.*

In 1986 I clearly hadn't gotten Fassbinder's death, nor even Pasolini's, out of my system. As I write this in the winter of 1998, a full retrospective of every single Fassbinder work imaginable has appeared in town, fresh from runs in New York and other centers, and the canonization of RWF is complete.

*   *   *

In January 1977 I was responsible for a rather hyperbolic feature in these pages, alerting TBP readers to a new gay radical star on the movie horizon, Rainer Werner Fassbinder. As a champion of Fassbinder's brutal dramas of love and victimization, I was faced even then with people whispering to me about Fassbinder's private life, about how he'd driven this or that lover to suicide; beaten up this or that actor; was a racist, misogynist, and dope fiend. After the filmmaker's death in 1982, from an accidental OD at the age of 37, the whispers became a roar.

I was never sure how to deal with this information about an artist who continued to rise in my estimation with each successive new release among his more than forty films. I always suspected the straights among the whisperers of wanting to chip away at a great gay idol out of pure envy, and I felt like sending them off packing to meditate on Hemingway or Belushi. But at the same time, I somehow knew it was all too true. Should I repudiate the films on the grounds that "the personal is political" and an artist who couldn't run his own life and treated people like shit couldn't make good films? Should I genuflect before the shrine of the *artiste maudit* and mutter the credos about tormented gay genius sacrificing life and love to the higher calling of art, recycling his suffering as raw material for the mills of creativ-

Fassbinder and me (c. 1981). Photo Concordia AVD.

ity? Or was the "autonomy of art" the only rejoinder, the irrelevance of an artist's life to the ultimate meaning of his or her work?

I always resisted falling into any of these traps, not because they're all false but because they're all a bit true, and all a bit insidious. So I've kept sitting quietly on the fence, preferring to explore the inexhaustibility of the films themselves rather than trying to relate them to the myth of the exploiter who drained his collaborators' blood out onto the screen, the self-destructive loser who couldn't apply any of his artistic wisdom to his own life.

Now we have a "tell-it-all" biography that endeavors to dislodge the fence-sitters: *Fassbinder Film Maker*, by Ronald Hayman, a British biographer-critic and former theatrical actor and director. The book is a "serious" addition to the small industry around Fassbinder's biography (another item is a fascinating feature film *A Man Like Eva*, starring the Fassbinder actress Eva Mattes in a drag portrait-à-clef of Fassbinder). Hayman's detailed chronicle of the filmmaker's personal life and artistic evolution follows him from his lonely childhood through his wunderkind days in the Munich theatrical avant-garde to his final years as the workaholic international superstar. Based primarily on interviews with the main collaborators, the book's only obvious imbalances come from the absence of perennial cast members Hanna Schygulla, Gunther Kaufmann, and Irm Hermann and perhaps too great a reliance on Kurt Raab, one of Fassbinder's cast-off collaborator-lovers.

The danger of the biographical myth, especially for artists who create better than they live, is that the life often becomes a marketable and inextricable part of the art. Just as with Pasolini's murder in 1975, Fassbinder's tragic death somehow becomes a culmination of his artistic vision, a kind of metaphorical punishment for his success and, inevitably, for both his sexual nonconformity and his refusal to accept the world as it is.

I'm afraid that Hayman's contribution ultimately falls into this trap. His theme is explicit from the very beginning: Fassbinder's "importance as a film maker depends on his ability to translate his neurosis into cinematic fiction." No doubt most artists translate the dynamics of their personal lives into their art, some like Fassbinder closer to the surface than others. The problem is that Hayman reduces the complexity of this translation to a simplistic and literal one-to-one grafting of life onto art. Again and again crude equivalences are established between biographical anecdotes from Fassbinder's life and plot details from the films. Furthermore the connections are often deployed in a web of superficial intellectual references or in a grating language of pop psychology. At one point we are asked, for example, to swallow "the female half of his psyche"; at another point we are led into a discourse on loneliness and the "Angst (with a capital A) that ensues from it."

Worse, the endless psychologizing takes on too often a latently homophobic tone, with quotations from straight "authorities" and discussions of Fassbinder's sexual relationships, especially with men of color, in clinical and pejorative terms. I am uncomfortable, for example, with the way Hayman finds in one script echoes of "the blandishments [Fassbinder] used to entice attractive young men into his orbit and then to keep them in it," as if gay relationships intrinsically involve seduction and exploitation. His repeated descriptions of how Fassbinder would build a film around his current lover make you forget that straight artists have been documenting every

passing lust and liaison for centuries. Even more seriously, Hayman down-
plays Fassbinder's own estimation of the contribution of his gay identity to
his work, most blatantly with his final two works, *Querelle* and *Berlin Alex-
anderplatz*, preferring his own dime-novel Freudian interpretations.

Part of the problem may be that Hayman does not fully understand the
films. Hayman may be perceptive (but long-winded and repetitive) about
Fassbinder's handling of the dynamics of power within all love relations
(and within director-actor relations). But he is in over his head whenever he
dares beyond the terrain of character profiles and literal plot synopses to the
crucial issues of style and sensibility: Fassbinder's brutal humor, his self-
reflective visual language, his postmodern indulgence in camp and pastiche, his comic-strip framing and staggered timing, his performance style
that blends minimalism with Grand Guignol.

These shortcomings segue into another major argument I have with
Hayman's book. The author continually underestimates the political dimension of Fassbinder's work, both the explicit political criticism of West
German society in particular and capitalism in general, and his interroga-
tion of the mechanics of oppression around class, race, sexuality, and the
family. This dimension is at its most lucid and explicit in Fassbinder's least
autobiographical films, such as *Fear Eats the Soul*, and in the historical films
like the "Economic Miracle" trilogy: *Maria Braun, Lola*, and *Veronika Voss*.
Predictably, Hayman finds these films less successful or interesting and
even misreads them, burying their political astuteness under the weight of
his Freudian analysis; Fassbinder's political anger comes across as being ultimately oedipal. Take as an example of Hayman's laundering Fassbinder's
episode in *Germany in Autumn*, a collective work denouncing the increasing abuse of state power in the late seventies (which Hayman characterizes
as some vague response to a cluster of terrorist incidents). It's a brilliantly
succinct dissection of the relationship between the political and the personal, the temptation to fascism in our dealings with our loved ones and
with authority. Executed through semifictional encounters among Fassbinder and his real-life lover and his mother, the episode is a pretext for Hayman to dwell almost exclusively on Fassbinder's real-life relationships, with
the conclusion that his "domestic habits must have been a strain on anyone
who tried to live with him and keep house for him"! The last straw is a con-

cluding generalization that Fassbinder shifted from working-class themes to middle-class themes as his career progressed in order to increase his audience, a reversal of the complex process that actually happened.

In conclusion, it could be added that *Fassbinder Film Maker* does not lack technical problems such as miscaptions and factual errors, sexist and racist usage, and inadequacies in the structure and index. But these are minor compared to the way Hayman's middlebrow snooping arouses appetite without satisfying. We must of course be grateful for the accumulation of raw personal documentation in the book, including new light on Fassbinder's childhood, valuable background information about most of the films, and a wonderful collection of stills (lots of the "gay Fassbinder"—on the set or at parties, relating tenderly or campily to friends and collaborators, even in drag). Hopefully other biographers will make use of Hayman's data to provide us with what we're still waiting for: a convincing exploration of how Fassbinder's psychology and social experience distilled a given historical setting, and of how this distillation intersected with his artistic intent and political vision and translated to the viewer with such an enduring wallop. In the meantime, I'll take Rona Barrett any day.

The Body Politic, no. 126 (May 1986): 32–33

Ashes and Diamonds in the Year of the Queer:

Decline of the American Empire, Anne Trister,

A Virus Knows No Morals, and *Man of Ashes*

*   *   *   *   *

The Montreal film festival may have been in decline but the American Empire wasn't, and there was still lots to write about. And now much to cringe about in this my last piece for TBP. *How glibly I spoke of many things, but especially "our identity": was this a self-aware compromise for the journalistic forum or the simplistic way I really thought in my late thirties before social constructionism became hot and then a cliché? And how fickle my opinions were, dismissing tearjerking here and extolling it on the next page. And as for dreading the next decade of straight filmmakers' stereotypes of* AIDS, *did that take a rocket scientist (the year after* An Early Frost)?

Some parts I do still like, however, namely the treatment of Man of Ashes, *by Nouri Bouzid, a strongman of Maghreb cinema who has maintained a steady production level over the last dozen years, by the way. Recently revived at a Montreal festival,* Man of Ashes *still occasions total avoidance on the part of critical voices.*

This article is a vivid reflection of an international upswing in queer-themed cinema (the original heading for the piece was "Year of the Queer"): in fact, was the New Queer Cinema already here in the mid-eighties on an international level before the trend watchers noticed its belated American branch? That the Quebec cinema in my backyard seemed to be going through a little queer cycle that year with a lineup of several strong films tended to be overshadowed. My favorite was Passiflora, *around which I led a quixotic battle to break damage control censorship by the* NFB *(the government studio). I won the battle, dragging the whole issue onto the CBC National News, but lost the war: the Quebec film critical establishment simply didn't go to bat for this blasphemous* cri de coeur—*whether because it was too experimental, and not very auteur focused, or because there was too much male-male kissing, we'll never know.*

* * *

Ten years ago, when the Montreal World Film Festival began, each new "gay" feature that came along seemed like a milestone in the consolidation of our identity. Now, despite the ever precarious status of our political and social gains, gays and lesbians seem everywhere on both sides of the camera (except perhaps behind the camera in Hollywood). Mere identity or visibility no longer seem a preoccupation. Individual filmmakers now take our identity for granted, exploring instead our history or, not surprisingly, confronting our health crisis or the relation of sexuality to power. Now that we have the luxury of films like *My Beautiful Laundrette* or *Desert Hearts* playing at the local cineplex, speciality gay film festivals are now less urgent than they used to be when they started up in the mid-seventies. Still, old habits die hard, and I haven't yet gotten over the compulsion to inventory each new image of ourselves, like a new millionaire who still hoards string. Is famine around the corner again? Just in case, the following is not a "review" of this year's trends in the noisy marketplace that unfolds annually in Montreal. Rather, it is simply an updating of the gay-image stockpile.

Some local film gluttons were caught looking enviously west at festival time again this year. For the second year in a row, Toronto snared the major gay-lesbian films of the international crop (last year it was *Desert Laundrette*, this year *Doña Caravaggio*). But the consolation prizes were varied and abundant enough here to keep me from complaining. They included new features from Rosa von Praunheim and Werner Schroeter, two of the German gay Big Four (Lothar Lambert and Frank Ripploh didn't make it this year); a promising gay biopic from Greece; a saga of lesbian nuns set in medieval Spain; a New York feature embodying a lesbian perspective of prostitution (Lizzie Borden's *Working Girls*); an intriguing entry in my favorite ongoing category, "Sexual Ferment in the Third World" (last year the Philippines, this year Tunisia . . .); plus major gay male characterizations of the s/m variety in two prizewinning productions from France.

Von Praunheim's *A Virus Knows No Morals* is only one of a rush of features about AIDS to appear recently in West Germany. A hideous melodrama called *AIDS: Too Young to Die* was the first to arrive in Montreal theaters last spring. *Virus*, like von Praunheim's other works, is an acquired taste. A frantic and uneven assemblage of sketches, the film satirizes reactions to the epidemic within both gay and straight society. Von Praunheim lashes out at the army of therapists, medical practitioners, politicians, journalists, clergy, relatives, and gay politicos who exploit the panic and victimize people with AIDS. Grotesque caricature is the main strategy. Von Praunheim himself plays a gay sauna-owner who finds his business threatened by "the American safe sex fad," until his own positive diagnosis. "Please blow me," he whines to his now-threatened lover. "I'll put on three rubbers." *Virus* is brilliantly shot in von Praunheim's garish expressionist mode and played cabaret style by a boisterous young troupe, including a genderfuck chorus line called Thilo von Trotta and the Three Tornados.

In the end gays are all shipped off to a quarantine dystopia called Hellgay-land, from which they are rescued by an underground cell of gay radical zappers. Unfortunately, I didn't meet anyone who responded even as lukewarmly as I did to von Praunheim's excesses. Some objected to the film's odd misogynist tone (the result I think of the circumstantial typecasting: because the male players tend to play gay men with AIDS, women collaborators end up playing gargoylish representatives of homophobic society). Whatever the case, von Praunheim is undeniably right about one thing: rabblerousing is a better means of confronting the epidemic than tearjerking. Let's hope he keeps refining his recipe.

Werner Schroeter shares von Praunheim's morbidity, his admiration of the masculine form, his orientation toward specialized audiences, and of course his nationality—but otherwise they're very different. *The Rose King* is a luxurious parable of roses, desire, and suffering, offering gorgeous Mediterranean teenagers undressing and torturing each other amid gorgeous Mediterranean landscapes. Someone told me it's a retelling of the Christ myth, which is as plausible I guess as the slow-motion oedipal soap opera that is the most obvious layer of meaning. The soundtrack partly compensates for whatever disorientation may ensue, with its rich collage of opera, popular music, and speech in several Mediterranean languages. Though *King* is now playing commercially in Montreal, this spectacle of languid aestheticism left my friend who likes nonviolent linear plots frothing at the mouth and may not last very long in the theaters. If it does, it will be a first, for this pioneering gay artist who influenced everyone from Fassbinder to Syberberg has never been able to get North American distribution.

The versatile Schroeter was also represented in Montreal by a feature-length documentary called *About Argentina*, an essay on political changes in that country that is no less smothered in opera and high camp than *The Rose King* (for example, endlessly indulgent demonstrations of Evita's gowns and jewelery). Bold and profound, it's the only film in the current wave of fresh air from Latin America to explicitly discuss gay political dimensions of fascism, patriarchy, and liberation.

Films like *Doña Herlinda* and *Laundrette* seem so fresh because they hail from those small national cinemas (like our own) that trickle in from outside of the Hollywood axis and inevitably bring together new perspectives on (homo)sexuality that undermine the unquestioned cultural assumptions of our own North American sense of it. Spanish cinema has been one of the gayest in Europe since the death of Franco a decade ago, but *Extramuros* is one of the rare films to deal with lesbianism. Although male-directed, this ascetic potboiler of convent intrigue, religious extremism (runny stigmata and all), and class conflict constructs its nun lovers with integrity and depth and frames them with rich period detail.

The same can be said for the poet hero of the Greek *Meteors and Shadows*, a gentle and moving biography of Napoleon Lapathiotis, a contemporary of Wilde and Cavafy who died in 1944. The film's image of the willowy and effete gay artist leisurely strolling arm in arm with his beloved through a cruisy public garden has been with us since the very beginnings of gay cinema (*Different from the Others*, 1919). Here the stroll proceeds through history as well, as different political contexts weigh down on the man who persists throughout in claiming his right to difference, commitment, and creativity. *Meteors and Shadows* echoes the melancholy rhythm of the stroll, but once the spectator accepts the pace, the rewards are everywhere, from intriguing glimpses of nocturnal subcultures, to rare images of friendships that ripen over decades and poem fragments that beckon beyond the border of the frame.

I've seen only a few films from the Arab world with any substantial references to intermale sexuality (*Adieu Bonaparte* and *Alexandria Why?*, by Egypt's cosmopolitan Youssef Chahine), and these pointed primarily to European affinities. Tunisian director Nouri Bouzid has hardly changed all that with *Man of Ashes*, but at least he has shattered the Arab cinema's silence about, let us say, a certain cultural reality in its backyard. Bouzid's hero, a twenty-four-year-old woodcarver on the brink of an arranged mar-

Man of Ashes (1985): serious sexual anxiety and honest exorcism. Publicity still.

riage, has always had as his best friend a coworker named Farfat, and their relationship, from childhood skinny-dipping and penis comparing to adult philandering, is heightened to a level of sacramental intensity. Both men were raped as boys by a craftsman to whom they were apprenticed, and this, the dramatic flashbacks tell us, has led to serious sexual anxiety for both of them.

Man of Ashes reminds me of all those closety Western films from the sixties in which homosexual themes are buried under respectable male bonding (drunken touching, communal bathing, and boyish sparring), lots of innocent beefcake, heavy-duty identity stress, and the displacement of explicit homosexual references onto a villain (who invariably ends up dead) or a secondary character. *Man of Ashes* uses all of these options, and Farfat is a clear candidate for gay sainthood. The specific question of what it is to be a man is raised repeatedly, even by queer-baiting graffiti, and it's never really resolved—even after the two buddies do in the nasty rapist. Hachemi proceeds to the altar, but Farfat, miraculously avoiding dead-queer status, makes good his escape from their small provincial town to the big city. It is clear that this escape hatch serves not only the character (like some fifties Fellini hero) but also the director and his irrepressible gay text. *Film Comment* has dismissed *Man of Ashes* with the racist sneer, "couscous psychodrama," but the Taormina Film Festival jury thought otherwise and gave it the prize.

I prefer Bouzid's honest exorcism any day to the jaded and violent portrayals of gay power relationships in two cynical French films that have been heaping up raves and prizes. The better of the two is by Claire Devers, a young film school graduate from Paris, who has based her film, *Noir et blanc* (Black and White), on the Tennessee Williams story "Desire and the Black Masseur." This (uncredited) source is a parable of masochism-to-the-death that has a strong erotic tension because of its context of U.S. race relations and black religion. Devers jettisons both Williams's social context and his dream-like allegorical aura, replacing them with a hip, amoral Parisian graininess that robs the story of its social and erotic anchor. Still, I liked the subtlety and humor of the start of the film, in which Devers establishes her passive hero's obsession with the silent black masseur who will knead (some great shots of strong hands manipulating muscles) and then crush his body. It was only when the denouement turned more and more mechanical (literally and figuratively) that the audiences and my attention started streaming for the exits.

Ménage (Tenue de soirée) is an interminable fag joke of a film in which Gérard Dépardieu adds a few more gimmicks (sadism and hooker drag) to his repertory of macho vulnerability and nudity-at-the-drop-of-a-hat. Director Bertrand Blier is famous for beating up female characters, and this film is no exception. The "sluttish" Miou-Miou gets repeatedly knocked around as macho Dépardieu seduces, humiliates, and commandos her "wimpish" little husband. The *Tenue de soirée* poster has been plastered all over town, shouting "Putain de film" (literally "a whore of a film"). "A Pimp of a Film" would have been more appropriate.

Of the above eight films the only film with guaranteed distribution in English Canada is, predictably, the last one. The Canadian festivals racket may have had its best year ever in Vancouver, Toronto, Montreal, and elsewhere. But we will only get real cultural dividends from our huge subsidies when

Canadian distributors are motivated to bring us these seven other small revelations of difference as well—once the festivals hoopla is over and life in this Hollywood hinterland gets back to normal.

The Year of the Queer from Quebec

On the whole 1986 has been a bumper year for Canadian features in both languages, and it's about time. Québécois papers also noticed, with some amusement, another milestone: a whole parcel of Quebec films were not only programmed in Toronto but actually stand a chance of catching on at the box office (instead of garnering the occasional polite response by Anglo art-house audiences and the usual not-so-polite response by the Ontario Censors). One of the new Quebec films, Denys Arcand's *Decline of the American Empire*, was honored at Cannes and at Toronto and is turning out to be the first-ever real commercial hit from Quebec in English Canadian theaters.

What interests me, predictably, about the Quebec showing at Toronto is its rich inventory of images of sexuality in flux and its strong stable of full-blooded lesbian and gay-male characters—characters conspicuously absent from Anglo features these days.

Decline, as every Canadian who has been reading the papers now knows, shows a group of academics of the baby-boom generation (four men and four women) talking about the wars and the truces of the sexes for two hours over dinner. It's the kind of film you're sorry has to end, cynical and melancholy yet tender. Spiced with enough humor, eroticism, and melodrama to make it marketable, *Decline* seems to have perfectly matched the mood of its audience in postreferendum, postmodernist, postfeminist, postpopulist, and neo-Bourassa Quebec.

Decline has star charisma also, with a sizzling performance by TV comic Dominique Michel as the expert on the decline of civilizations who, having slept with all the men in the history department, has abandoned her contemporaries for the firmer pastures of graduate students. Her motto is "Words are cheap, baby."

Gay spectators seem divided about whether they like Claude, the gay male art historian (of course) in the group. He's sympathetic and Yves

Decline of the American Empire (1986): Claude, the art historian (right), in Montreal's Mountain cruising area "like an alley cat on the prowl." Publicity still.

Jacques's portrayal is finely nuanced, but not everything about the role rings true. His description of his compulsive cruising on "the Mountain" for example didn't seem exactly right ("like an alley cat on the prowl"), nor did Arcand's stilted accompanying images. What is more I found Claude's completely unguarded frankness about his sexuality with his hetero male colleagues as inconceivable as their full unproblematic acceptance of him as peer. On the other hand, his trusting intimacy with the women was truer and very moving. No one knows what to make of Arcand's giving the gay character an AIDS-like non-AIDS illness (he pisses a very dramatic toiletful of blood early in the picture). I like the film so much (I'm partial to films about gay teachers), I'd rather not think about that one, but if we're in for a decade of AIDS stereotypes from straight filmmakers, I'll pass.

Many feminists have had similar reservations about Arcand's rendering the woman part-time lecturer as a masochist (played by the very unsubmissive rock singer, Louise Portal). At the very least, it's a cruel in-joke, since under-financed Quebec universities depend heavily on underpaid woman part-timers at the bottom of the pecking order. In fact the question of the representation of women sparked an angry debate in the letters column of *Le Devoir*, in which the gay male issue didn't get very respectful consideration (one reader reputedly even asked what an AIDS patient was doing preparing dinners for others). I've never had any delusions about Arcand being profeminist or progay, so I wasn't disappointed with his coming halfway with strong likable portraits of both women and gays. In fact I'm glad that one of Quebec's most talented filmmakers has finally got the opportunity to speak his piece and to get the praise he deserves, not to mention an audience in Wasptown-the-Good.

Yves Simoneau's *Pouvoir intime* (Intimate Power) has none of Arcand's ambitions of pronouncing on generations and civilizations but has the still-enviable merit of being a small-scale heist movie that delivers on its promise of pure delight. Because the audience continuity necessary for a genre tradition is completely missing in Canada (except for Quebec TV melodrama), fully realized genre movies are a rare treat. Of course, we again have a heterosexual male viewpoint of the world, but if anything, Simoneau's gay male characters are even more striking and unexpected than Arcand's. Martial, a burly security guard (Robert Gravel) and his "chum" Janvier (Jacques Lussier), a slight blond waiter, get caught up in a bungled Brinks-style caper by a gang of lovable, small-time thugs (which includes film star Marie Tifo in a tomboyish part whose sex-role reversal complements the refreshing nonstereotype design of the film). Even the straight men are loving and affectionate in this one. Unfortunately, things go very badly for everyone. Suffice it to say that the gay relationship is privileged among the network of caring relationships that seem to be the only thing our losers have going for them. I can't resist mentioning the magically satisfying ending in which for the first time in film history the queer actually gets off with the loot.

Although Léa Pool is somewhat reserved about her public identity, her two prizewinning features, *La Femme de l'hôtel* and this year's new *Anne Trister*, are strong women-identified films that have played in lesbian film series and just can't avoid the label "lesbian cinema." In *Anne Trister*, the heroine, a young European painter (Albane Guilhe), immigrates to Montreal to sort out her identity and her art and in the process encounters and falls in love with a fortyish psychiatrist (Louise Marleau), who both resists and succumbs. Mother/daughter overtones inevitably complicate this intergenerational fling, and both partners emerge transformed. Although by general consensus *Anne Trister* doesn't quite rise to the expectations generated by the phenomenally successful *Femme*, Pool's delicate orchestration of layers of symbols and searchings confirm the thirty-six-year-old director's place as a major Quebec filmmaker of the eighties.

Passiflora is an anarchic semi-/anti-/post-documentary on two mega–media events that hit Montreal in September 1984, the papal visit and the Michael Jackson Victory Tour. Though there is no obvious potential here for gay male representation, *Passiflora* may be the gayest film ever made in Canada. National Film Board veteran Fernand Bélanger codirected it with feminist newcomer Dagmar Gueissez-Teufel. The gay male subversion of the sanctimonious hype fits in so well with the feminist viewpoint that it's as if our natural compatibility proclaimed in all those seventies demonstrations has finally sunk in somewhere. The two filmmakers surround the slickly orchestrated unanimity of rock and religion with fictional sketches of all the "marginal" characters it excludes, gay men and lesbians, women who undergo abortions, transvestites, assorted "neurotics," and even heterosexual lovers. A kiss between two men becomes a refusal to participate; a parade of "papettes" in clerical drag becomes a claim of difference.

So does the film, which may explain why the N F B was reputedly nervous about releasing *Passiflora* and has softpedaled its distribution. My pet peeve for years has been the N F B's arrogant silence toward its gay-lesbian constituency: now that this triumphant and hilarious document of defiance has suddenly emerged as if in penance for decades of contempt, we may not get to see it in English Canada—despite its obvious translatability (didn't we all have to put up with Michael and John Paul that year?). Perhaps a little pressure may make the bureaucrats release it countrywide.

One might well ask why the four major Quebec films of 1986 should offer such a positive balance of gay-lesbian characters and sensibilities. It may not be too surprising that Quebec films are relatively together about sexuality, considering that we are graced with the least neurotic history of film censorship of any province, virtual abortion on demand, and the only provincial human rights legislation protecting sexual orientation. Still, things should not be construed as being hunky-dory—I've been ranting for a full year about the virulent homophobia of last year's festival offering, Claude Gagnon's *Visage pâle*. Regardless of whether next year's output continues the present trend or shows it all to have been a fluke, having four such bonuses appear in our own backyard has made this year's event seem like a real festival of festivals for once.

The Body Politic, no. 132 (November 1986): 25–26

The Kiss of the Maricon, or Gay Imagery

in Latin American Cinema

*   *   *   *   *

This essay came at an explosive moment in the North American lesbian and gay politico-intellectual trajectory: its discovery of the Latin American continent—rather, universe—in its backyard. As Brazilian and Argentine cinemas were testifying in their political and sexual energies to those societies' recent emergence from dictatorship, the anti-Castro documentary Improper Conduct, *codirected by closeted Cuban exile cinematographer Nestor Almendros, was polarizing queer communities along ideological lines as never before. This polarization was exacerbated by the Reagan administration's genocidal contra war on the Nicaraguan revolution (1979–89) and most recently by the infamous Supreme Court decision of June 1986,* Bowers vs. Hardwick, *a major defeat for American lesbians and gays as a political constituency. Meanwhile the first gay-authored Latin American feature film in North American distribution, "out" in the North American sense,* Doña Herlinda and Her Son, *had just appeared and seemed to herald a new frontier in Latin sexual politics and culture. Even Hollywood had jumped on the bandwagon with the first—and last—Oscar-winning Latino-scripted and -directed melodrama about (queer) sex and (left) politics in South America,* Kiss of the Spider Woman.

It was time to take stock of the astonishing ferment that seemed to be coming out of nowhere, and yours truly responded to the summons. Not that I had any expertise in the field whatsoever, but if no one who knew the scene and the languages was going to break the silence, then I was. All the more since the presentation was to kill two birds with one stone: the otherwise heterocentric New Latin American Cinema conference at the University of Iowa, and the otherwise U.S.-centric LA Lesbian and Gay Film Festival. Perhaps some of my brazenness was because, along with a couple of gay politico fuckbuddies from Toronto and LA, I had tasted Cuba firsthand at the Havana Festival in 1985 and knew that much more was happening than reached the screens. . . . (Neither of the major Cuban directors Sergio Giral or Humberto Solas had yet come out, though we knew they were gay through the usual means. We also knew that another major new Cuban epic of beefcake and homosociality, a kind of socialist Pretty in Pink, *was by a closeted gay director and featured his boyfriend in the leading role.)*

In any case, the continental ferment wasn't coming out of nowhere, of course, and needed more precisely to be termed ferments *rather than the monolithic phenomenon and teleological readings that my cross-cultural surveys and list-making tendencies tend to construct. As for my critical vocabulary,* homosocial *was a word that had apparently only recently appeared, but it was clear that it was indispensable to dealing with the new queer Latino cinema. A decade later it is hard to imagine how we could ever have done without it.*

Unfortunately, in retrospect, the promise of the moment was exaggerated: all of this so that we could have the halfhearted time-capsule romanticism of Tomás Gutiérrez Alea's Strawberry and Chocolate *(which I am sure was at least partly the result of the tongue lashing José gave Marta Ibarra, Mrs. Alea, and the film's lead actress, on an earlier visit to Montreal at the height of the* Improper Conduct *controversy)? The disappointment would result of course more from the collapse of the Latin American national cinemas before the onslaught of* Batman *and* Die Hard *than from any internal political developments (although the Nicaraguan Contras' simultaneous recriminalization of homosexuality and deactivation of the Sandinista cinema, once they regained power, did offer an unfortunate symptomatic symbolism . . .). The lively video scene of the nineties, however, both diasporic and domestic, testifies to a continued energy and promise south of the Rio Grande.*

As a final testimony to its time (and to my taste for dramatic dedications), I should mention that this paper was dedicated to transvestite sex workers recently murdered by death squads in São Paulo, to the thousands of victims of cleanups in Mexico and pre-Papal sweeps in Peru, to queer "gusanos" who left and stayed during the Mariel exodus from Cuba, and to lesbian and gay Sandinistas fighting against U.S. imperialism in Nicaragua.

*   *   *

The following survey of Latin American cinemas from the eighties offers a generic inventory of gay men's voices and images that have recently been challenging the patriarchal foundations of the so-called New Latin American Cinema. Indeed in this decade there have emerged small but recognizable gay (or protogay or cryptogay) cinemas in Brazil, Argentina, Mexico, Cuba, and a few other countries, in tandem with oppositional, antipatriarchal and feminist cinemas but not always or necessarily in step with them. My corpus consists primarily of male-directed, male-content narrative features, though a few women directors and a few documentary, short film, or experimental film or video artists are of interest.[1] In general, in terms of simple visibility, it is male homosexuality that is most represented on the screens and in the streets. This is hardly surprising because sexual expression is the traditional prerogative of men within Latin American patriarchy, gay or straight, inside or outside of the family, provided that the institution of the family is maintained.

Only one of the feature films treated can make any claim to "gay authorship" in the North American "gay lib" sense of a declared gay authorship and constituency: Jaime Humberto Hermosillo's *Doña Herlinda and Her Son*. Six or seven other films in the corpus, mostly Brazilian and Argentine, reflect varying degrees of gay input and authorship, representation and enfranchisement, varying combinations of honesty and closety ambiguity, utterance and retraction.

When looking at gay representation in Latin American cinema, it is important to avoid the imposition of northern models of gay liberation, just as we must avoid imposing northern models of feminism or of film theory. (Remember that Sandinista gays and lesbians interviewed in the North American gay media put a chastening low priority on gay movement concerns, in the limited sense.) The difficulties of factoring cultural differences into readings of discourses of gender, marginality, and homoeroticism are brought out by my baffled review of the Brazilian *The Intruder* in 1980, a series of questions in the face of the utter unintelligibility of the film:

> How do you deal with a raunchy cowboy yarn in which two brothers quarrel fatally over their woman slave (fatally for her, that is) because what they really love is each other? What do you do when you discover that the movie is a faithful adaptation of a Jorge Luis Borges parable (faithful even down to the contradictory echoes both of Cain and Abel and of David and Jonathan?), faithful that is except for sundry additional homoerotic frissons such as the brothers' daily nude swordplay practice at bedtime and a threesome culminating in a long, lusty male-

to-male kiss? How do you react when you think you are being told that homosexuality is at the base of machismo or vice versa, or maybe even that homosexuality must be behind any challenge to patriarchy (someone in the film says that any man who looks at a woman for more than five minutes must be a faggot), and then a Latin American woman friend tells you how thrilled she is to see machismo finally crumbling on the screen? Shall we wait until next year's festival to see if you're really onto something promising or just a Brazilian Friedkin?[2]

Such images and the problems of interpretation they pose are only the tip of the iceberg of my eighty-film corpus.[3] The challenges to the gay critic are huge, all the more so because of my outsider cultural status: how does one sort out the perennial tension between transhistorical essences of sexuality and their social construction; the strong national differences, both political and cultural, that exist in Latin America; the interplay of representation and self-representation?

Granted, many of the same issues of gay representation appear to be raised as in northern gay cultural politics and criticism. There is the same ambivalence about the competing attractions of marginalization and integration, visibility and invisibility, even of stigmatization and "positive images." One feels the same betrayal at recognizable patterns of censorship, for example the bowdlerization and compromises that come with literary adaptation (e.g., *Kiss of the Spider Woman*, *City and the Dogs*). One recognizes the same avoidances and deploys the same subtexting strategies in the face of "nongay" works (e.g., those by Giral and Solas). One recognizes also familiar generic patterns: the male-male-female triangles of *Adios Roberto*, *Kiss of the Spider Woman*, and *Pixote*; the all-male institutional settings of *The Intruder*, *City and the Dogs*, and *Los chicos de la guerra*, entailing the safety valves of both male-male violence and intimacy, as well as endless other subterranean dynamics; associations of homosexuality with moral depravity or bourgeois decadence, for example the predatory gay Somozista officer in *The Uprising*, the stereotypes of clowns, transvestites (the most marked of gay characters in the corpus, e.g., the effeminate "gusano" seen in long shot boarding her exile boat in the Cuban documentary *Mariel*[4]), rigid active or passive roles, and of course the dead queer (*Opera Malandro*, *Pixote*, *Kiss of the Spider Woman*). Finally, one recognizes, at least in the Brazilian context, where gay community institutions and networks seem most developed—including an active and articulate gay paper, *Lampião*—the vocation that community-based criticism assumes in confronting the cinema's barrage of negative stereotypes.

Ironically, no film problematizes the northern readings of Latin America more than the exile documentary *Improper Conduct*, a denunciation of the abuse of human rights for gays and lesbians in Cuba, aimed as it is not at domestic audiences but at middle-class Europeans and above all at the society that, with the Hardwick decision, has just entrenched its own sordid record of human rights abuse at the Supreme Court. Ironic also, in the sense that, beyond its certain (but uneven) testimonial value as a film allegedly defending homosexuals, it violates every ethical and political principle of gay rights and civil rights movements in the northern societies it addresses. As the most egregious example, it sets up a hierarchical distinction between its subject groups, that is white middle-class intellectuals, often closeted but well integrated into the social order, whose role it is to theorize and analyze vs. lumpen or working-class queers, often of color and flamingly public in their embrace of social marginalization, whose role it is to emote and experience. Not to mention the dichotomy the film sets up between the smugly visible heterosexual coauthor and the invisible closeted gay coauthor, a dichotomy that bolsters the patriarchal system allegedly being questioned (without even dealing with the film's scurrilous queer-baiting of Castro). Ultimately, the oppression of gays and lesbians, according to the rhetoric of the film, is a metaphorical figure, a stand-in for the failure of marxism rather than a representation of real historical subjects in their own right.

For the rest of this chapter I would like to look at several key films from my corpus, using this general framework, suggested unwittingly by *Conduct*, of opposition between integration and marginalization and of the metaphorization of homosexuality. For *Conduct*'s two basic terms are deployed throughout the corpus, as elsewhere, for the representation of gayness, whether we are talking about sexual identity as an attribute of the self or of the other: first, the term of sameness, belonging, assimilation, in short, integration; second, the term of difference, opposition, in short, marginalization.

Doña Herlinda and *Adios Roberto*, the 1985 features from Mexico and Argentina respectively, are films of integration, echoing in many ways the mi-

Adios Roberto (1985): Argentina's alternative family and open ending. Publicity still.

nority discourse of the mature gay and lesbian political movement of North America. The discourse around their images of middle-class values and style is that "we are like you." In the former film, Rodolfo, a gay neurosurgeon, lives with his wealthy mother. Doña Herlinda wants her son to establish a nuclear family so marries him off to Olga and orchestrates at the same time the absorption of his lover, Ramon, into the extended family and its villa. And a climactic anal penetration scene between the male lovers is intercut with Olga's birthing scene that ensures the continuation of the family line. All live happily ever after. In *Adios Roberto*, a thirtyish male office worker abruptly leaves his family and ends up with a gay roommate who soon becomes his lover. The accent is on the nonthreatening ordinariness of the gay hero, the arbitrariness of his sexual choice, and the formation, despite the open ending, of an alternative family with the new lover. Both films are gently satiric. *Roberto*'s target is intolerance and conformity, and *Herlin-*

da's slightly more sophisticated target is the ease with which the bourgeois family can accommodate nontraditional sexuality, provided its economic and social role is unchallenged. In both films the basic formula is transformation back and forth between straight and gay, between familiar and unfamiliar, between having your cake and eating it too. Both are predicated on the stability of the affectional bond within the couple as a familial unit, and none of the other possible variables of class or gender are challenged. Difference is reconciled, erased.

In a way this is also true of *Spider Woman*, in the sense that the middle-class couple of radical straight intellectual and apolitical gay cinephile is affirmed and that each character is transformed by this bond, Valentin learning to love and dream, Molina learning to care and commit. Nevertheless Babenco and Puig's queen character is also the standard icon of marginalization and otherness in the Latin American corpus, the figure of the transgression of cultural and biological gender coding, of social stigma.

Unlike Rodolfo and Roberto, the queen has no possible recourse to camouflage or closet. In *Pixote*, the passionate and brave, strong and beautiful teenager Lilica is resigned to her persecution: one lover is murdered, the next is stolen. She is the most marginal figure within the marginal proto-familial gang to which she belongs and disappears unceremoniously before the end of the film. As for *Spider Woman*, its queen character, Molina, brings acting prizes to the straight actor who stiffly incarnates him and redemption to the straight fellow prisoner character who uses him sexually and politically. In *Improper Conduct* it is Caracol, the black drag queen exiled plaintively in Miami, who plays a similar role. In *Alem da paixao* the drag queen role is simply a temporary preliminary phase for the straight gold digger who liberates and redeems a middle-class straight woman. The basic dynamic of interclass encounter in all such films is consistent: in the encounter of the bourgeois sexual conformist with the lumpen pervert, the Other operates as a safety valve for repression, as an inoculation against polymorphous perversity, as a catalyst for straight self-discovery and redemption. In *Pixote* the reformers, bureaucrats, and the persona of the humanist filmmaker stand in for the straight elements encountering the redeeming margins, whereas in both *Spider Woman* and *Improper Conduct* it is the middle-class intellectual who confronts the queen. These are not comedies of inte-

Pixote (1980): Director Babenco (center), star Pixote (right, under Babenco's arm), and cast. Queen Lilica is missing. . . . Museum of Modern Art Film Stills Library.

gration, rather tragedies of separation—at last from the point of view of the Other—in which the encounter is so terrifying that the fulfillment of the straight usually comes at the expense of the life of the queen.

Can the image of marginality become appropriated, can it pass beyond redemptive voyeurism and assume a role of enfranchisement and opposition, and if so when? Perhaps only when that image acquires a voice of its own. No doubt *Pixote* comes closest to this ideal, with its successful incorporation of semidocumentary casting; its exposé stance; and its contextualization of the queen as part of a spectrum of outcasts constructed by race, gender, economics, and culture, as a voice that speaks of historical and personal specificity, embodying collectivity, humor, emotion, theatricality, loyalty, and defiance.[5]

It is not surprising, considering the political history of Latin America, that there should be a strong tradition of interlocking the private spheres of sexuality and the public spheres of politics through metaphorical statements. Remember how the sexual proclivities of the Peace Corps volunteers, partying all night, were the characteristics that distinguished them definitively from the traditional aboriginal villagers they were trying to sterilize in *Blood of the Condor*? More recently, think of the whole genre of post-junta Argentine films in which sexual relations stand in for political ones: *Malayunta, Chicos de los guerra, Funny Dirty Little War*, and the two best known, *The Official Story* and *Spider Woman* (Argentine by nationality of its source novel and screenwriter). If the hero of Glauber Rocha's 1967 *Land in Anguish* had to choose between sex and politics and ends up miserable and dead, the updating of this impossible either/or choice in *Spider Woman* is that sexuality *is* political, and you can't choose one without the other. More common is the "woman's awakening" genre, of which *Official Story* is the best known example. The sexual fulfillment of this heroine who finally lets her hair down, à la Jane Fonda, is parallel to and symbolic of her political awakening. If the explicit gay awakening variant of this formula is quite rare—and may be limited to *Spider Woman*—there is a protogay variation in which the victimization of a gay or marginal character is symbolic of political oppression, homophobia standing in for larger, more generalized repressions. I am thinking of *Malayunta*, a Boudu-like fable about repression in which a sterile, meat-eating petit bourgeois couple displaces a young marginal artistic landlord, coded as possibly gay, from his apartment. Nestor, the victim, is a vegetarian and an artisan in theater production; hence his apartment is full of significant masks. The heterosexual couple burns his icons, including a Caravaggio painting on the wall, takes over his space and makes him prisoner, then tortures and kills him after elaborate sadistic sexual games. The victim may not be explicitly gay, despite the Caravaggio, but is sufficiently countercultural and intellectual to allow this reading. In the Brazilian *The Kiss on the Asphalt*, a Nelson Rodrigues story adapted twice for the screen,[6] a man is falsely accused of being gay, is persecuted legally and socially, and loses his job, his wife, everything. This thriller of paranoia, celebrated in gay film festivals around the world for its rare understanding of homophobia but described by one gay critic as devoid of all gay sensibility,[7] at first appears to have a standard "dead queer" ending. But instead, the queer discourse is displaced onto the protagonist's villainous father-in-law, allowing a reading of this parable along the hoary lines of the homophobe as repressed queer.

Less explicit than these two clearly parabolic narratives is a generic tradition of films about masculinity, some with only minor or nonexistent homosexual references, in which unspoken anxieties about machismo—about violence, rigidity, conformity, the refusal of feeling—effectively constitute a critique of the patriarchal system. This happens most vividly in films about all-male institutions, such as *A Time to Die*, *Memories of Prison*, and *City and the Dogs*, in which the relationship of homosociality to homosexuality almost automatically undergoes scrutiny. It is not only that anti-*maricón* abuse overwhelms even the bowdlerized adapted scenario of films like *City*, set in a military school, but that the affective relationships formed in these institutions, alternative families effectively replacing heterosexual marital units, are constructed with even more evasions, subtexts, and complacencies than their Hollywood male bonding equivalents like *Scarecrow*, *Thunderbolt and Lightfoot*, and *The Deer Hunter*. Here, culturally different definitions of masculinity and heterosexuality enter into play. The mechanics of sexuality are in fact situated at their center, namely, the issue of getting fucked. In *Pixote*, for example, the teenager Dito is not gay, though he fucks Lilica. In *Doña Herlinda*, shifts in penetrational practice signal a climactic joke (Rodolfo receives a gift of Nivea Creme from his lover, the more powerful partner begins to get fucked, and the narrative balance of the film and the whole structure of Mexican bourgeois masculinity are challenged). In Arnaldo Jabor's *Love Me Forever or Never* the estranged husband battling with his ex-wife and trying to get her back delivers a triple whammy confession: not only has he been unfaithful, but it has been with a blond transvestite, and to top it off, he has been fucked, enjoyed it, and fallen in love. (She replies, "You're charming when you're weak.") Western gay lib ideologues may have found the somewhat simpler penetration politics of *Spider Woman* objectionable, but director Babenco's reaction to this criticism was telling:

> I think one of the things the movie has to offer is a definition of sexuality. Why define everything in terms of roles? You can get and give pleasure in certain ways without reversing the roles of your life. A man who is not a homosexual can have a homosexual relationship and still

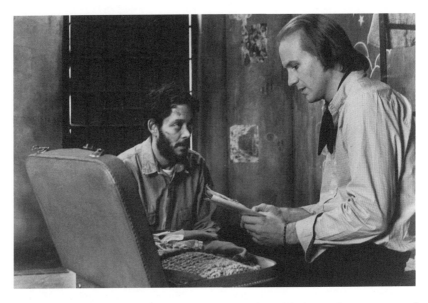

Kiss of the Spider Woman (1985): fucker Valentin (left) and fuckee Molina. Museum of Modern Art Film Stills Library.

be heterosexual. At the end of the movie, Valentin has a heterosexual dream, but who gave him the capacity to dream? . . . I received a strong and fascist letter from a gay community association in LA (the Alliance for Gay and Lesbian Artists in the Entertainment Industry). . . . They wanted me to make serious and dangerous alterations to please their gay point of view—such as "If William Hurt is being penetrated by Raul Julia, it's necessary to have another sequence in which William Hurt is making love to Raul Julia." I thought, "Oh my God, I'm in Germany in the 30s." I'm not doing a Bible or a guide of how to be gay with more or less pleasure; I'm making a movie about something I consider more deep, more humanitarian than just a gay relationship.[8]

This extreme defensiveness may have been personal, but it also represented a wall of intercultural confusion. The LA positive image prescriptions come from a northern post-Stonewall ethic in which the basic dialectic is identity vs. the closet. Within this ethic, "coming out" is the basic political ritual, as well as the dramatic hinge of movement-influenced narratives such as *Mak-*

ing Love, Consenting Adult, and *An Early Frost*. The confessional moment becomes the assertion of public identity and claim of public space. In the
Anglo-Saxon tradition, with its criminalized sodomy statutes and history of
public trials, purges, and panics, sexuality is regulated, defined, categorized,
medicalized but endlessly spoken. The politics of Stonewall and coming out
stems from a political tradition of individualism, pluralism, and liberal democracy—to thine own self be true. The Anglo-Saxon insistence on labels
and the sexual-role egalitarianism that Babenco found so fascistic was a response both to this state regulation and to the commodification of sexuality
that evolved first in northern countries, where capitalism first invaded the
private sphere of desire and where consumption first emerged as a vehicle
of both community identification and political mobilization. The Latin
American tradition, in contrast, derived from the Napoleonic code of un-
criminalized sodomy, is based on an ethic of sexual conduct, not spoken but
understood—*entendido*, that is, *non se dice nada, pero se hace todo* (as opposed to the Anglo-Saxon equivalent that sometimes seems like *se dice todo
pero non se hace nada*[9]). North American interpreters of this ethic, like B.
Ruby Rich, the most vocal critic of *Improper Conduct*,[10] were explaining this
sociospatial discourse separate from the public sphere and attempting to lay
the groundwork for understanding more generally the social construction
of all sexual ethics, something that both Babenco and the Los Angeles positive image activists seemed beyond comprehending. "Out" is not a relevant
category within this ethic, as João Trevisan explains, but an intricate and unspoken network of gradations of behavior, and codings, and understood
boundaries defy categorization, above all an assumed dichotomy between
the private sphere of sexual *ex*pression and the public sphere of sexual *re*-
pression. Cinema, being part of the public sphere, is also a sphere of repression. The drag queen, in asserting a public identity and saying everything,
is a key figure in the assault on the patriarchy, the martyr at the barricades,
liberty leading the people. Her importance in the popular cinemas especially from Brazil and Mexico cannot be overestimated (e.g., the Mexican
Place without Limits or the Brazilian *Republic of Assassins*). In contrast to
North American ethics of private consumption, in third societies where
scarcity is the rule, above all scarcity of private space and housing, the dichotomy of the public street (the domain of the drag queen) and the private

bedroom (a bourgeois privilege) is crucial. Whereas many of the films of marginality feature queens acting out (and dying) in the public streets, *Doña Herlinda's* resolution of homosexuality is through private space, the integration of the gay lifestyle, and even of feminism into the upper-class hacienda, with the familial definition altered no more than its traditional procreative function.

It is no accident that the films discussed in this chapter come largely from those national cinemas situated in Mexico, Brazil, and Argentina, three societies with large unorganized urban gay subcultures and more recent histories of both gay organization and U.S.-style gay commercial ghettos intruding on the public sphere. These small but lively gay cinemas, it could be argued, derive much of their resilience from the cultural and political confrontations arising from these histories. Yet the political import of these cinemas must not be misjudged, all the more so because two of them appear in the turbulent wake of military dictatorships. Moreover, although it would be wishful thinking to attribute much of the bravado of the films I have been discussing to the presence of organized gay and lesbian political movements, it is important to listen to voices from within these movements, and a cautionary note is necessary. In reading these films, these narratives of integration and marginalization, these figures of liberation and repression, these images of desire, it would be best to listen first to those voices who know from recent and direct experience the relative and varied significations of liberation:

> . . . This crucial preoccupation with affirming one's identity makes the gay character the object of some holy cause in an attempt at exorcism which ends up in fashionable clichés. . . . This heroicization is less a gesture of subversion through art than an attempt at integration in the market; the gay boom becomes something new for the system to consume.
> . . . In this era of artificial flavoring, permissiveness is a magic spell by which liberation is put on display so that in reality nothing changes. . . . The arts have been amazingly naive in raising the veil from the world of gay men and lesbians and judging that to be in itself a gesture of liberation. . . .

Contrary to the naive dreams of certain activists, subversion is not latent in gay lifestyles as the Greeks lurked in the Trojan Horse. Nor does sexuality in itself have the gift of guaranteeing solidarity among the oppressed—desire obeys neither principles nor ideologies.[11]

Unpublished conference presentation, 1986–87

Filmography

Adios Roberto, Enrique Dawi, Argentina, 1985.

Los chicos de la guerra, Bebe Kamin, Argentina, 1984.

City and the Dogs (La ciudad y los perros), Francisco Lombardi, derived from the novel by Mario Vargas Llosa, Peru, 1985.

Doña Herlinda and Her Son (Doña Herlinda y su hijo), Jaime Humberto Hermosillo, Mexico, 1985.

Funny Dirty Little War (No habra mas penas ni olvido), Hector Olivera, Argentina, 1985.

Happily Ever After (Alem da paixao), Bruno Barreto, Brazil, 1985.

Improper Conduct, Nestor Almendros and Orlando Jiminez-Leal, France, 1984.

The Intruder (O intrusa), C. H. Christensen, Brazil, 1980.

Kiss of the Spider Woman (O Beijo da mulher aranha), Héctor Babenco, Brazil-U.S., 1985.

The Kiss on the Asphalt (O beijo no asfalto), Bruno Barreto, Brazil, 1981. Previously adapted in 1964 by Flavio Tabellini.

Land in Anguish (Terra em transe), Glauber Rocha, Brazil, 1967.

Love Me Forever or Never (Eu sei que vou te anar), Arnaldo Jabor, Brazil, 1986.

Malayunta, José Santiso, Argentina, 1985.

Mariel (documentary), Cuba, 1984.

Memories of Prison (Memórias Do Cárcere), Nelson Pereira Dos Santos, Brazil, 1984.

The Official Story (La historia oficial), Luis Puenzo, Argentina, 1984.

Opera do Malandro, Ruy Guerra, Brazil, 1986.

Pixote (Pixote, a lei do mais fraco), Héctor Babenco, Brazil, 1980.

The Place without Limits (El lugar sin limites), Arturo Ripstein, Mexico, 1977.

Republic of Murderers (Republica dos assassinos), Miguel Faria Jr., Brazil, 1979.

Strawberry and Chocolate (Fresa y chocolate), Tomás Gutiérrez Alea and Juan Carlos
 Tabio, Cuba, 1993.
A Time to Die (Tiempo de morir), Jorge Ali Triana, Colombia-Cuba, 1985.
The Uprising, Peter Lilienthal, Nicaragua-West Germany, 1978.

Notes

1 Directors and works of interest outside my largely male-authored feature film corpus include most notably: Maria Luisa Bemberg, who presented the first Argentine
   gay male character in *Señora de nadie* (1982); the Brazilian Marisa de Rosario, who
   depicts a lesbian couple in *Marcados para Viver* (1976); the Brazilian lesbian Adele
   Sanpião, director of *Amor Maldido* (date unknown); and the 1982 short documentary *Profissão: Travesti* (director unknown), downbeat and lively.
2 *The Body Politic*, no. 68, November 1980. The final reference is of course to William
   Friedkin's *Cruising* (1980), the notorious film that occasioned gay liberation's first
   major run-in with Hollywood.
3 More than half of the corpus is from Brazil, thanks to the excellent documentation
   provided by João S. Trevisan, editor of the Rio de Janeiro gay paper *Lampião*, in one
   of my major secondary sources, *Perverts in Paradise* (London: GMP Publishers,
   1986).
4 A documentary presented at the Havana Festival of 1984, *Mariel* offered a Cuban
   point of view on the flood of exiles and refugees that left and were expelled from the
   Cuban port of Mariel in 1980. The *Marielitos* were called *gusanos* (worms) in Cuban
   propaganda and included many homosexuals.
5 Trevisan's *Perverts* provides an excellent history of transvestism in Brazilian popular culture.
6 Nelson Rodrigues, the Brazilian playwright, d. 1980, was often adapted for film,
   and his stable of marginal characters is of great interest to Trevisan and other gay
   Brazilian commentators.
7 Elliot Stein, *Village Voice*, January 21, 1986.
8 Kate Walter, "Interview. Hector Babenco: Powerful Dreams Woven in *Kiss of the
   Spider Woman*," *The Advocate*, August 20, 1985, 51.
9 Literally, "do everything but don't say anything" and "say everything but don't do
   anything," respectively.
10 See B. Ruby Rich, "Bay of Pix," *American Film*, July–August 1984, 57–59. See also
   Rich and Lourdes Arguelles, "Homosexuality, Homophobia, and Revolution:
   Notes toward an Understanding of the Cuban Lesbian and Gay Experience, Part I,"
   Signs 9.4 (summer 1984): 683–699; Part II, 11.1 (autumn 1985): 120–136.
11 João S. Trevisan, *Perverts in Paradise* (London: GMP, 1986), 125, 130, 151.

Laws of Desire: *Maurice, Law of Desire,* and *Vera*

* * * * *

All this gushing would never see the light of print, for Epicene, *the Toronto magazine and self-styled* Body Politic *replacement, folded after only one issue. The history of queer journalism is littered with such short-lived dreams and broken young wings.*

Too bad, for it's one of my few pieces on what would become canonical queer films, from Maurice *to* Law of Desire, *and a mix of populist style and intellectual rigor that I would rarely thereafter get a chance to exercise.* Maurice *had a profound impact on me: I never recovered from Hugh Grant having hurt Maurice so much and have not been able to stomach him to this day, star or martyr to lust or whatever. Rupert Graves has of course gone on to dreamboat heaven, at least in my books. I do stand by my intemperate praise of the film, incidentally, despite the trashing it would receive as heterocentric melodrama by Mark Finch and others.* Maurice *and this piece's other feel-good melo,* Le Coeur découvert *(which went on to win the audience prize at the Los Angeles Gay and Lesbian Festival), are examples of queer narrative, mainstream but uncompromising, which we academics disparage at our peril.*

Reading all these reviews at once, I'm afraid, will out me as a skinny-dipping fetishist. So be it. At the same time, one has to acknowledge that nude bathing has been one of the most obsessive motifs of gay male narrative since its beginnings, and would I not be remiss as a critic if I didn't harp on it ad nauseam?

* * *

Bereavement was not a very conducive mindset for attending the eleventh Montreal World Film Festival last August. But, sampling this year's international crop of gay cinema, I couldn't forget that the two leading lights of American gay cinema had just been extinguished by AIDS, Curt McDowell and Artie Bressan. Life continues, and the cinema staggers on, but would I ever feel again that combination of tears, laughter, arousal, and insight as offered by those two very different artists? Farewell, Curt the jubilant (and lusty) cynic, Artie the angry (and lusty) romantic.

Of course both McDowell and Bressan were either too raunchy or too marginal for the wff, but enough of the romantic sensibility was present in the gay films I saw—from Britain, Quebec, Spain, and Brazil—to make me think that Bressan was more prophetic of the pulse of this end of the decade. Not that Bressan would have ever been content to tackle anything so respectable as E. M. Forster's *Maurice*, the most eagerly awaited mainstream gay film of the season. Producer-director duo James Ivory and Ismail Merchant had already tackled lesbianism in their series of literary adaptations over the last couple of decades, most notably in the tragic but grand Vanessa Redgrave character in *The Bostonians*. And they carefully succeeded in keeping some of Forster's gay sensibility in last year's *Room with a View*, something that went considerably deeper than the skinny-dip sequence, immortal as it was (*Maurice* also has a nude bathing sequence delicately inserted into the spare narrative of the original). In short, *Maurice* has more than met expectations and may just turn out to be a mainstream consolidation of last year's breakthrough, *My Beautiful Laundrette*.

Written in 1913 after Forster's encounter with the pioneer gay sexologist Edward Carpenter, *Maurice* never saw the light of day until 1971, after Forster's death. I remember devouring every word immediately on its publication, being devastated by Clive's abandonment of the hero and being transfixed by the gamekeeper Scudder's stealthy entrance through the window into the hero's bed. The novel may have been a trifle earnest and discursive, but its wonderful (s)wish-fulfillment ending perfectly matched the afterglow of Stonewall. Now, on rereading *Maurice* I was surprised to discover that it's even better than I remembered, having easily endured with a layer of irony that the glow may have obscured (I can't explain the twenty-five-year-old men I've encountered who couldn't even get through it).

Merchant and Ivory seem to have recognized a virtue in the novel's deceptive simplicity—boy meets boy, loses boy, and meets another—which lends itself perfectly to their style of leisurely and literate cinematic adaptation. They may even have calculated that its modest couple-oriented romanticism and positive coming-out imagery would respond to the mood of the aids generation. In any case, they have approached the property with fastidious faithfulness, and every detail of performance and design is lovingly

Maurice (1987): (clockwise) gamekeeper heartthrob Rupert Graves (seated), stockbroker James Wilby, and treacherous coward Hugh Grant, whom I have never forgiven. Museum of Modern Art Film Stills Library.

controlled. The three young actors are handsome, talented, and restrained: in particular, Rupert Graves (Lucy's younger brother in *Room with a View*) will now reach the summits of heartthrob-dom as the gamekeeper who ends up in Maurice's arms despite everything.

At 135 minutes, *Maurice*'s indulgent pace may have caused some squirming during the stretch between the hero's two greatest passions. And its darker sensibility may prove to be less popular than the sunny affability of *Room with a View*: its key moments, romantic and sexy as they are, take place during rainy evenings and in melancholy London hotel rooms rather than amid Italian wildflowers. But for me the measured unfolding of the final euphoric glimpse of liberation, the hero's "reckless climb" as Forster put it, was to be savored, true both to the original novel and to the lonely dynamics of individual salvation as Forster's generation—and ours?—knew them.

The filmmakers' major departure from the novel is a subplot involving

Risling, an unpleasant aristocratic classmate of Maurice's and Clive's who is entrapped with his hands in a guardsman's pants, tried, convicted, and sent to jail, his promising career in ruins. This echo of the Oscar Wilde trial, of which Forster's unconsummated readers of 1914 would have needed no reminder, means that the social and political context of the story are much better focused for today's ahistorical nongay audience. Clive's abandonment of his lover is thereby more the result of cowardly capitulation to social pressures than the obscure biological voice that Forster originally described. The scriptwriters' license is more than vindicated. Aside from the reminder of oppression, there is also a nuance added to Forster's not-so-dated world of interclass relationships, a sobering qualification to the utopian concluding fantasy in which servants live happily ever after with Cambridge-bred stockbrokers.

Not that the happy ending needs any qualification for gay audiences, I suspect. What Forster said had been "imperative" in 1914 worked fine in 1971 and all the more so in 1987: the decades haven't changed our occasional need for wish fulfillment. As for Merchant and Ivory, honored with a retrospective at this year's festival, let's take the liberty of bestowing on them henceforth the honorary label of "gay filmmakers": though they've never made a Fassbinder-style big deal about their private lives, the usually reliable *People* magazine's profile of the pair last year made no bones about their long-standing cohabitation. And after all, with *Maurice* now in place as one of the most moving and honest gay films of the decade, and a faithful adaptation of one of the most important gay novels of the pre-Stonewall era, the record stands unassailable.

The problematic of the couple is also at the center of the homegrown romanticism of the Quebec film *Le Coeur découvert* (The Heart Exposed). Radio-Canada's Jean-Yves Laforce has directed this made-for-TV film from Michel Tremblay's scenarization of his recent novel.

Since Tremblay became Quebec's literary superstar and moved to shady well-heeled Outremont, some of his work has lacked the punch of the earlier plays situated in the Plateau Mont-Royal, the *quartier populaire* of his childhood. Tremblay simply never convinced me that the dowagers and French professors of Outremont were as interesting as Oncle Édouard, the Duchesse de Langeais. Although his four memoiresque novels appearing between 1978 and 1984 returned to the Plateau and to his earlier pizzazz, I found his 1981 play, *Les Anciennes odeurs*, a melancholy portrait of a gay college professor, stiff and hesitant. The same was true, though less so, of his 1986 novel, *Le Coeur découvert*. Still I was eventually won over by its upbeat and sympathetic narrative of Jean-Marc, a very similar thirty-nine-year-old Outremont French professor, now more textured, who sets up a relationship with Mathieu, a twenty-five-year-old would-be actor, only to discover that he must welcome Mathieu's five-year-old son Sébastien into his life and co-op for the same price.

I found the film adaptation to be a refreshing improvement on the novel. This made sense when I later learned that the script had actually come first and was only novelized when producers failed to nibble. In any case, the life-and-blood characterizations of the very likable and skillful cast add color and warmth to Tremblay's scintillating dialogue of the novel. Indeed the cast, composed mostly of old Tremblay hands, is uniformly excellent: in particular Gilles Renaud, hero of *Anciennes odeurs*, who plays Jean-Marc, and is excellent at showing the nuances of a too-settled life's being stirred up; and Amulette Garneau, Mathieu's hesitant but conciliatory mother, who has been in practically every Tremblay work ever mounted, but whom I will never forget as the taciturn lesbian Bec-de-Lièvre in *Il Était une fois dans l'Est*. Newcomer Michel Poirier almost steals the show as Mathieu, however, with his defensive innocence and wiry energy. As for child actor Olivier Chasse, Laforce has extracted a strong understated performance with only the occasional lapse into the cuteness syndrome.

Best of all, the primary relationship at the core of the film is entirely believable, from the currently fashionable extended courtship to the final domestication. My only reservation was that Laforce apparently let the constraints of television (self-?) censorship muffle the physical dimension of their relationship, mysteriously absent: the two go to bed, not like passionate lovers but like the chaste Hollywood couples of the fifties, complete with dry peck on the cheek on parting. I don't expect the cbc to show penetration and ejaculation, but the hockey miniseries *He Shoots He Scores!* isn't quite so prudish in hetero territory. On other counts, however, Laforce doesn't hold back. Straight critics were terribly nervous about the novel's exploration of adult-child relationships, parental and nonparental. A scene bringing Jean-Marc and the little boy together in a shared bathtub set off some real critical twitching—in unconscious imitation of the macho uncle in the novel who harasses the new "family" with his homophobic terror of "touching." Laforce goes one better, giving us not one but two adult-child bathtub scenes and confronting the issue of gay parenting of children with humor, subtlety, and defiance.

The only other criticism I have is of the film's design, which has a little too much of that boutique-y Radio-Canada flavor, the Outremont setting notwithstanding. Although it may be a bit excessive to go on and on as some of my friends did about how no self-respecting lesbian would go walking in Parc Outremont in a little straw hat, in general the look of the cultural milieu in question is slightly off. On the other hand, the location shooting provides a witty and authentic backdrop in that same milieu: my archivist friend is ecstatic that the oldest gay bar in Montreal, dating from the thirties, the old Café Lincoln, has now been documented on film, colored glass globes and all.

But I digress. The ultimate pleasure of seeing this warmhearted, polished little gem is to be relished all the more because of its positive and complex representation of gays in this year when everyone in Quebec is gushing about a violent misogynist derivative little queer-basher of a film, *Night Zoo*, and because one of our finest writers has made another all-too-rare visit to the screen. There are presently no plans to broadcast *Le Coeur découvert* on the English CBC network, another instance, I'm afraid, of the conspiracy of that institution to keep the best programming in either language from the other constituency. They'll bend over backwards to bring the Anglos *He Shoots He Scores!*, but forget about the occasional productions of real quality.

Speaking of very fast and very witty, I won't say much else about Pedro Almodovar's *The Law of Desire*, since Torontonians have been treated to a complete retrospective of this hotshot young gay Spaniard's work at the Festival of Festivals. It is enough to say that *Law of Desire* is a film that McDowell would have loved (and Bressan too) for its anarchic taboo-shattering embrace of lust *fou*. Almodovar has the ability to compress all of the neuroses, trips, and explosive release of post-Franco Spain into a single film. What he did for the nuclear family in *What Have I Done to Deserve This?* and for machismo in *Matador* he does in this comic erotic thriller for artistic creation, sex, religion, gender, love, and childhood. It's as if all of the structures of repression that Maurice has to battle have fully evaporated in Spain in the mere decade since the Caudillo kicked off. Next to Almodovar, Eloy de Iglesias, the Spanish gay sensation of a few years back (*The Deputy*), may seem somewhat sanctimonious, but do we have such a dazzling choice within any other comparable national cinema?

Recrossing the Atlantic to another outpost of Iberian acting out/up, my roster finishes off with two films from Brazil. *Vera* is a well-made open-ended social issue feature from São Paulo about an angry young man trapped inside a woman's body, or rather an angry young woman who thinks she is but who in the end thinks she might be a woman after all. However, the film is not so much about trans-vestism/sexualism as it is about love between women, about women's nonconformity and revolt, and society's institutions for containing those threats, from the prison to the family. *Vera* reminded me a lot of *Pixote* in the earnest social compassion it focuses on an institution for marginal young people and its even-headed oscillation back and forth on the limitless spectrum of sexual choices, so I was not surprised to learn that director Sergio Toledo had worked with Héctor Babenco. Featured in this year's San Francisco Gay and Lesbian Film Festival, *Vera* rises better than might be expected, I would say, above its inherent liability of being a "lesbian film" directed, written, and photographed by men. Like *Pixote, Vera* is best at showing the networks of loyalty and self-defense, with the jail-like "orphanage" where the heroine must spend her formative years, and at getting dazzling performances from its cast of unknowns and marginals. Ana Beatriz Nogueira is superb as Vera and I'm sure had the jaded sisterhood of San Francisco writhing in their seats. However, like *Pixote, Vera* loses its footing when attempting to resolve all the questions it raises in the outside world. At least it has the authenticity to end on a question: the terrorized young woman, having lived a rocky relationship with another woman and a traumatic defeat in the workforce, locks herself in a bathroom. Instead of the tragedy the conventions of the genre have led us gullibly to suspect, Vera rediscovers her womanhood—or *I think* that's what happens, for this is a *very* open ending.

Anjos da noite (Night Angels) fits closer to the stereotype of Brazilian cinema with its two hours of beautiful people screaming, fucking, and putting on makeup, although it too is from staid middle-class São Paulo rather than the *tropicalista* Rio milieu that originated the stereotype. Set in the racy milieu of the theater and the streets, Wilson Barros's film shows its intense characters darting in and out of every cinematic style from pop-Brechtianism and postmodern quotations to on-the-street vérité. Despite some very entertaining moments, and a scene-stealing performance by Marila Pera (*Pixote, Mixed Blood*), it's far from a great film. At the very least, however, it's an enjoyable reminder that Brazilian gay popular culture, with its seething menagerie of bisexual hustlers, transvestites, and horny individuals of every stripe, has enough unplumbed depth to keep foreign audiences panting for generations.

It's no accident that missing from the above survey is good old Hollywood, and it's not only because the studios don't throw all their pearls before Montreal festival moguls. Year after year, despite an occasional flash in the pan like *Kiss of the Spider Woman*, we are reminded at these festivals that if we're searching for mature and interesting reflections of ourselves on the screen, we can't look at the 99 percent of our screens controlled by Tinseltown—there we range from the gross homophobia of *No Way Out* to the irritating minor homophobia of *The Fourth Protocol* (the biggest Hollywood film in the Montreal festival). Instead, we either have to wait for the occasional Bressan, McDowell, or Almodovar film that slips through the cracks of the distribution cartel, or else we have to overdose once a year or so at the festivals. If we're really, really lucky, *Maurice* will change all that, but don't hold your breath.

Unpublished review essay, 1987

Two Great Gay Filmmakers: Hello and Good-bye

*   *   *   *   *

This elegy for Norman McLaren and Claude Jutra, the two great queer film-makers from my adopted hometown of Montreal, was written for another short-lived Toronto gay tabloid known for ideological rigor. This is one of the few Cana-dian pieces retained for The Fruit Machine's *American-targeted selection but one that I hope will transcend borders of nationalist sentimentality.*

This was my only excursion into biographical criticism of the eighties, and it wasn't easy with two such private artists, both dead. I'd tried to meet McLaren's lover Guy Glover for an interview, but he was cloistered off by an officious NFB *sycophant; as for Jutra, the stories of his dragon-lady sister, snorting litigation threats to protect her brother's "privacy," are rife in Canadian journalism. In any case, the films say it all. Especially a 1957 film I unaccountably omitted in 1988 but that I've focused on more recently:* A Chairy Tale, *the pixillated com-edy about a topsy-turvy relationship between a man (Jutra) and a chair that in-sists on reciprocality. A relationship film entirely free of gendered pronouns, inci-dentally,* Tale *was codirected by Jutra and McLaren and thus moving evidence of a relationship of mentorship and collaboration.*

As I write this in 1998, Jutra's Mon Oncle Antoine, *once praised by Pauline Kael and enthroned as the best Canadian film of all time, has just been revived to an indifferent and amnesiac response on the part of Canadian audiences. On the other hand, his* A tout prendre *gets better with every viewing and now stands, among other things, as the first Canadian feature film about race. As for McLaren, the* NFB *continues to beatify its in-house genius, with best-selling video packages, and a full-length artistic biography on film,* The Creative Pro-cess, *which contains an oblique passing reference to his life relationship. Glover died shortly after this piece came out in 1988, and ten years later his own forty-year career as a producer increasingly looms as another subject for queer archeol-ogy in its own right. If I were to write this now, it might be about the three of them.*

A Chairy Tale (1957): a pixillated relationship without gendered pronouns. Ciné-mathèque québécoise.

*   *   *

Many Canadians learned the names of filmmakers Norman McLaren and Claude Jutra last winter at their deaths. It is true that all of us have flickering grade-school memories of the work of McLaren, the National Film Board's great animator. It is true also that in Quebec there is hardly anyone who has not caught Jutra's *Mon Oncle Antoine* (My Uncle Antoine) at some point or other on TV, and never forgotten what is generally believed to be the best Canadian feature film ever made. But in Canada, even our two greatest filmmakers do not become household words, like Hitchcock or Spielberg, and too often we learn of the achievements of our culture in the obituaries.

But even in the obituaries we did not learn that our two most honored filmmakers were gay. Unless of course we're experienced obituary subtex-

Mentorship: Norman McLaren (left) and Claude Jutra (c. 1950s). National Film Board of Canada.

ters, in which case a light would have come on while we read about McLaren's male companion of many years or about Jutra's devoted sister and the void of his personal life.

It was a coincidence of course that the two men died within a few months of each other. Except for the fact that the same city and the same cold winter were the setting, the two deaths couldn't have been more different.

There was nothing tragic in the death of the world-famous animator at the age of seventy three after a forty-three-year career and sixty films, crowned with distinctions (including the Order of Canada, the Oscar, and the Palme d'or), surrounded by friends, adoring colleagues, and his lover, NFB producer Guy Glover. Jutra, on the other hand, took his own life at the relatively youthful age of 56: after years of box office failure and exile, Jutra

Lovers Guy Glover (left) and Norman McLaren (center) at an airport parting (c. 1965). National Film Board of Canada.

had recently undertaken his first film in almost a decade in his beloved Quebec only to discover, while still on the set, the slow approach of Alzheimer's disease. As the debilitation spread, Jutra made a brave decision that the time had come, and as reporters who had never seen a Canadian film in their lives kept reminding us, the body was missing for more than four months before washing up on the shores of the St. Lawrence. Serene old age vs. dramatic suicide, the media blathered on. Theaters and festivals were dedicated to either or both of the departed artists; in the two filmmakers' festival-mad hometown, Montreal, there were even competing retrospectives of their work.

One thing you can be sure of: the media never got into homosexuality, probably not so much out of Canadian tact as out of Canadian inertia. Neither McLaren nor Jutra was Jean Genet, and sexuality has never had anything to do with Canadian cinema anyway (until *Decline of the American Empire* came along), so what would have been the angle?

In fact what *is* the angle? Both McLaren and Jutra were private men, and neither was a "Gay Filmmaker" in the sense that Fassbinder or Pasolini were, *poètes maudits* of the taboo and the carnal. What is the importance of the filmmaker's life in dealing with movies in general and with these movies in particular? To me in each case the biography is essential for a full appreciation of the films, no matter how nonsexual they may seem, no matter how discreet. The closet doesn't extend over the grave, and their lives are also part of our lives, part of gay social history, part of Canadian cultural history. We have an obligation to make connections that the obituaries and the tributes have suppressed.

So far so good, but there's one more essential detail: both McLaren and Jutra did in fact make one Gay Film, each in his own way. McLaren's, called *Narcissus*, was his last, completed two years before his death, and thus acquires the aura of a testament. It was without a doubt the most autobiographical work of an artist whose films were famous for being playfully abstract. Jutra's Gay Film, *A tout prendre* (Take it all, 1963), was his first major work, as well as his most autobiographical and, according to some, his best. Though neither Gay Film was recognized as such by the critics or by the obituary writers, one essential task of this article is to restore these films in this light and to claim these artists as—besides everything else—ours.

In many ways Norman McLaren fit one stereotype of the gay artist perfectly—not the tormented self-destroyer but the sensitive, fastidious, and solitary craftsman and visionary. One colleague commented on his "soft, sad, watching eyes, that sometimes searched me furtively and then left me for his heart of hearts." Others found a similar sense of mystery and unstated sexual tension in both his work and his personality:

> So complex is McLaren that people who have worked with him for decades say frankly they don't understand him. The symbolism of his movies offers a fertile field for psychoanalytic interpretations. His humanitarianism, which led one writer to call him "a saint," has a touching child-like quality to it, of one reaching out to be loved as well as to love. He dresses like a college boy, looks twenty years younger than his age, and has kept the youthful innocence and enthusiasm common to great artists. Far from taking seriously any thought he might express about giving up filmmaking, one shudders to think of what life would

be for him without it; the necessity brings him in to work sometimes when he is so mentally depressed and physically ill that he frightens those around him.

McLaren had been at the NFB since almost the very beginning, recruited by his fellow Scotsman John Grierson in 1941. He very quickly established a worldwide following for his lively un-Disneyesque abstract choreographies and radically innovative techniques of scratching and painting right on celluloid. He maintained his status as the NFB prestige artist until his retirement.

McLaren was not the only homosexual at the board, needless to say. A picture is only beginning to emerge of the NFB's role as Ottawa's own small Bohemia in the forties and fifties: who would have ever thought that about the staid producer of documentaries on salmon hatching? Scandals resulting from police raids on the Chateau Laurier, narrowly averted by Grierson's deft string-pulling, became in-house legends, and McLaren and Glover's fresco-covered apartment became another. There is also the story of the Halloween party of the early fifties, when McLaren and Glover both showed up in full Spanish senorita drag, complete with white lace mantillas. No wonder that an NFB administrator is said to have claimed that one reason for the NFB's historic move from Ottawa to Montreal in 1956 was simply "to get the sandal- and ascot-clad fairies off the banks of the Rideau Canal." The fairies were no doubt just as eager to move. There are also grimmer stories, however, about how, as late as the sixties, the administration kept the salaries for Glover and McLaren and other homosexuals down to the bare minimum because of their presumed vulnerability. The NFB may not necessarily have been a hotbed of homosedition, but its place as one of the more interesting corners of Canadian gay social history is definitely a subject for further research.

In the mid-sixties, after more than a quarter-century as principal practitioner of his brilliant rhythmic abstractions, McLaren turned to a new series with a photographic style that would celebrate the human body with an unprecedented sensuality. The three films in the series, *Pas de Deux* (1967), *Ballet Adagio* (1971), and eventually *Narcissus* (1984), all used ballet as the basis for haunting evocations of movement, gesture, and dance and through the use of various technical procedures magnified the ballet's inherent celebration of human grace. In *Ballet Adagio*, slow motion transformed the romantic lyricism of the balletic pas de deux convention into an ethereal erotic dream (all the more so because the skimpy male costume revealed the sexualized male body more than the comparatively chaste getup of his female partner). Ultimately though, *Ballet Adagio* is a dissection and elaboration of a ritualized convention of heterosexual mating. Twelve years later with *Narcissus*, McLaren is less cautious and goes much further.

Narcissus, the self-absorbed dreamer, is one of the classical myths that has always served as a cover for male eroticism. Ganymede, Endymion, and Hyacinth are others that have been pressed into service over the centuries to legitimize gay fantasy within a hostile social context. Some version of the Narcissus myth had been on McLaren's drawing board for over thirty years. But it was perhaps a good thing that it took so long to come to fruition, when the social climate and McLaren's unassailable status would permit a relatively explicit exploration of the sexual signification of the story.

McLaren offered a simple three-part narrative structure in which a dreamy and exquisite youth engages in two romantic pas de deux, first with a female partner, a "nymph," and then with a male partner, "a hunting companion" (according to the ludicrous official summary). The two pas de deux may be equally luscious, but the male duet has a stunning effect as an unprecedented representation of gay male sexuality. Of course McLaren covers himself by equating the two gender options for the tragic hero, and both options are equally rejected, but there is no doubt what side the weight of centuries of wish fulfillment is leaning toward. In keeping with the story, the ending is tragic: the hero rejects his two lovers, dances with himself (in another breathtaking pas de deux!), and is finally revealed to be imprisoned by iron bars and a brick wall.

It would be too easy to dismiss this film as yet another arty piece of closet beefcake and to see McLaren's lavish stylization as yet another mechanism of avoidance. Still, the prison-bar ending comes across as an image not so much of the tragedy of self-absorption but of sexual repression, even of the thwarted self-realization of the closet. *Narcissus* would be false if it were not as tragic as it is beautiful. As such, it stands up well as the statement and the yearning of one of the more isolated contemporaries of Visconti, Cadmus, and Burroughs, of the shy Scottish-Canadian civil servant who lived light-years from Greenwich Village and even from the Main.

Narcissus (1983): tragic and beautiful. National Film Board of Canada.

The irony is that it was the puritanical homophobes at the Board who financed some of the loveliest homoerotic imagery in Canadian cultural history. Claude Jutra had to leave the board to produce *his* Gay Film. The freedom of financial autonomy (as well as poverty) is apparent in *A tout prendre* and thus also, because the film appeared twenty years earlier than *Narcissus*, the recklessness of an imagination ahead of its time.

I first met Claude Jutra through a mutual friend at one of Montreal's glitziest male strip clubs. Though we passed an hour or two together enjoying the show and met a few more times over the years, he never remembered me. This was more a function of shyness I think than the onslaught of his disease. In any case, I heard that he had liked a piece I wrote in 1981 in which I praised his pioneering role in gay cinema in Quebec and called him the E. M. Forster of Quebec film for the problematic silence that followed the bravado of *A tout prendre*.

When he made *A tout prendre* in the early sixties, Jutra was scarcely thirty but had already established a name for himself as one of the figureheads of the lively young Quebec cinema. *A tout prendre* was the most personal and autobiographical of a highly original group of films at the forefront of the Quiet Revolution. In step with, if not ahead of, the best achievements of the French Nouvelle Vague, it well deserved its Best Film honor at that year's Canadian Film Awards.

The protagonist-narrator is a young artist-intellectual, similar to Jutra, played by Jutra, and named Claude. The story recapitulates the filmmaker's ill-fated love affair with a black woman model named Johanne, played by the real Johanne Harel. At one point, after their delirious courtship, Johanne caresses Claude on the forehead. Claude is unreceptive so Johanne quietly asks if he likes boys.

This shocking question is permissible in 1963 only in the social and artistic context established by the film. The social context—bohemian and artistic—was one of the few in which lesbians and gays could live relatively openly before Stonewall, though the gay artist was a more common figure in Paris and New York than in English or French Canada (the very out Jean Cocteau had been another of Jutra's mentors). The artistic context—the gay confessional work of art—has been a continuous fixture of Gallic culture from Verlaine to Genet and beyond.

But Montreal was not Paris but a still very Catholic island in a puritanical Anglo-Saxon sea. So Johanne's question is accented by a dramatic echo effect, a crash of percussion, an abrupt insertion of an extreme close-up of the hero, and a confessional whispered voice-over by Claude: "I don't say yes any more than I say no. Thus the secret gets out that I had been hiding longer than my earliest memories. Johanne did that. With her woman's hands, she lifted off the heaviest part of my burden. She made me confess the unconfessable and I was not ashamed and it didn't hurt. And now everything is changed, for that driving desire that was never satisfied, that torment, has taken the form of a ray of hope." Suddenly Claude is on a film set directing two players:

> Actress (voice off): It's not me that you loved, but an image that you had invented.
> Actor: No, it's you because you delivered me from all images.

The lines patently apply, not to the film within the film but to Claude and Johanne, both fictional and real-life. Claude is infatuated not with Johanne, the black Montrealer, but with an exotic Haitian fantasy. He is also infatuated with Johanne as his deliverer from the "burden" of his homosexuality. Can she be the proof of his "normality" to straight society? to himself? The implied answer is negative, for the next image shows Claude staring intently into the eyes of the actor who is staring back, an exchange of looks loaded with signification and concluded with Claude's additional offscreen line, "At last!"

Claude's sexual anxiety and self-hatred spur a series of fantasies throughout the rest of the film, including three in which he is killed by male assailants (one is a virile, leather-decked biker), as well as recurring images of muscular tropical harvesters (male, significantly) evoked by Johanne's supposed origins. Claude's anxiety also leads him to drop Johanne, now pregnant, with no word of explanation but a check in the mail. The explanation, however, has already been offered to the spectator by the single moment of revelation, of "coming out." Johanne's woman's hands do not relieve him of his burden after all but only compound the shame he feels because of exploitation of her.

The closet door has been flung open but is then quickly allowed to swing back. After all, the confessional elements in the film are all sound and editing effects added in the privacy of the lab and not in the public space of the set (the straight cameraman was later to describe the work as a "bathroom film"). Jutra instantly recoiled from this guarded avowal, never returning to it in explicit terms for the rest of the film—or for the rest of his career. In a way the narrative working out of Claude's dilemma is as isolated a breakthrough and as problematic politically in its atmosphere of pervasive guilt as McLaren's guarded eroticism twenty years later. But in the context of 1963, *A tout prendre* was a flash of daring lucidity.

Does the pattern of revelation and hasty retreat also explain much of Jutra's subsequent career? After Jutra's triumph *Mon Oncle Antoine* (1970), what follows but two misunderstood films on heterosexual passion and marriage, then exile in English Canada, a few commissions, silence, and then one final film on native soil?

Jutra paid the price for his daring. None other than Denys Arcand was the most public of the gay-baiters, reacting to the film in the pages of indépendantiste journal *Parti pris* with an incoherent smear (twenty years before the appearance of the sensitive gay blood-pisser in *Decline of the American Empire*). Arcand took his colleague to task for his claim to "the right of homosexuality," asking whether homosexuality is "a solid form of sexual activity" and how it can have "a special status of self-affirmation in view of our global context of existence in regard to artistic expression." That was not all: Claude's fixation on a black woman is also a "refusal to coincide with his collective identity" and an inability to achieve an "everyday sexuality." The general principle is that "the fruits of the flesh can be tasted only in freedom" and that a free cinema for Quebec will only appear when filmmakers will be able to "serenely undress their neighbor Yvette Tremblay or Yolande Beauchemin in full sunlight with a well-focused wide-angle lens." Of course Arcand was not the first homophobe blinkered by the confusion of nationalist cause and sexual fulfillment. In linking the collective Québécois identity to heterosexual conformity—and even more incredibly to heterosexual partners of prescribed racial origin (!)—Arcand was still ensnared by the Duplessist Catholic narrowness that his generation was attempting to leave behind. In the light of such bigotry, Jutra's moment of truth seems like the manifesto of a political principle that the nationalist consensus had not yet assimilated, that the personal is political, that collective liberation is tied up in individual liberation.

My original Forster label was perhaps too severe in downplaying Jutra's subsequent films, for although they are never as explicit as *A tout prendre*, they extend his earlier preoccupations in a very interesting way. For example, the critique of the constrictions of the bourgeois family in *A tout prendre* can be seen evolving in such films as the costume epic of rebellious desire, *Kamouraska* (1973), in the bittersweet marital comedy *For Better or Worse* (1975), and even in his "lesbian" comedy *By Design* (1981), with its parody of straight family planning.

More important to me is another group of films that deal with young people growing into maturity—principally but not exclusively boys. The young subjects are handled if not with eroticism then with a kind of sensuous identification that is also part of Jutra's gay sensibility. His second full-length feature, *Wow!* (1969), was the NFB's tribute to the late-sixties youth revolt. Using a semidocumentary format, the director let his grass-smoking young protagonists express themselves, do their own thing, perform their own fantasies, and all go together to a big protest demonstration in Washington. Although obviously a document of its time, the film shows that Jutra listens to his glowing and earnest subjects with the utmost sensitivity, respect, and

Claude Jutra (left) directing Benoît and Oncle Antoine (1969). National Film Board of Canada.

tenderness, and the result is a moving durability. Needless to say there is lots of glowing and earnest flesh as well, including a psychedelic nude trampoline romp with one of the heroines, and even more abundant beefcake.

The subjects of the famous *Mon Oncle Antoine*, made the following year, are even younger but painted with the same glow. The adolescence of the hero who discovers death, sex, and human frailty in the snows of rural Quebec is a time of curiosity and innocence that is idealized and down-to-earth at the same time. Played by a nonactor discovered by Jutra on location in Thetford Mines, Benoît had eyelashes that have entered film history. The next youth film, *Dreamspeaker* (1976), produced for the CBC's *For the Record*, is by far Jutra's best English-Canadian film and, some argue, one of his best works. Here the age-frame is lowered even further: the runaway blond hero is lovingly depicted in a paradisiac wilderness refuge with a wise old native protector and the latter's affectionate but silent grown-up son. But white civilization, from which all three have escaped, relentlessly reimposes its order, and the film ends tragically when the boy is locked up in one of the institutions of "civilization." Again, Jutra's identification with the tormented boy is as intimate as it is compelling. Jutra's final film, *La Dame en couleurs* (1984), pursues a similar theme, with a group of orphans burrowing out of yet another repressive institution, this time run by nuns, to encounter another kind of refuge, the visionary frescos of a subterranean painter that contrast sharply with the children's constricted lives.

Though the quixotic protogay rebel of *A tout prendre* is no longer present in this fifteen-year series of intense and poetic youth films, another aspect of the artist's sociosexual imagination is almost as vivid, his compassion for the flame of childhood struggling under the weight of society. It is significant that this theme echoes Narcissus's prison and the vision of Jutra's mentor McLaren. Our two great gay filmmakers were allied in their art, after all, just as they were in their careers and as they were in the season of their deaths.

Rites (Toronto) 4.10 (April 1988): 10–11

Beauty and the Beast, Take Two

* * * * *

This personal ramble mixes a little institutional politics from the educational conglomerate where I teach—polyglot, low budget, progressive, urban—with my engagement with anticensorship politics in the larger arena, and my personal trajectory of reconnecting with India, almost two decades after I had left a two-year volunteer stint of English-teaching and self-discovery in Punjab. Somehow they all held together.

Now I detect just a little dash of arrogance in the mix (which my little sister tells me is my major problem), not only in the anecdote of the Calcutta interlocutor whom I failed so miserably, but also perhaps in its "talking down" pedagogical stance. Arrogance was certainly part of how I badgered the editor to run a safer-sex comic frame as illustration, over her objections that a volatile condom and hard-on drawing would distract from the larger theme of the volume. Of course this turned out to be one of many, many scuffles around sexual images that had been dogging me since Kinsey (and Hard to Imagine *was still eight long years away!).*

As for the sex wars, my note of mitigated optimism toward the end of this piece was short-lived. Despite the confident profile of media activism at the Montreal AIDS Conference the following year, safer sex campaigns continued to be marginalized and invisible in the public sphere, and the sacrifice of a whole generation of gay men continued unabated. And in 1992 our "Butler Decision," handed down by the Supreme Court over a porn video case, would make the Tories' Bill C-54 seem like a paper tiger: Canadians ended up with the worst imaginable application of Mackinnon-Dworkinism enshrined in our criminal code, and the scapegoating of minority sexual images through the courts and customs harassment could now proliferate throughout the nineties with impunity.

* * *

In March 1987 I participated, in a kind of presabbatical swan song, on the Concordia Fine Arts Status of Women Committee's panel "Beauty and the

Beast, Art and Politics." Speaking about sexual representation in the arts, I tried to raise the alarm about state intervention in sexual discourses. The Tories' Bill C-54, outlawing all sexual representation, was looming large on the horizon. I warned against comfortable academic isolation from the political wars over sex, culture, and artistic freedom outside in the real world. I showed various slides, including a nude shot of American feminist performance artist Linda Benglis sporting a huge erect dildo, asking the audience to pretend they're the patriarchal state deciding whether or not to censor each image. The audience seemed to enjoy playing out all the contradictions of censorship.

Soon after, I made my getaway from Concordia for a one-year sabbatical leave. I was to continue my book project on sexual representation, *Hard to Imagine: Gay Male Eroticism in Photography and Film from Their Beginnings to Stonewall.* I was embarking also on an apparently unrelated new direction: a four-month research project in India devoted to independent documentary film in that movie-mad country. My original commitment to documentary film art stemmed from convictions about the role of the filmmaker in political change: here was a chance to scout out these old ideals in the Third World.

But no getaway was possible from the never-ending war over art and politics, sex and culture. As a contribution to this volume on "Critical Paths," I offer the following fragments of a pseudodiary of continuing skirmishes in that war during my late lamented sabbatical.

MONTREAL, AUGUST 1987. I attend a press conference at the Montreal World Film Festival held by a Quebec group called Le comité pour la défense de la liberté d'expression, mobilizing against Bill C-54. On the platform are a filmmaker and an art museum director alongside a representative of the Canadian Periodicals Association. Politics make strange bedpersons, I wryly note: the last gentleman holds a monopoly on magazine distribution and has made millions handling *Playboy* and *Penthouse*. His eyes light up when a reporter asks the implications of the impending North American Free Trade Agreement for the Canadian "adult magazine" market.

Two months ago I talked to my friend Ralph in Los Angeles, who said he had been diagnosed with AIDS-Related-Complex. Now I learn he is dead.

TORONTO, NOVEMBER 1987. At the Grierson Documentary Seminar, we show *Passiflora*, a brilliant, anarchic Quebec documentary inspired by the simultaneous visits of John Paul II and Michael Jackson to the Olympic Stadium. This film by Fernand Bélanger and Dagmar Gueissaz-Teufel uses graffiti as both image and method. The NFB has quietly dumped the film because of its "sensitive" images of organized religion, abortion, and sexual and social marginality, refusing to bring out an English version. We succeed in raising the issue of NFB censorship on *The Journal* but know that this breakthrough is only graffiti on the twenty-four-hour-a-day unperturbed surface of consent.

AMSTERDAM, DECEMBER 1987. I'm on my way to India, but first a conference entitled "Homosexuality, Which Homosexuality?" bringing together over five hundred gay and lesbian scholars from around the world in the Dutch gay mecca. The debate is between the social constructionists (sexualities are historically determined by social contexts) and the essentialists (there have always been gay people and lesbians in every society and every historical period). I give a paper taken from my book-in-progress on gay mail-order erotic cinema of the 1950s, talking about how our flickering libidinal imprints were constructed in the dark postwar era by societal censorship and shame. I'm paranoid about transporting "research materials" through international customs.

Everyone at the conference is outraged about Clause 28, Margaret Thatcher's new antigay legislation, which epitomizes the state's threat to cultural expression by sexual minorities in the age of AIDS. The law will prohibit local governments from "promoting" homosexuality, whatever that means, in cultural and educational contexts, affecting everything from libraries and arts and film funding to the employment of teachers who discuss human rights and sex education in the classroom. The self-censorship by artists, educators, and cultural administrators, all relying on public funding, could be even worse. Opposition to the clause includes the largest gay-rights demonstrations ever seen in Europe, raids by lesbian guerrillas on the BBC and the House of Lords, and threats by David Hockney to withdraw his works from British galleries.

CALCUTTA, MARCH 1988. My lecture on Canadian documentary film seems to have interested an eager sellout crowd despite the stifling hall. Afterwards, I am asked a very pointed question not about Canadian documentary film. My questioner has dug up my 1985 *Jump Cut* article on gay erotic film. (Who would have thought that *Jump Cut*, that "commie-lesbian rag" from Berkeley and Chicago, would have made it through Indian customs? Perhaps it's because the editors, somewhat edgy about my illustrations, had processed a few tumescent penises through five generations of xeroxing.) "How can homosexual cultural expression be considered political beyond the obvious level of minority civil rights?" is the question. I am taken aback because I have kept this aspect of my personal and intellectual life in the background here, if not in the closet, out of deference to a society whose sexual ideology I find inscrutable at best and conformist and familial at worst. It is an excellent and impossible question. Are gay liberation and the cultural and political issues entailed a luxury that only the wealthy individualistic "First World" can afford? Is the personal less political in a so-called Third World society organized along collective lines?

Outside the hall I see a *hijra* (member of a wandering caste of eunuchs, transvestites, and hermaphrodites with ancient ritual functions) in the crowded bazaar. He/she winks carnivorously at me and lifts her/his skirt, but I don't linger to see whether essence or construction is dangling beneath.

Many Indians are fiercely committed to the struggle against gender oppression. Interestingly enough, within the independent film circuit I am researching, feminist directors constitute a unique and vital core, addressing issues not only of gender politics but of all vital issues confronting Indian society, from casteism and communalism to the environment. One of the most stunning films I see is a documentary on "dowry deaths" (murders of newlywed women by greedy in-laws). Another woman's film tackles the interface of bonded labor, prostitution, and untouchability, first from the perspective of caste and economics and then from the unsettling perspective of gender.

Meanwhile, a gay male friend, a cultural historian, shows us around Delhi, including the tomb of Jamali Kamali, a Mughal poet-saint buried alongside his male lover, a gleaming architectural treasure in white marble and blue tiles, an essentialist's dream. Zakir adds something that amazes me, that the political context is more friendly to gays in India than in Montreal, where as a student he was arrested in one of the notorious bar raids of the late seventies and terrorized in legal limbo for years. Not that the choice between a Delhi closet and a Montreal jail is any choice at all.

Censorship is a very current issue in India, where the "democracy" of repressive tolerance functions less smoothly than in the West. Censorship is sexual: commercial films are monitored for any explicit sexual signs, including kissing, until recently, resulting in the most erotic (and most neurotic?) cinema in the world—ingenues in minimal saris brushing tree trunks with fluttering lips, etc. Censorship is also more conventionally political—several of the "oppositional" filmmakers I meet have had to battle the censors all the way to the Supreme Court—to say nothing of the inherent censorship of the film distribution system itself, which will never let them into the theaters or on TV. Sounds like home.

MONTREAL, JUNE 1988. I'm back, and there is a bit of good news about censorship. A temporary reprieve has spared us Bill C-54, thanks in no small way to lobbying by feminists, artists, and cultural organizations (including the Concordia Cinema Students Association). While we're waiting for the next federal initiative, constant vigilance is required, particularly over local police, provincial film (and increasingly video) censorship bodies, and Canada Customs (who confiscated books by Proust, Gide, and Yourcenar in Toronto last year).

I learn of another provisional victory. The owner of the Duluth St. Galerie Fokus is acquitted of charges of indecency (under section 171 of the Criminal Code) for having displayed a photo of a naked woman holding an erect penis between her legs in a show on birth and reproduction. Still the police got even through a conviction on a municipal bylaw when the gallery placed a protest board reproducing the seized photo on the sidewalk.

Is this the same bylaw used a few years ago to browbeat the Shadow Project participants for having sketched silhouettes of vaporized Hiroshima victims on Montreal sidewalks? Concordia Fine Arts students and faculty were among the accused, but their peers often subscribe to a naive mythology of free cultural expression in Quebec. My 1986–87 class on the Arts in Canada was surprised to hear about Mayor Drapeau's administration's bulldozing (literally) of "Corridart," a huge public art event only ten years earlier. In court the city's art historian henchmen argued that art should be beautiful rather than political.

Of course all of these clashes are in the shadow of larger, darker censorships. The North American Free Trade Agreement seems to be lurching more or less relentlessly ahead. Cultural workers' lobbying has been much less successful here than with the obscenity bill. Have we won the obscenity battle only to lose the right to all indigenous artistic expression and the whole culture war?

Speaking of Free Trade, I learn that my New York publisher has dropped my book because they would "simply not be able" to market the vintage "illicit" photos ("sucking and penetration—even erections would be very iffy").

Meanwhile the new *Jump Cut* has come out. I am moved to see that they are running an eight-page editorial statement on "Representing AIDS" that includes a long piece on "Safer Sex Guidelines." Last fall the U.S. Senate amended an appropriations bill to prohibit federal AIDS education monies from being made available "to provide AIDS education, information, or prevention materials and activities that promote, encourage, or condone homosexual sexual activities" and to require such monies to be used to "emphasize" "abstinence from homosexual sexual activities." This literally fatal amendment has effectively cut short the work of the most effective AIDS prevention organizations in the United States, such as the Gay Men's Health Crisis (New York). *Jump Cut* defiantly reprints the *GMHC Safer Sex Comix No. 4*, depicting condom use. The *Jump Cut* policy on tumescence has evidently evolved.

Censorships and Tories and erections all rouse and droop, but meanwhile Registration is coming up fast and is a fairly constant variable. Looking back at my stock-taking of a year "outside," it is clear that the separations of inside and outside, art and politics, culture and smut, First World and Third are false . . . and sometimes true. The critical path for teachers in Fine Arts in the nineties will be to dislodge false separations and other fictions and censorships and to keep graffiti and guerrilla tactics alive in the studios and classrooms.

Essay published in Renée Baert, ed., *Critical Paths: A Collection of Essays and Artworks from the Faculty, Staff, and Students of the Faculty of Fine Arts, Concordia University* (Montreal 1988), 39–41

Whipping Up a Cinema

*   *   *   *   *

Writing an intro to the latest lesbian and gay film festival for our local cine-matheque audience, I felt I was again preaching to the unconverted. In this translation from the original French, my reference to the revolution of '89 was of course to the French Revolution (I hope the other local references will not be an obstacle to international readers), and my explanation of Stonewall was still necessary for the linguistically insulated heterosexual readership. My defense of queer cinema and video events still seems valid a decade later, and in fact the phenomenon is still growing after more than twenty years of development.

*   *   *

Homosexuality shocks less, but continues to be interesting; it is still at that stage of excitation where it provokes what might be called feats of discourse. Speaking of homosexuality permits those who "aren't" to show how open, liberal, and modern they are; and those who "are" to bear witness, to assume responsibility, to militate. Everyone gets busy, in different ways, whipping it up.—*Roland Barthes*[1]

Nineteen eighty-nine marks the anniversary of more than one revolution. For three days in June 1969, an enraged mob of drag queens and gay bar customers fought off police in the streets around the Stonewall Tavern in New York's Greenwich Village. The repercussions of "Stonewall," this gay Bastille, weren't really felt in Quebec until 1971, when the brave *Front de libération homosexuel du Québec* started appearing at "indépendantiste" rallies with slogans such as "Vive le cul libre!" [Long live free fucking] and "Il faut se libérer soi-même avant de libérer le Québec!" [We have to free ourselves before freeing Quebec].

On the twentieth anniversary of Stonewall, and the two hundredth anniversary of the decriminalization of sodomy in the French Republic, yet another gay-lesbian film series unfolds at the Cinémathèque. It is thus a good time to take stock briefly of this mysterious entity that is the gay and lesbian cinema (do gay movies love other movies of the same sex?).

Looking home first of all, one discovers in the *cinéma québécois* of the eighties a modest but robust "whipping up" of alternative sexuality, striking in its contrast to the famine of the seventies. On the surface it is what many of us have always wanted: banality, a situation where "feats of discourse" hardly seem necessary any longer. How else to describe a situation so ordinary that three Quebec features appear at the Los Angeles Lesbian and Gay Film and Video Festival—*Firewords, Salut Victor,* and *The Heart Exposed*— the latter acclaimed as most popular feature. And to this everyday discourse of TV movies are added such major voices as Léa Pool and Yves Simoneau (both are also well represented at foreign gay-lesbian festivals).

Nevertheless, homosexuality can never be quite as banal as all that. In Quebec as elsewhere, sexuality stubbornly refuses to lose its profoundly political import, as unwilling martyrs from Pierre Lacroix to Joe Rose, from Sylvie Lamothe to Chantal Daigle[2] keep reminding us. In this tense climate even the tenderest parables of awakening and reaching out, like *Salut Victor* and *The Heart Exposed*, become bold manifestos.

As for *Passiflora*, which the "damage control" strategy of the NFB's PR office has almost succeeded in making us forget, this whimsical anarchist dystopia now clearly emerges in retrospect as one of the most important Quebec films of the eighties; its gay-feminist perspective is all the more prophetic in the dark summer of 1989 as the Jean-Guys join the Jean-Pauls as the smotherers of the liberated body.

In comparison, Michel Langlois's luscious short, *Exit 234,* the only 1989 gay male entry from Quebec in the Cinémathèque series, seems oddly classical, even retro. In Langlois's spectacle of unconsummated desire, the Quebec countryside becomes the pre-Stonewall past; this sensibility of tense triangles was previously enshrined in the cinéma québécois of the sixties, appropriately enough, in Claude Jutra's still misunderstood *A tout prendre* and in the stuttering work of Michel Audy, revived in last year's series.

Such are the films, politely ignored or misinterpreted in the heterosexual media, which the perennial gay-lesbian series have the important role of reclaiming, of reconnecting to a vital cultural tradition. The present series is the eighth to take place in Montreal over the last decade, if I've counted correctly, echoing those everywhere throughout the West. True, the Patricia Ro-

Curt McDowell, manwatching in *Loads* (1980). Frame enlargement.

zemas and the Lizzie Bordens, the Derek Jarmans and the Merchant-Ivorys all now show up on commercial screens and in the video stores, and the Ottingers and the Schroeters regularly appear at Montreal's hetero festivals and retrospectives. Yet this impulse for gay-lesbian audiences and programmers to affirm difference, to name a cinema that still too often dare not speak its name, continues to proliferate (despite the discriminatory refusal of funding bodies, I might add).

I have not yet mentioned the pandemic that has proved the most important factor in shaping international gay-lesbian cultures in the eighties. Barthes could not have predicted a decade ago the devastation that has led homosexuality to shock a great deal more in the eighties. Yet, except for Arcand's hideous metaphor of blood-red urine in *Decline of the American Empire*, Quebec film- and video-makers have succeeded in sleeping rather comfortably through the AIDS crisis, including the filmmakers of the NFB. If René Lavoie's pioneering programming on AIDS over the last two years did nothing else but fill in for our media community's criminal negligence, his work is still indispensable. This year there are few works that address AIDS directly, no doubt because of the glut of films and video presented during the Conférence internationale sur le SIDA last June. Yet the traces of loss and of resistance are everywhere below the surface. One remembers filmmakers who have participated in previous gay-lesbian manifestations in Montreal and who have since fallen to the Syndrome: Guy Hocquenguem, Curt Mc-Dowell, Arthur Bressan. Bressan's question-and-answer appearance in the hall of the Cinémathèque after his presentation of *Buddies* in 1986 took place a few months before his death. Not knowing that Bressan's spirited responses masked his sense of his own mortality, the audience was still moved beyond tears by his energy and humor and by the simple emotion of his film, a challenge to death and complacency, an exaltation of sexual love.

On the fortieth anniversary of Stonewall, our Holocaust will hopefully be behind us, but I hope that the Cinémathèque will still be lending its screen to the celebration of difference and of desire, to whipping it up.

Original publication in French as "Billet," *La Revue de la cinémathèque* (Cinémathèque québécoise, Montréal), October–November 1989, 14

Notes

1 Renaud Camus, "*Tricks*, an Excerpt from the novel by Renaud Camus," with a preface by Roland Barthes, *Christopher Street* 5, no. 5 (March/April 1981): 14.
2 Joe Rose was fatally gay-bashed on a Montreal bus by a gang of punks; Chantal Daigle was successfully sued by her estranged boyfriend Jean-Guy to prevent her from aborting their child; Sylvie Lamothe was fired from her job for being HIV positive; Pierre Lacroix was a priest implicated in a sex scandal with an underage male.

Erotic Self-Images in the Gay Male AIDS Melodrama

*   *   *   *   *

First presented at a "Representing AIDS*" conference at the University of Western Ontario and at an American Lesbian and Gay Studies Conference in 1988, this piece of cultural analysis by a tired academic never seemed as urgent as the activist video work that was catching the energy and anger of the time. Narrative genres simply didn't have either the short-term efficacy or the glamour that the context demanded, so I had the impression of being beside the point alongside the brilliant leadership offered by Simon Watney, Douglas Crimp, John Greyson, and Jan Zita Grover, among others whom I was meeting at the conferences. Spreading myself out within the local Concordia* AIDS *committee and the video programming committee for the Fifth International Conference on* AIDS, *held in Montreal in 1989, I was aware of the tremendous potential of the wave of video activism by then at its peak but was mostly a user rather than an organizer. In fact I must confess that I was sitting exhausted and shamefaced in the audience when the* ACT UP*-ers in* T*-shirts, mostly from the States and Toronto, butchly stormed the stage at the conference (and I've never worn a baseball cap in my life).*

Still, the guilty conscience of the critic and historian aside, when the piece finally came out in the Canadian anthology in 1992, it did seem to have been a little prophetic alongside the melodrama cycle of the nineties: Longtime Companion *(1990),* Zero Patience *(1993),* Philadelphia *(1993),* Savage Nights *(1992),* Silverlake Life *(1992), and* It's My Party *(1996). And retroactively, if this chapter is the only record of those stirring early independent films like* Buddies, *mostly disappeared from circulation, then that alone is a gesture against forgetting. My point about activism and its relationship to popular culture and narrative mythologies is of course still an interesting and unresolved one—not to mention that between activism and academia. And* An Early Frost *no longer looks as bad as it once did, despite all the energy that went into dismantling it— so sue me.*

*   *   *

This article was first presented in embryonic form at "Pedagogy and Politics," the Second Annual Yale University Lesbian and Gay Studies Conference in October 1988. Also on the agenda at Yale was a "gays in the media" panel of the kind that have become second nature to lesbians and gays over the last two decades. Three scholars in a row embarked on familiar tirades against the made-for-TV gay melodrama, focusing principally on *An Early Frost*, one of the earlier major fictional representations of AIDS on the U.S. commercial networks. It is a movie we have all come to love to hate but one over which many of us secretly wept copious tears. The panelists were of course correct in their dissection of *An Early Frost*, and I am certainly not about to defend it or the made-for-TV melodrama. Yet in their blanket dismissal of the melodrama per se, I wonder if the panelists were involved in a somewhat careless, ahistoric, and even elitist negation of the heritage and current arsenal of gay popular culture.

In this essay I would like to defend that much stigmatized genre, melodrama, which has in fact been the format, I would argue, for some of the most important gay male cultural responses to the epidemic. Specifically, for two or three years, starting around 1984, when the first fully developed cultural responses to AIDS started appearing, melodrama was the principal vehicle in independent gay male fiction in film and video (and theater as well, though that is beyond my territory for the moment) for our dealing culturally with the trauma, fear, bereavement, and sacrifice that AIDS has occasioned in our community.

Melodrama is the genre that popular culture has traditionally drawn on to work out the strains of the nuclear family under patriarchy. This form that evolved for the orchestration and resolution of the conflicts of the emotional sphere and the domestic realm, constructed on the dynamics of hopeless passion and inevitable societal repression, undeserved suffering and impossible choices, has historically had special contextual relevance for the women's audience. The melodrama—the woman's film, the weepie, the tearjerker, the soap opera—has been traditionally opposed to the male genres of effective action and rationality in the outside world, from the western to the whodunit, and, until the feminist renovation of the discipline of film studies, was unjustly stigmatized by film historians for this reason. Gay

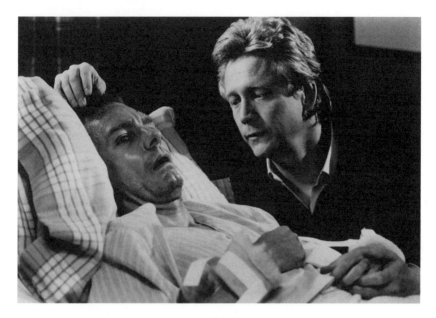

Longtime Companion (1990): the climax of the eighties' AIDS melo cycle. Museum of Modern Art Film Stills Library.

An Early Frost (1985): the AIDS melodrama we hate to love and love to hate. Museum of Modern Art Film Stills Library.

critics have often followed this pattern, batting about pejorative terms like *sentimental, maudlin,* and *Rodgers-and-Hammerstein* to dismiss one of the special if not essential forms of gay popular culture. They follow, as Richard Dyer has pointed out, our culture's putdown of forms too closely allied to bodily responses, like horror, arousal, belly-laughs, and weeping.[1]

The 1984–86 cycle of film and video melodramas may already be familiar to the reader: William Hoffman's *As Is,* adapted in 1986 by Home Box Office for pay-TV and the home video market; the two New York indie feature films, Arthur Bressan's *Buddies* (1985) and Bill Sherwood's *Parting Glances* (1986); Stewart Main and Peter Wells's New Zealand television film *A Death in the Family* (1986); to this list I would like to add two safer-sex porno-melodramas that express an undeniable continuity with the "legit" works: *Inevitable Love* (1985), produced within the U.S. sex video milieu and directed by a man named "Mach," who I am told is a prolific writer of erotic fiction; and *Chance of a Lifetime* (1985), produced by the Gay Men's Health Crisis (I am speaking primarily of the third episode, "Hank and Jerry").[2]

These works remind us, as has often been argued, that the melodrama has had a privileged relationship with gay men as well as with women, both as audience and as producers, situated as we are, like women, if not outside patriarchal power, in ambiguous and contradictory relationship to it. It is not surprising that the community that enshrined *Camille, Dark Victory, Brief Encounter,* and *A Star is Born* in the gay pantheon (and incidentally made major artistic contributions to those films as well) should have confirmed the melodrama as the key gay film genre of the period between Stonewall and the Epidemic: think of *A Very Natural Thing; Sunday, Bloody Sunday; Fox and His Friends; The Consequence; Making Love;* and even *The Times of Harvey Milk.* The pattern continues with films like *Maurice,* situated outside of the AIDS problematic (inasmuch as that is possible).[3] As the epidemic entrenched itself, it was no accident, I'm sure, that one of the first major documentary features on AIDS, Nick Sheehan's *No Sad Songs* (Toronto 1985)—a portrait of a man with AIDS taking leave of lover and family—echoed in its title *No Sad Songs For Me,* a 1950 Hollywood melodrama in which a terminally ill Margaret Sullavan prepares her children and husband to go on without her. The melodramas *Parting Glances, Chance of a Lifetime,* and *Inevitable Love* may all briefly play with male action genre iconography in the form of fantasy interludes (cowboys, Indians, GIS, and jocks), but the effect is to accentuate all the more their hasty return to the vale of kisses and tears, their proper genre home. The melodrama became the first and foremost fictional form for independent filmmakers addressing the health crisis within a popular constituency in the mid-eighties.

My emphasis in drawing up the list of AIDS melodramas is of course on self-representation, gay men's images of ourselves.[4] My corpus presumes by and large, for better or worse, the context of independent cinema and video. (The examples of the New Zealand television film *Death* and HBO's adaptation of *As Is* both confirm the continuing sad necessity of our reliance on gay-controlled independent media for our representation of our lives: although in both cases, the gay point of view is maintained and gay input is determining, material relating to the gay community's political response to the crisis was deleted along the road to broadcast.)

For independent gay artists to elicit tears as a response to the crisis is a worthy aesthetic strategy, especially when the tears are accompanied by the political lucidity that is also a feature of these films (to varying degrees, it can of course be argued) and, perhaps most important of all, when the tears are accompanied, as I would like to demonstrate in this article, by other bodily secretions.

Secretions and sexuality are in fact at the center of the discourse of the AIDS melodramas, and this I would argue is one of their great merits. The framework of sexual desire and love is so essential to the generic energy of these works that they should perhaps be categorized more precisely in terms of a sub-branch, the romantic melodrama. In the romantic melodrama the problematic is not so much the crisis within the family, the nuclear family or the alternative surrogate family, as the impediments to the sexual founding of the romantic unit or the family itself. The independent gay filmmakers who produced the collective articulation of caution, mourning, and consolation constituted by the melodrama cycle have insisted on affirmative representations of our sexuality, on its celebration. In fact they organize the dramatic structure of the works around moments of sexual union and release. As *Buddies*'s person-with-AIDS hero, Robert, declares, "Sex is the part that makes you in or out." In that film as an act of sexual comforting, David, the volunteer buddy, gets alongside Robert, the PWA, in the hospital bed and cradles him as he masturbates. The act becomes an affirmation of Robert's identity, a bond between him and the world, an assurance that he will not die alone. It is also a reversal of an earlier scene of great pain in which Robert masturbates compulsively and without pleasure as he looks at a picture of his ex-lover. "It was terrible," he told David. "I jerked off. Oh, everything worked out. I hadn't fallen apart yet. My cock came but I didn't feel it. There's more to sex than the orgasm grabbed in the dark. I started alone and I finished alone. I don't want to die."

This opposition of "bad/solitary sex" reversed and transcended through "good/mutual sex" provides the dramatic framework for several other works, including both *As Is* and "Hank and Jerry." In *As Is*, one of several works patterned on the separation and reconciliation of lovers, the first sexual encounter is derailed by the discovery of a Kaposi lesion on protagonist Richard's back. At the end Richard has evolved from his former anger and denial, and a final act of sexual sharing in the hospital bed between the reunited lovers signifies their serenity in the face of the crisis and the rescue of sex from its association with disease. In "Hank and Jerry" the PWA's masturbatory dream, though not signified as traumatic, is supplanted by a long sequence of sexual play and consummation with his lover, orgasm dissolving into embrace, the lovers trembling and sobbing with emotion. In all three works sexuality is a sacramental charge, impelling and resolving the melodramatic moment, as well as signifying the force of renewal, healing, and comfort.

The sexualization of the person with AIDS in these films, his conception as an active sexual agent, constitutes a defiant articulation of desire and sexual identity in the face of the stereotypes, the taboos, and the death we know so well. It is also a gesture toward incorporating the point of view of the character into the discourse of AIDS, a reversal of the process of silencing, inoculation, and ridicule that has occulted the reality of these figures in the media. The person with AIDS is shown not only as sexual but also in several instances as downright sexy.

Characters peripheral to the key person with AIDS participate in this sustenance of an erotic narrative universe. The buddy protagonist of *Buddies* is seen more often in his underwear in the single film than Clara Bow was in her entire career, participating in an idealized and fulfilled relationship with his lover, as well as in his increasingly sexualized ministry to Robert. In *Death* also, though less explicit, a diffuse sexual camaraderie is seen as the cement holding together the group of gay male mourners. As for the safer-sex films, needless to say, they do not hesitate to follow the prescriptions of the porno genre, investing every character, line, and situation with an overstated sexual potential.

The transformational operation of sexual exchange attains a particular complexity in *Buddies* through an iconographic opposition of "before" and "after," images of the previously healthy character with AIDS being inserted into the unfolding of the narrative. This is true also of Stash Kybaratas's admirable 1987 video, *Danny*, and of course of the majority of the PWA documentaries. Unfortunately it is equally a gruesome feature of mainstream media representation of AIDS, as several commentators have pointed out, the foundation of the medical pornography of the doomed homosexual and deserving victim. Bressan's orchestration of the structure, relying on both stills and home-movie images of Robert's sunny California past as a countercultural beach hunk, evokes a sexual history in the company of previous lovers that occasions no regrets, no retroactive dynamics of inevitability or morality. It is a past to be celebrated, not to be paid for. As buddy David's personal and sexual commitment to Robert grows, he begins to inhabit that flashback past; fantasizing himself as Robert's beach companion, he begins to claim it as part of his own sexual identity. His idealized and never seen lover accepts this sharing of his lover's erotic energy with a third man, who is nevertheless not felt as a rival. A further dimension is added during Robert's climactic scene of sexual reaffirmation: as he masturbates he is watching on the VCR that David has brought him the 1974 porno film *Passing Strangers*, by none other than Arthur Bressan. A private self-referential conceit no doubt, but in retrospect this autobiographical insert is moving beyond words as the late artist's incorporation of his own past, his sexual and artistic history, even his testament, into the text. But even for the spectator unaware of this poignant extrafilmic significance, the short clip connotes our history through the performers' rippling hippy hairstyles and their aura of San Francisco and gay liberation, a utopian vision of sexuality reclaimed and restored from the past. An affirmation of our cultural heritage of eroticism, epidemic or no, the insert is also an exploration of the erotic component of individual and collective memory. Robert's individual home movie becomes paired with this collective home movie that Bressan's porno film represents, and the gay liberationist heritage is conjured up to bolster us in the midst of crisis.

Parting Glances (1986): not so affirmative of gay sexuality? Museum of Modern Art
Film Stills Library.

In contrast, *Parting Glances*, a film unanimously acclaimed on its release,
now seems to offer by and large a sexual discourse that is somewhat less
affirmative of gay sexuality than may have at first appeared. Here sexuality
seems to be less transformational in both its personal and dramatic operation than a dramatic pretext and a psychic plateau to be left behind. The
main protagonist, Michael, is seen emerging from a lover relationship in
which sex has a teasing, coercive quality. The melodramatic transformation
that occurs is not the renewal of this relationship—though the open ending
does not rule out this possibility—but the strengthening of his relationship
with Nick, his AIDS-stricken buddy, a character for whom he has always had
an unacknowledged and unrequited love deeper even than his sexual love
for the *Gentlemen's Quarterly*–style heel he lives with—shades of Scarlett
O'Hara's love for Ashley Wilkes. Michael's relationship with Nick, like the
relationship in Bressan's *Buddies*, grows and deepens, evolving from adolescent arm wrestling to cathartic dish smashing, platonic embraces and visions of open-ended voyages to be embarked on together, but it never becomes sexual in the genital sense. Though Nick maintains a kind of gaunt

rock-star sexual glamour in the present (he admits to his buddy that he's a thrice-daily masturbator) and a kind of punkish friskiness in the fantasy sequences, sexual exchange seems to be out of the question. *Parting Glances*, otherwise abounding in deceitful or perverse heterosexual relationships and unconsummated gay flirtations, ultimately articulates an attitude toward sexuality that is ambiguous at the very best and at worst symptomatic of a cynical distrust of sexuality that has been reinforced by the health crisis.

Another recent gay melodrama with a not dissimilar pattern of the abandonment of traitorous and illusory sexual passion in favor of platonic friendship is Dick Benner's Canadian sequel *Too Outrageous* (1988).[5] Though AIDS is a minor theme in this film, Benner's profound and unresolved AIDS scars are less smoothly camouflaged than in the New York equivalent: an appealing secondary character suddenly starts a Camille-like cough and is given first the scriptwriter's trapdoor treatment, then is overmotivated retroactively through misleading and didactic fast talking. *As Is* gives occasional evidence of a similar disturbance, though it is ultimately patched over. In addition to *As Is*'s symptomatic connotations of the first lovemaking scene privileged as the occasion for the discovery of the lesion, already mentioned, other aspects contribute to an undermining of the positive vision of sexuality that Hoffman may have been attempting. One scene offers an uncompassionate satire of a pickup in a leather bar, retained from the play even as the health crisis hot-line scene was dropped. The secondary characterization of Chet, the most recent lover of the character with AIDS, is especially problematic. The only figure in the work constructed in terms of conventional erotic codes of nudity, Chet is seen splitting up the originally happy couple and deserting his new lover after the diagnosis; then he himself gets the AIDS trapdoor treatment in the next act, implicated by simple inference as the adulterous source of the hero's infection.

Inevitable Love, one of the two safer-sex videos that are part of this melodrama corpus, is successful in almost entirely avoiding the naming of AIDS (there is a single reference).[6] Nevertheless, AIDS is a structuring absence, accentuated by the conspicuous emphasis on safer sex and condoms and by the occasional passing lecture on condom use. It deploys very much the same transformational structure of sexual meanings and positive perspective of sexuality as *Buddies* and *Chance*. Two closeted roommates, unaware of each other's love, must suffer an ordeal of separation and bad sex (safe and hot, but bad) before finally being reunited, sexually this time, with the line "Forget about the past." The melodrama of unspoken passion has always been a basic formula for the porno industry, with *Navy Blue*, Francis Ellie's mid-seventies classic, providing the basic plot formula for this variation that substitutes college jocks for sailors. The final sex scene risks being anticlimactic, given the intensity of the various "ordeals" and adventures along the road to the lovers' reunion. The editor comes to the rescue with an interpolated flashback of the lovers' original crotch-grabbing wrestling scene from their innocent sublimated past. The effect, in its endearingly trashy way, lacks neither erotic power nor melodramatic transcendence.

A Death in the Family is the only one of the AIDS melodramas to confront through full dramatic representation the death of a major character with AIDS. Surrounded by his alternative gay "family," Andrew lapses in and out of consciousness as the last sixteen days of his life parade by. The transformational sexual structure of the other melodramas is nevertheless still recognizable, now altered, however, by the circumstances of the plot. After his death the ritual of sexual renewal is taken over by two of the mourners who have been brought together by the death. The two men, who have been seen exchanging meaningful looks throughout, are shown kissing, tentatively at first, as much out of mutual consolation as desire, and their eventual sexual union is only implied.

As for the PWA, like the characters with AIDS in *Buddies*, *As Is*, and *Parting Glances*, Andrew's moribund figure is still eroticized in his way. I am speaking on one level of a certain element in his visual conception that consigns an almost ethereal beauty to his face, body, and limbs.[7] At the same time, through the mise-en-scène of nonverbal communication, Andrew's body is constantly maintained in sensuous tactile contact with his grieving friends. Comfort is implicitly shared back and forth through caresses, touching, looks, and smiles. The bathing scene, a traditional format for the erotic representation of the body, is particularly eloquent in this regard, luxuriating in the textures of skin and fabric, in the light reflected in the movement of water, and above all in the simple childlike pleasure registered on Andrew's face. At another point Andrew plays with his doctor's baby, enriching the atmosphere of pansexuality (as well as inserting an important didactic message about contagion). Even after his death, Andrew's corpse continues to be an erotic icon, like the bodies of martyrs in the Baroque painterly traditions evoked continuously by the filmmakers' composition and lighting; his body continues to be touched, even caressed, with the classical imagery of candle flame, flowers, and sky now adding to the sensuous luminosity.

It is Wells's and Main's insight into the erotic nature of comforting and receiving comfort, of the human body even in abject humiliation and pain, of the sexual dimensions of the act of mourning itself, whether solitary or communal, that particularly distinguishes *A Death in the Family*. This insight is present in a more diffuse way in all of the melodramas under discussion by the very nature of their generic construction and address: all melodramas invoke after all the contradictory beauty and pleasure of suffering. In *Danny*, the video maker's grieving voice makes this point explicitly as his camera lovingly scans in tight close-up both of Danny's bodies, before and after AIDS-related chemotherapy. Eroticism is clearly a potentially creative phase in the trajectory of the responses to dying and death, an embodiment of acceptance and affirmation of the body. As Michael Bronski has argued in his moving personal reflection on this unconventional association of sex and death, eroticism is, for the mourner, as in this context for the artist and the spectator, "a constructive way to regain a sense of self and strength in a world that is too difficult to bear at the moment. . . . The primal act of sex seems to mock death by reaffirming the feeling of being alive."[8]

What about safer sex? The space remains to inventory and reflect only briefly on the discourse of nuts-and-bolts sexual behaviors within the framework of the melodrama genre and in reference to the political imperative of the films' context. The "legit" films (i.e., nonexplicit ones) tend to privilege relationship sex, as the current fashion and the generic demands of the melodrama would have it, though they do not close the door on what the lovers of *As Is* nostalgically call "non-committed sex." Masturbation is acknowledged to exist and to be a valid dimension of the sexual spectrum, as is group sex, but ultimately the couple is the locus of the positive incarnations of sexuality that are envisioned. Except for *Buddies*, none of the legit films depicts orgasm directly, and this may testify to an evolving conception of sexual behavior in our community, the dispersal of the cult of come. The safer-sex videos support this hypothesis, not only through the almost total banishment of the close-up "money shot" from the iconographic register (the defetishization of the infested discharge?) but also in the opening up of the spectrum of sexual behaviors. Of particular interest is the legitimation of a sexual union in which one or even both partners may not come. Otherwise heavy scrotal licking and on-the-belly and between-the-legs frottage are on the ascendent. Condoms are surprisingly rare, except in *Inevitable Love*, where they are everyone's "favorite thing to wear" (to quote John Greyson's safer-sex rock video). *Chance* eschews anal fucking, even protected, but *Inevitable* goes all out. It is ironic that kissing rather than fucking remains the litmus test of sexual politics, as it was before AIDS: its absence from *As Is* calls into question the good faith of the Home Box Office apparatus and the straight-identified actor in the lead role, just as its delirious presence throughout the safer-sex films and *Parting Glances*—and of course its climactic function in *Death, My Beautiful Laundrette, Maurice, Torch Song Trilogy*, and even *Kiss of the Spider Woman*—indicates a new maturity in our sexual self-representation. Kissing, with the romantic, even transcendental, semiotic baggage it has acquired in our culture, returns us to the subject of melodrama, where the nitty-gritty of condoms unfortunately seems ill suited to the spiritual union of two hearts. Did Rock Hudson wear a condom in *Magnificent Obsession*?[9]

The mechanics of love and orgasm are thus evolving in the domain of our self-representation. Our melodramas have reflected this to a greater or lesser degree. Perhaps more important, their resurgence in the mideighties may have helped keep in view a certain continuity of cultural tradition and sex-positive erotic energy, mingling the "positive image" ideology of seventies gay-lib aesthetics with the cathartic function of narrative fiction to help us in the crisis of the eighties to communally mourn the dead, comfort the living, and imagine the future. None of the films or videos I have discussed is without ideological tensions and elisions, yet they have participated in a kind of cultural healing process within the framework of gay popular culture. To the extent that they have succeeded in flowing through the channels of ghetto distribution, they have been at the center of our evolving political and cultural consciousness.

Nevertheless, the melodrama cycle may now have spent most of its force, and its mythic concerns may be resurfacing within other generic forms. A possible indication of future directions is the German Rosa von Praun-

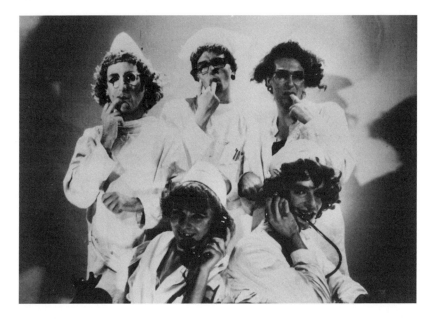

A Virus Knows No Morals (1986): replacing comfort with assault. Museum of Modern Art Film Stills Library.

heim's *A Virus Knows No Morals* (1986), a film that replaces the aesthetics of comfort and eroticism with one of assault. Toward the end of the film, the principal character (played by the filmmaker himself), an unscrupulous gay sauna owner who thinks safe sex is bad for business, is wandering amid the flower beds of a cemetery, thinking about the epidemic, his sex life, and a departed employee, organ music sobbing in the background. "This disease makes me horny . . . ," goes his voice-over soliloquy. "Sex is life and I believe in life."

One might think out of context that this is a conventional scene of the melodrama genre: von Praunheim might have been Shirley Maclaine at the end of *Terms of Endearment*. Yet the context in *Virus* disallows this reading: elsewhere, this "black comedy" (as it is tactfully labeled by distributors to ward off audience uprisings) is a bleak nihilistic dystopian farce in which every possible implicated constituency is scornfully satirized—medical researchers, health-care workers, tabloid reporters, people with AIDS, AIDS activists, Christian celibates, gay profiteers, AIDS therapists, bureaucrats, mothers, widows, and babies. Everyone gets AIDS and ends up in a concentration camp called "Hell-gay-land." In short, *Virus* is an antimelodrama. A long series of melodramatic situations is shredded with gleeful Brechtian savagery: in addition to the hospital-bed suffering scene's exploding in a murderous assault with an infected syringe, there is also a tearful reunion with a mother figure that degenerates into a raucous screaming match and a poignant diagnosis that quickly slides into slapstick.

What about sex? Sex is a halfhearted ritual in an empty sauna littered with shit or in a cruising park where condoms dangle from the trees and used Kleenexes cover the earth. It is hesitatingly approached by naked young innocents wandering around at the end of the world. Sex becomes what Arthur Kroker would call cynical and parodic, panic sex, sex without secretions by bodies in ruins at the postmodern end of the simulacrum of the world, the pleasure of catastrophe. Eroticism is as impossible as is melodrama itself. Is von Praunheim engaged in a clever political tactic for stirring up our profoundest cultural response by turning the melodrama upside down, or is his work simply a way of dealing culturally with the epidemic, an artistic embodiment of the stage of mingled rage, paranoia, and suicidal self-pity that many of us have gone through or will go through? It is only our knowledge of the context of *A Virus Knows No Morals* and its use within its author's tireless AIDS activism in Germany that allows us to infer some level of sincere commitment from the graveyard credo. It is interesting that the film, despite a few enthusiastic reviews, has to my knowledge not really struck a responsive chord outside of Germany.

The antimelodrama is not the only alternative: Canadian video maker John Greyson has evolved from a 1985 coming out melodrama, *The Jungle Boy*, to a new feature film, *Urinal* (1988), a political sci-fi parlor mystery, as playfully sex positive and studiously camp as it is lucid and angry, situating the health crisis on a spectrum of other gay political issues and beyond. This, we can hope, may be part of a larger pattern. Will the gay melodrama expand its role of conscience, consolation, pillowbook, and elegy, crossfertilizing with those other resilient cultural forms of our heritage, comedy and camp, as they adjust to the imperatives of the current political emergency? Can the deconstructive froth of the camp response and the visionary

anger of the activist documentaries absorb the depth of feeling and affirmation of desire that the AIDS melodramas articulated?[10] Should we ask for
both the moon and the stars?

[1988] In James Miller, ed., *Fluid Exchanges: Artists and Critics in the AIDS Crisis*
(Toronto: University of Toronto Press, 1992), 122–134

Notes

1 Two book-length historical studies of the film melodrama that appeared in 1987 are
Mary Ann Doane, *The Desire to Desire: The Woman's Film of the 1940s* (Bloomington: Indiana University Press), and Christine Gledhill, ed., *Home Is Where the
Heart Is: Studies in Melodrama and the Woman's Film* (London: BFI), which includes several of the pioneering individual articles on the subject that have appeared since 1970. A similar re-estimation of the importance of the melodrama is
taking place in literary studies, as Geoffrey Rans mentioned to me at Western,
pointing me to such works as Philip Fisher, *Hard Facts: Setting and Form in the
American Novel* (New York: Oxford, 1985), and Jane P. Tompkins, *Sensational De-
signs: The Cultural Work of American Fiction* (New York: Oxford, 1985). Dyer's comment is in "Male Gay Porn: Coming to Terms," *Jump Cut* no. 30, special section on
"Sexual Representation" (March 1985): 27–29.

2 Paul Vecchiali's 1988 French film *Encore* (Once More) may also be added to this list,
but I will not come back to it because I have not ascertained its cultural context and
cannot say whether the producers are merchandising AIDS to the dominant culture
as yet another morbid metaphor or whether this problematic and disturbing work
can be situated as an authentic utterance from within the gay community; outside
the purview of my audiovisual corpus, Larry Kramer's theatrical play, *The Normal
Heart*, it may be noted, also has a strong melodramatic line, involving a traditional
teeter-totter between the demands of love and vocation and culminating in a death-
bed marriage ceremony.

3 Mark Finch and Richard Kwietniowski have commented on the melodramatic
affinity of *Maurice* in an astute and acerbic article ("Melodrama and *Maurice*:
Homo Is Where the Het Is," *Screen* 29.3 [summer 1988]: 72–83), but it is a film that
I am not ashamed to admire. *Maurice* belongs to an impulse toward literary adaptations from the pre-AIDS universe that admittedly signifies in some ways an escape
from the demands of the present, but, notwithstanding its *Masterpiece Theatre*–
class aura, Ivory's work has importance in terms of a popular project of the restora-
tion of gay historical memory.

4 For this reason I do not consider such made-for-television melodramas as *An Early Frost*, regardless of how much gay input may have been present, since their emphasis on the heterosexual point of view moves this work over into the problematic of media representation of AIDS, a topic that is currently receiving the lion's share of gay cultural analysis.

5 Both star Craig Russell and director Richard Benner would die shortly hereafter of AIDS, as would Bressan and his *Buddies* PWA star Geoff Edholm.

6 There is no space here for a tirade about the thriving porno industry's avoidance of the epidemic (except for a few exemplary figures like Richard Locke). It's unfathomable to me why there has been so little debate about the industry's utter bad faith in its masking of whatever safe sex the performers are fortunate enough to be allowed to practice on the set and above all in its abundant glamorization of risk behaviors. Apart from perfunctory printed guidelines scrolling here and there, and some producers' self-righteously pronounced avoidance of internal ejaculation (when did the come-shot trade ever show internal ejaculation?), the industry's culpability in this matter is a baldly stated matter of record. Nor is there space to savor the irony that our arguments about the difference between individual consumer fantasy and the collective politics of sexual practices, advanced in the porn and censorship wars of the early eighties, are now coming back to haunt those of us who are very disturbed about the foot dragging of the porno sector.

7 Of course, this has left *Death in the Family* open to the criticism (not long in coming in today's vigilant climate) that the ugliness of AIDS deaths is thereby trivialized, a criticism that if valid is equally applicable to all the works under study. However, unless we insist that fiction's aims are to provide medical documentation, rather than to operate mythically on some level, this criticism does not invalidate the films.

8 "Death, AIDS and the Transfiguration of Grief: Thoughts on the Sexualization of Mourning," *Gay Community News* (Boston), July 24–30, 1988, 20, 13.

9 Cindy Patton is developing some interesting analysis of the representation of sexual intercourse in mainstream material, heterosexual as well as lesbian-gay, since the onset of the epidemic. A promising installment is "The Cum Shot: 3 Takes on Lesbian and Gay Sexuality," *Outlook* (San Francisco) 1.3 (fall 1988): 72–77.

10 One listener's response at the conference at Western reminded me that my discussion is open to the misreading that I am arguing an "unproblematical return to the melodrama" as a useful activist cultural strategy. This is certainly not the intent of this historical assessment of various works within gay popular culture of the mid-eighties. If there is any implied tactical prescription in this analysis, it would simply be that activist artistic initiatives need to harness positive erotic energies, as well as incorporate existing momentum from within gay popular culture(s), as opposed to some of the inaccessibly avant-gardist and deconstructivist efforts in which our

community resources have been invested (which fortunately remain in the minority). It would also seem appropriate for the activists that the crisis has brought to the surface to profit from the lessons learned by the earlier seventies generation of cultural activists, on the left as well as within the gay-lesbian movements, namely the importance of a wide range of cultural responses within a broad-based culture of resistance—including pleasure, humor, eroticism, fantasy, and pathos—and that anger, denunciation, and reactive media critique cannot be the sole cultural diet of a community in for a long haul.

In Memoriam: Vito Russo, 1946–1990

* * * * *

Here I am writing again for the popular press, this time for Xtra, *Toronto's market-savvy defanged version of* The Body Politic. *This was clearly not the forum for me—having to eulogize Vito in four hundred words would never do. In retrospect the obit seems bitchy and begrudging about the man who'd come sick, grinning with generous complicity, to my talk at some gay conference or other, crouching on the floor because the usual porno-title effect had crammed the hall. But then I know he'd agree with my instinct not to sanitize the dead. . . .*

* * *

Vito Russo, author, activist, and supreme chronicler of lesbian and gay aspirations—and betrayals—on the silver screen, died November 7 in New York after a five-year struggle with HIV. Vito will be remembered as the author of *The Celluloid Closet: Homosexuality in the Movies*, one of the most influential books on film of the eighties; as an *Advocate* columnist who got complacent gay consumers to really care about Hollywood's crimes of representation; and as an indefatigable champion of anger, caring, and humor in the Epidemic wars.

To be sure, some of us in academia may have wondered about aspects of Vito's work: his cranky resistance to theory, left politics, and alternative film/video production, his American-centered cultural framework, his omission from *Closet* of the history and dynamics of gay fandom (no mention even of his beloved Judy Garland!). Yet without exception we were indebted to the visionary populism at the root of these idiosyncrasies, to Vito's grassroots political instincts, his encyclopedic knowledge and keen eye.

In addition to his impact as a writer and a speaker whose fierce and campy lectures packed them in around the globe, Vito was a pioneering gay militant, a founding member of New York's original Gay Activists' Alliance in 1969 (for which he used to program all-night film festivals). Fifteen years later, during the second generation of gay activism sparked by AIDS, Russo was still a whirlwind of energy and rage, helping to found ACT UP and the Gay and Lesbian Alliance against Defamation, and becoming one of the most eloquent spokespeople for people living with AIDS.

Vito's ideas always vibrated with lucidity, perceptiveness, and respect for his audience. In one of his last interviews (with one of my students, Matt Hays, to whom the unwell yet busy activist didn't stint a precious long hour), Russo raised these principles to the level of a credo: "You have to trust your audience. To trust that they'll be intelligent and sophisticated. And to have a little guts. I approach everything with the idea that gay men and lesbians are going to have courage."

Vito himself had more than a little guts and courage; he's probably up there in queer heaven right now, slugging away at negative stereotypes.

Xtra (Toronto), no. 162, XS supplement (January 1991): 8

We're Talking, Vulva, or, My Body Is Not a Metaphor

*   *   *   *   *

This piece was commissioned by The Banff Centre for the Arts for a volume following up on their controversial show "Much Sense: Erotics and Life," in 1992–93. It had been controversial because Banff is an alpine oasis of the artistic and cultural avant-garde in the Texas of Canada, our wealthy redneck Bible-belted province of Alberta, which only this year has been forced by the Supreme Court to add sexual orientation to its charter of rights. Right-wing media and troublemakers had reacted hysterically to the explicit sexual imagery in the show, in particular performance work by the Vancouver lesbian collective "Kiss and Tell," and threats of provincial defunding were in the air. Curator Sylvie Gilbert conceived of the book to synthesize and assess, for a half dozen authors to pursue the themes of the show in words and ideas.

Well, it turned into another saga of censorship and demogoguery. Culturecrats and printers alike got cold feet, and my own illustrations for this reflection on the film and video components of the show somehow ironically became a testing ground of political will. Even my backing off on the queerest and most explicit of my illustrations didn't help, and the anthology went into a holding position limbo that lasted more than four years. As I wrote this in 1998, I was not holding my breath about the anthology, entitled Arousing Sensation, *ever appearing: the latest version had continued to show monkeying around with the pictures in a volume that is ostensibly about the politics of art, sex, and censorship (deleting a video still from Katie Thomas's 1990 biographical video* Francesca Woodman, *showing a female torso and pubic area, for example). (Flash update: as of press time 1999,* Arousing Sensation *is on its way after all!)*

As it stands, the piece represents an important new direction of my work, attempting to situate queer imagery within a larger context of homosocial and feminist cultural discourses. It was dedicated to a courageous Montreal PWA video artist, Esther Valiquette, who died as I was writing the piece, author of Récit d'A and two tapes not in the Banff show, but all indelible luminous images about sexuality, the body, identity, and history.

* * *

Sylvie Gilbert's selection of five films and eight videotapes entitled "Much Sense: Erotics and Life" must have been strong stuff for the ethereal mountain atmosphere of the Banff Arts Centre. Almost four hours of bodies being pummeled, pressured, prodded, probed, pierced, penetrated, and pissed on, as well as prized, petted, proffered, and proudly pumped, left even this jaded viewer from Down East not only alliterative but gasping for oxygen.

Women's bodies, lives, and sexualities are the substance of this remarkable show. Leading women artists in film and video are presented alongside the upcoming generation: from Canada, Lisa Steele, Midi Onodera, and Lorna Boschman alongside Katie Thomas and Stasie Friedrich; from the United States, Peggy Ahwesh and Paula Levine, alongside Sadie Benning, Greta Snider, and Leslie Asako Gladsjo; from the United Kingdom, Pratibha Parmar. Also included are Toronto video artist Colin Campbell and Ahwesh's collaborator Keith Sanborn. Gender is so much the organizing principle that this particular male author, my specialty being relatively tame representations of men loving men, feels somewhat of an outsider, slightly confused but honored by the challenge to write much or little sense about it all.

The thirteen films and tapes can be looked at from two different angles, first as documentary and only then as eroticism. (And who knows which angle was the most scary for arts funders?) An unacknowledged documentary tradition has been of primary importance for the feminist and avant-garde cinema and video of the last generation. Half of these films and tapes are structured more or less on the documentary idiom that my Spielberg-suckled directing students would pejoratively call "talking heads." Of course sex doc poses very distinct aesthetic and ethical problems for talking heads: accordingly, heads in the show may be disguised by masks (*Mirror, Mirror*), below-the-shoulder framing (*Scars*), silhouettes (*Khush*), and actresses (*Skin*). Yet the testimonial impulse of the political cinema launched in the late sixties (the New Left, the women's movement, minority rights, and lesbian-gay liberation) is present all the same. Interestingly, even Benning and Snider, two artists that operate furthest from documentary codes—the baby dyke with her toy camera reinventing Hollywood in her bedroom (*Jollies* and *It Wasn't Love*), the all-hung-out California urban commune members reinventing Sodom in theirs (*Shred O'Sex*)—both seem to spend half their time in gigantic head-on close-up, fogging up the camera lens as if in tribute to the talking head. However histrionic, the status of this self-portraiture as documentary truth value—whether by baby dykes with painted mustaches or by skinheads who fuck their skateboards—is without a doubt. I think we will never be tired of listening to new voices emerging from silence or of discovering new faces crystallizing in the shadows of invisibility and stereotype.

But something else is going on in these works, and not just heads talking of the new marginalities, demographies, and epidemiologies that Gilbert invited to Banff (women living with AIDS, South Asian lesbians and gays, institutional survivors . . .). The testimonial impulse migrates down the treasure trail from the talking head to the talking body: talking arms (*Scars*); talking labia, nipples, and frenula (*Stigmata* and *My Body Is a Metaphor*); talking organs and orifices (*Shred O'Sex*); talking skin (*Francesca Woodman*). If the original sixties and seventies documentaries of solidarity, consciousness raising, and coming out privileged the gifts of speech and hearing, Lisa Steele realized as early as 1974 (*Birthday Suit—with Scars and Defects*) that the bodily sense of touch and feel was also emerging within the iconography of liberation, that the body was becoming a new organ of speech, a new performative apparatus of survival, empowerment, and communication. That she did so the morning after the partial decriminalization of sodomy, abortion, and prostitution in many Western countries—a full dozen years before the earliest other work in this exhibition—was prophetic. Steele's conceptual adaptation of body and performance art may have been taped deadpan in a rarefied white studio in the seventies, but it anticipates the gritty real world inhabited by the palpable, malleable bodies that are the raw material of the eighties and nineties.

Steele's tape is also the link between the more conventional documentary works in this show (*Mirror, Mirror*) and those stemming from entirely different formal directions and cultural roots: the erotic tale (*The Deadman*), the porno film (*Shred O'Sex*), the home movie (Benning's two tapes), the comic sketch (*Ten Cents a Dance [Parallax]*), and the found footage mosaic fleshed out with the medical microfilm (*My Body Is a Metaphor*). The heads may talk compellingly and proudly in all of these works, but it is the bodies that *really* speak. It is no accident that the last decade has seen dialoguing penises in European features (the French *Marquis*, Henri Xhonneux, 1989, and the German *Me and Him*, Dorris Dorrie, 1988), not to mention singing assholes (*Zero Patience*, John Greyson, 1993) and all-singing, all-dancing vulvas (*We're Talking, Vulva*, Shawna Dempsey, 1990). Bodies pulsate in the universe of the spectacle to claim authenticity and pain; bodies ask the order that invented cyberspace, Schwarzenegger, and mammary implants, do we not *really* bleed, scar, throb, and swell?

Bodies, yes—genitals, orifices, epidermises galore—but erotics? What exactly is meant by the title "Erotics and Life"? Did anyone actually get turned on up there in Banff other than the bigots in the media and the Alberta cabinet? A pity that the local audiences for the film and video screenings were not larger, for one would expect that Albertans whose annual tourist extravaganza is the binding, spurring, racing, harnessing, whipping, taming, and barbecuing of large mammals would find the branding and harnessing of humans (*Stigmata*) pretty hot. In any case, I might otherwise have been tempted to pronounce prematurely that for most viewers most of Gilbert's films and tapes are *about* erotics without *being* erotic. Even these works that most blatantly borrow the familiar textual conventions of visual eroticism (*Shred O'Sex, Khush*) might be thought too self-reflexive, too jokey, or too just plain ideological to get the juices flowing in any sustained way (can politics ever fortify desire?). Granted, erotic art usually builds on the tension between documentary grain and oneiric mist, but can erotic dreams handle Brechtian interruptions without getting flaccid?

On second thought, well, yes. Having just finished an out-of-control book on gay male eroticism in photography and film from their nineteenth-century origins up to 1969[1]—a book that finds love in all the least familiar places, from ethnography and exercise instructions to crime detection manuals—I know that any sweeping generalization about the art of desire is asking for trouble. In every audience-text interaction bloom a hundred turn-ons.

If we compare "Much Sense: Erotics and Life" to those twentieth-century traditions of film, photo, and stage eroticism that an amnesiac culture and Canada Customs want us to forget, echoes and continuities abound. Indeed most of the artists in the show use tried-and-true erotic vocabulary. The great theatrical tradition of burlesque, for example, was based on the exhibi-

It Wasn't Love (1992):
Sadie Benning's
"burlesque" exhibitionism.
Video frame grab.

Stigmata (1992): reinventing
seventies West Coast lesbo-
erotica and winking at *Penthouse*. Video frame grab.

tionist strutting, wisecracking, and self-conscious staring down of the audience that Snider and Benning sewed into *Shred* and *It Wasn't Love* respectively. As for the radical body alteration of *Stigmata*, it mimics the obsessive
body sculpting of the physique pose films that used to turn on our gay ancestors in the fifties and sixties; at the same time, its sense of women's bodies
reinvents the seventies West Coast lesbo-erotica of Tee Corrinne and Barbara Hammer but also winks at the gynecological hyperrealism of *Penthouse*-style centerfolds. The talkfests like *Mirror Mirror, Scars,* and *Ten Cents
a Dance [Parallax]* all unwittingly recall a short-lived genre of the mid-sixties
when the censors allowed words to outpace images and strange dirty-talk
movies (women talking about their below-the-frameline bodies) briefly became a staple of the U.S. soft-core industry. Of course one of Onodera's cun-

ning set pieces targets the phone-sex trade, an industrialized revival of that dirty-talking tradition. Even Parmar, in many ways the most chaste but also the most sensuous of the Banff artists, explicitly reclaims earlier genealogies of eroticism, not underground this time but mainstream: swirling veils, stamping anklets, filtered light, and tropical homosocialities via the Bombay-Madras film industry of her ancestral homeland.

There are also memories of the underground. Everything from the earnest masks of *Mirror, Mirror* to the artisanal spontaneity of Snider and Benning, complete with tacky Magic Marker title cards and low-definition black and white, remind me of pre–sexual revolution clandestine traditions in which signifiers of shame, hand-developing, and toy technologies were the norm. In fact, as I argue in my book, such undergrounds were fundamentally political in their formation of oppositional community. Who could deny that the sleazy Polaroids and murky 8mm films of the pre-Stonewall fifties anticipated the new women's media and performance arts of the eighties in their enactment of taboo desire?

As for the avant-garde, sex has always been too important to leave to the underground and the mainstream: cycles of utopian erotic obsession have marked avant-garde history. Thomas's luminous black-and-white epidermal landscapes recall more than one prehistoric avant-garde film, for example Willard Maas's *Geography of the Body* (1943). Ahwesh and Sanborn include affectionate homages to two vintage epics of sex and death that epitomize earlier golden ages of the erotic avant-garde, the anarchist surrealism of Bunuel's *L'age d'or* (1930) and the East Village flower child hysteria of Jack Smith's *Flaming Creatures* (1965).

Finally, *Penthouse* is not the only artifact from after the so-called sexual revolution to be appropriated and transformed in this show. Ahwesh and Sanborn evoke in *The Deadman* not only the Sadeian universe of excess and satiation borrowed via respectable French pornographer Georges Bataille (author of the story they adapted). They have absorbed also, no less than Snider's lecherous roommates, the commercial hard-core films of the seventies that Linda Williams found safe enough for her scholarly feminist analysis fifteen years later in *Hard Core: Power, Pleasure, and the "Frenzy of the Visible."* In particular those two canonical narratives of insatiable "nymphomania," *Deep Throat* and *The Devil in Miss Jones* (both 1972), hover over the work, now turned on their heads (as it were) to become an oddly exhila-rating fable of a woman who shouts for whiskey and fucks her brains out. As for Friedrich's lurid microclose-ups of pulsating vessels and gaping valves, their erotic lineage seems closely related, with just a touch of Right-to-Life fetus pornography thrown in for good measure, just the kind the late Tory Family Caucus loved.[2]

I mentioned gender at the start of these reflections and somehow must come back to this unspoken organizing principle in conclusion. What does it mean that the few men represented in Gilbert's selection serve as accesso-ries or amanuenses? Campbell's *Skin* is atypical of his work in its dramatiza-tion of transcripts from women living with AIDS; and, other than Sanborn, the only other male film- and video-makers are Snider's male housemates, pumping and primping as uncredited supporting performers and coau-thors in *Shred O'Sex*. As for gay men, we may not be absent from the large and small screen in this panoply of bodyworks, but on reflection we're unex-pectedly scarce behind the camera (is it because of Canada Customs' ban on anal penetration, or is the government of Alberta right in claiming we don't exist?). In fact this scarcity is noticeable because the work of such gay artists as Bruce Labruce, Marc Paradis, and John Greyson—to name only a few Ca-nadians who come to mind—would have fit perfectly.[3] After all, gay male film- and video makers can be thought to have been pioneers in the arts of the body. Moreover, as Gilbert recognized in programming *Skin* and *My Body Is a Metaphor*, the AIDS pandemic has sparked corporal iconographies that bleed into other imagery of body exaltation, alteration, and mortifica-tion in the show. Mostly gay male HIV+ and PWA artists as diverse as Carl George, Andy Fabo, Greg Bordowitz, and the late Marlon Riggs, Tom Joslin, and Esther Valiquette (an amanuensis of sorts for a gay male PWA in her first work) have all demonstrated this continuity again and again.

Noticing such patterns is not to take away from the urgent priority of fo-cusing on the women's voices and images reshaping the vocabularies of bodies and sexualities in the eighties and nineties. It's about "taking our power back," says the tattoo artist from *Stigmata*, about dealing with "visi-ble stuff rather than internal stuff I can hide," says one of Boschman's scarred heroines. The last thing we need is yet another man griping about exclusion from women's space. Yet such a strict gendered focus can be hard to maintain in the current context. After all, Onodera, Ahwesh, Snider, Friedrich, and Parmar all could not resist incorporating male homoerotic imagery in their works in the show, and I for one am delighted with this "appropriation." Dialogue is continuing to open up as fast as the thighs in these works, and the Michigan Womyn's Music Festival, in this symbolic landmark year, has finally opened its gates to transsexuals. On some level, at least in terms of bawdy and body images, biological gender essentialism may make less and less sense.

Erotics and life, sex and documentary, the gendered and transgendered body theater of bedroom, street, and imagination are what this show is about. As it happened, the Alberta media lynch mob focused on the "Kiss and Tell" "lesbian performance" and symptomatically paid scant attention to film and video. No need to feel left out, for I have a hunch that some of the bad girl hetero stuff would have frightened the horses of the patriarchy even more (Ahwesh, Snider, and above all Gladsjo's shot of the phallus itself being pierced). Whenever our endemic crises in sexual politics converge with crises in sociocultural politics—sex radicals vs. family values, an urban "tiny coterie of grant-hungry artists" and "anarchists in the subsidized arts clique"[4] vs. populist, nativist, and rural politics within a downturned economy—the shit really hits the fan, and outlaws, marginals, subalterns, and so-called elites are scapegoated. It is ironic that while avant-garde artists are systematically exploring pop forms and while audience and distribution are becoming deep-rooted concerns of artist-run outfits, the polarization between artists and the so-called mainstream has been exacerbated.

It may be that the pandemic has widened the rift of fear and loathing. The new imagery of bodies—fluids, membranes of tissue and latex, cells, lesions, hollow eyes, and loose skin—is largely absent in most of the works in this show (although Ahwesh inserts a condom that wasn't in Bataille's original story . . .). But HIV is present as a profound shivering absence all the same. Is AIDS behind the propensity of several of these artists to link the eroticization of the body with its mortification, sex with pain and death? Whatever the reason, women artists' appropriation of sexual imagery, their use of the body as a blank screen and malleable clay, is a political ultimatum that the powers that be understood all too well. This body on which we carve our revolt and register every sensation, this body from which we squeeze every drop of pleasure and pain and reach out every gesture of community and autonomy, this body is a battleground—not only against the virus but also against censorship, conformity, and control. In the province of the hyperreal and the all too Real Women, our bodies are not metaphors.

In memory of Esther Valiquette

[1995] In Sylvie Gilbert, ed., *Arousing Sensation: A Case Study of Controversy Surrounding Art and the Erotic* (Banff, Alberta: Banff Centre Press, 1999).

Notes

1   *Hard to Imagine: Gay Male Eroticism in Photography and Film from Their Beginnings to Stonewall* (New York: Columbia University Press, 1996).
2   A network of ultraconservative Conservatives who gained the upper hand in the cabinet during the Mulroney administration of the eighties, influencing the government's hand on rights around freedom of speech, reproduction, and sexual representation, and succeeded in defunding various women's organizations. Affiliated with the far-right pseudo-women's lobby group Real Women.
3   The late Robert Flack's presence as one of three visual artists featured in the installation side of the show brought genders closer to balance, as well as stepping up gay male visibility.
4   Headlines in *Alberta Report*, March 1, 1993.

Walking on Tippy Toes:

Lesbian and Gay Liberation Documentary of

the Post-Stonewall Period 1969–1984

*   *   *   *   *

This is the longer, earlier version of my contribution to an anthology on queer documentary, first given as a paper at the Visual Evidence documentary conference in Boston in 1995 and trimmed—hatcheted, I thought—as it moved through an unusually rough tunnel on the way to publication.

Anthologies have been a big genre in the queer academic publishing boom of the nineties, and I have done my bit. Few realize the underside of the anthology industry, however, anchored disproportionately on the unpaid labor of impoverished graduate students and other unremunerated contributors and on shortcut, erratic, and ideologically zealous editing (a major struggle over my use of the second-person plural pronouns seemed to me symptomatic of a neurotic subculture of linguistic and cultural microidentity politics that had lost touch with the real world). In another recent anthology, French-language this time, I was forced to use "we" with a gun at my head, because that's the constipated French academic convention adopted. (At the same time, I wonder if my increasing bad temper in the company of editors is simply part of my midlife crisis, postbreakup, post–catastrophic flirtation with alternative parenting, post–Hard to Imagine birthing . . .). In any case, we're [oops] lucky to have a flourishing literature that we [oops] can complain about, and history tells us [oops] that it will probably not last. . . .

This look back at the seventies in fact echoes some of the process of The Fruit Machine itself. It is a special challenge for cultural historians to assess a period they have experienced. In such a process, of course, the temptation of mythologization is always present, and there's always a fine line between recycling and reviewing/rethinking. I hope that Fruit tilts decidedly toward the latter.

*   *   *

Camp is individualistic; as such, it relishes the uniqueness and the force with which personality is imbued. This theatricalisation of performance derives both from the passing experience (wherein, paradoxically, we learn the value of the self while at the same time rejecting it) and from a heightened sensitivity to aspects of a performance which others are likely to regard as routine or uncalculated . . . this awareness of the double aspect of a performance. . . .
—*Jack Babuscio, "Camp and the Gay Sensibility"*[1]

Mother: It started actually in high school. You were in the plays in high school and did a beautiful job. And that's why I think that speech and drama was a very good start for you. . . .

Father: Well, all I can say is I think that you get mixed up in the drama, the music and the arts of that type, I think it's a . . . most people have a tendency toward that type of thing that . . . Maybe I'm wrong. I don't know anything about statistics, I've never looked it up but most people who are in arts and drama are walking on tippy toes, a little fluttery, you understand what I mean. When I was a kid, the guys that played the violin, with the long hair, that kind of stuff, they were a little more effeminate than most people, so when you get mixed up with the arty people, that's it. You just join the gang, I guess.

—*from Tom Joslin's* Blackstar: Autobiography of a Close Friend

Years of Famine

I was a Film Critic for the Gay Revolution. Over a decade beginning in 1976, I must have written several dozen film reviews, mostly for the Toronto "Magazine for Gay Liberation" known as *The Body Politic*. I recently sifted through these once-urgent dissections of the state of gay cinema, denunciations of various capitalist-homophobe conspiracies from within and without, and overstated celebrations of each new "breakthrough." One 1980 pronouncement that "the famine is over" caught my eye.[2]

Famine? Did we ever feel the burden of representation back then! I'd forgotten what it felt like in those days before there were queer film and video festivals in every city and twenty-year-old queers with video cameras at every gathering. *Famine, drought, silence,* and *invisibility* had indeed been the words that cine-pinko-fags used to describe the audiovisual environment in the first decade after Stonewall. Perhaps my own frustration was exacerbated because the post-Stonewall famine had coincided, paradoxically, with an age of feasting for the 16mm social-issue documentary film. From *Harlan County, U.S.A.* (Kopple, 1976), to *Union Maids* (Reichert and Klein, 1976), from *The Sorrow and the Pity* (Ophuls, 1971) to *The Battle of Chile* (Guzman, 1977), what a thrilling trajectory it was for artists and audiences who wanted to change the world with images of reality! So why, as I assembled an anthology on "committed documentary" in 1980 (published only in 1984), could I not include a single gay male documentary in my "radical" corpus and manage to squeeze in only a single, discreet lesbian-authored short that addressed sexual orientation as part of a spectrum of feminist issues.[3] I remember not including the 1977 "breakthrough" *Word Is Out* (Mariposa Film Group, 1977) because I then agreed with ideological criticisms of the film's integrationist agenda and its soft-pedaling of transgression and activism. But for my next two attempts to assemble a more inclusive body of lesbian and gay documentary, a 1982 lesbian and gay film and video festival—the first in Canada—and a 1983 curriculum package, the pickings were still very slim. By then I could draw on the eclectic mixture of 16mm documentary shorts that was only beginning to accumulate in 1980–81, topped off by some uneven work in Super 8 and community video, and fleshed out by ambiguous films by feminists who were not willing or ready to claim publicly the L-word label (Margaret Wescott, Su Friedrich, Janis Cole and Holly Dale, Chantal Akerman, Michelle Citron). But why had there been no queer *Harlan County*?

My international working filmography for this article, about twenty pre-1980 titles, may now seem too respectable to justify the word *famine*. Famine is of course relative (African American documentarists were then an even scarcer breed than lesbians and gays), but the lesbian and gay corpus is indeed tiny, dispersed, and erratic compared say to the sustained wealth of women's movement image making in Europe and North America during the seventies. A 1978 review of *Gay U.S.A.* (Bressan, 1977) and *Word Is Out* by Lee Atwell, one of the decade's handful of visible gay critics of any stature, mentioned two obvious reasons for the six-year gap between the promising *Some of Your Best Friends* (Robinson, 1971) and *Word Is Out*: "Large segments of the gay populace feared any sort of public exposure that might mean loss of jobs, friends and/or family support. Simply getting an openly gay woman or man to appear before a camera was a primary difficulty. And secondly, the difficulties in financing a nonsensational (non-commercial) treatment of the subject was virtually insurmountable."

Aside from the lingering closet and the unorganized apparatus for financing, distribution, and criticism, other obvious factors were in play. With regard to the U.S. infrastructure, it took some time for Carter-era liberalism to penetrate the blackout in public broadcasting and in the funding bodies. The invisibility of lesbians and gays within the still largely homophobic Left/New Social Movements networks persisted,[4] and it was only in the eighties that the alternative distribution outfits, for example Toronto's DEC, would take on gay and lesbian titles. Meanwhile future leaders of eighties lesbian and gay documentary were tactfully present within leftist and feminist organizations: if Peter Adair and one or two other Mariposa Collective members were coming out of careers in progressive documentary to make *Word Is Out*, Richard Schmiechen and Margaret Wescott were still quietly at work at Chicago's Kartemquin Collective and Montreal's Studio D respectively. It was only on the tenth anniversary of Stonewall at the 1979 Bard College Alternative Cinema Conference that North American lesbian and gay media activists actually came together for the first time and surprised the straight left attendance with their unified demands, including that alternative distributors "seek out, distribute, and encourage the production of media made by lesbians and gay men."[5] The right-wing backlash of the late seventies fanned the new militancy all the more: Atwell thought that the 1977 Dade County catastrophe (Anita Bryant) had sparked socially conscious filmmakers like artsy porn-maker Artie Bressan to get on the bandwagon, and California's 1978 Briggs Initiative was the catalyst of what would eventually be *The Times of Harvey Milk* (Epstein, 1984). My own 1980 declaration of famine's end was probably inspired as much by the proletarian-butch Italian feature *Ernesto* (Sampere, 1979) as *Word Is Out*, but suddenly there did seem to be lots of documentary projects in sight at the turn of the decade, especially in the United States and Canada, films that finally had the right to be underfunded, mediocre, or single issue because they were no longer solitary voices in the wilderness.

In 1984 I came to write an overview article on post-Stonewall documentary, eventually called "Lesbian and Gay Documentary: Minority Self-Imaging, Oppositional Film Practice, and the Question of Image Ethics."[6] By the time it was published in 1988 my sampling had swelled to twenty-four documentaries from six countries, but most were postfamine titles from the first half of the eighties, and seven were dated 1977, 1978, or 1979. The only earlier film was *It Is Not the Homosexual Who Is Perverse but the Situation in Which He Lives*, the unique 1971 jeremiad by Rosa von Praunheim, the Berliner who (symptomatically) would go on to make the best documentary of U.S. Gay Liberation, *Army of Lovers or Revolt of the Perverts* (1978).[7] My overview, in addition to discussing particular problems around community accountability and (self-) censorship, argued that distinctive aesthetic strategies had evolved in response to the ethicopolitical challenges of our identity politics as an invisible minority and the volatile audience dynamics of a minority steeped in what Jack Babuscio called "the passing experience." Among these strategies I noted particular approaches to creative collaboration, such as collective authorship and consultative procedures, and, most important, performance-based techniques for incorporating the input of subjects into the process and for filling in gaps left by conventional documentary methods. These performance-based techniques included particular inflections of standard interviewing, editing, and expert testimony styles, "coming out" variations of consciousness-raising formats borrowed from women's movement documentaries, and expressive elements that were more theatrical than the standard documentary idiom of the day allowed: dramatization; improvisatory role playing and reconstruction; statements and monologues based on preparation and rehearsal; nonverbal performances of music, dance, gesture, and corporal movement, including those of an erotic and diaristic nature.

What I didn't realize in 1984 was that I was summing up the first generation of lesbian and gay documentary. Nor did I realize that by squeezing in the first works of 1984 and 1985 by lesbians and gays of color,[8] the first few references to AIDS, and *The Times of Harvey Milk* (whose 1985 Oscar symbolized once and for all the *real* end of famine), I was heralding the next period of what Richard Dyer calls "post-affirmation" cinema,[9] to be marked not only by the Epidemic and postcolonial voices but also by a discursive flux around issues of identity. It was only in 1990, with Dyer's definitive *Now You See It: Studies on Lesbian and Gay Film*, that it finally seemed possible to get a historical handle on the first-generation documentaries. Looking back now from the vantage point of 1995, I am struck even more that performance-based aesthetics was their distinctive contribution, as well as their most important link with the queer nonfiction of the late eighties and nineties. I would therefore like to devote the rest of this space to extending my reflection on performance as the crucial idiom of the famine years.

Performance and Performativity

> I pass, like night, from land to land
> I have strange power of speech
> That moment that his face I see,
> I know the man that must hear me:
> To him my tale I teach.
> —Coleridge, *The Rime of the Ancient Mariner*

First, however, I need to define more precisely what performance means as a documentary ingredient. I have argued elsewhere that, contrary to a layperson's commonsense notion of documentary as a window on an un-scripted, undirected, unrehearsed, and unperformed reality, performance and mise-en-scène have been a basic syntax of realist discourse throughout the *entire* one hundred–year documentary tradition: "Performance—the self-expression of documentary subjects for the camera in collaboration with filmmaker/director—was the basic ingredient of the classical documentary."[10] And not only of the classical documentary: throughout the modern phases of documentary as well—if we use Nichols's neat but useful categories, the *observational* impetus of the sixties, the *interactive* impetus of the seventies, and the *self-reflexive* impetus of the eighties—collaborative performance has maintained its centrality in the lexicon of documentary re-alism.[11] This has been consistently true of that vast majority of documentary productions, in which subjects have been aware, actively or passively, of the camera and by extension of the spectator.[12] Performance has been a constant regardless of whether the favored performance mode of the day is what I call *representational* (a mode imitating mainstream narrative, anchored in the performance of *not* looking at the camera) or *presentational* (a mode centered on the look at the camera, performing a direct address of the camera) or a mixture of the two (*Harlan County, U.S.A.; Hoop Dreams* [James, 1994]).[13]

But before showing how seventies lesbian and gay documentarists pushed performance beyond this standard realist lexicon of the day, I must acknowledge that perform-words are very popular in both gender/queer theory *and* documentary theory these days, and a few overlaps must be sorted out. Slippages between the two principal relevant dictionary senses of the word *performance*—"the execution of an action" and "a public presentation or exhibition"[14]—can be as confusing as they are stimulating. The term *performative*, deriving from the first sense and borrowed from speech act linguistics, defines a category of utterance that executes, enacts, or performs the action that is uttered, for example, *I apologize, I sentence, I promise, I welcome,* or the *I do* of the marriage ceremony. Hence Judith Butler's theory that "gender reality is created through sustained social performances," that maleness or femaleness are "*performative* in the sense that the essence or identity that they otherwise purport to express are *fabrications* manufactured and sustained through corporeal signs and other discursive means."[15]

Similarly, Bill Nichols posits performative documentary as a dominant of nineties documentary, reflected in such films as *Sari Red* (Parmar, 1988) and *Tongues Untied* (Riggs, 1989), which are not only referential (or *constative* to continue the speech act terminology) but primarily performative. Like an utterance that not only describes but executes a transformation in the relationship of speaker and listener, performative documentaries "address us . . . with a sense of emphatic engagement that overshadows their reference to the historical world . . . mak[ing] their target an ethics of viewer response more than a politics of group action or an analysis of the ideology of the subject. . . . Performative documentary attempts to reorient us— affectively, subjectively—toward the historical, poetic world it brings into being."[16]

However, as Eve Kosofsky Sedgwick explains with regard to Butler's gender theory, the term *performative* never loses the connotation of performance as exhibition and presentation—in short, theater—primarily because Butler maintains the "apparently unique centrality of drag performance practice as—not just the shaping metaphor—but the very idiom of a tautologically heterosexist gender/sexuality system, and the idiom also of the possibility for its subversion."[17] Nichols also maintains this connection, less explicitly perhaps, in the sense that most of his prototype performative films are documentaries relying on dramatization and self-conscious theatricality (including several, incidentally, that have become canonical paving stones of the new international queer documentary, by Pratibha Parmar, Isaac Julien, and Marlon Riggs). Nichols also names as an ancestor the tradition of autobiography in avant-garde film that anticipates the confessional quality of many performative documentaries and mentions as an example Kenneth Anger (though inexplicably omitting from his summation of that tradition two other precursors of queer documentary, that other autobiograph-performance artist, Jack Smith, and the performance-impresario Andy Warhol). Although Butler disavows the "reduction of performativity to performance" and calls a "misapprehension" Sedgwick's reading of the centrality of drag as both metaphor and paradigm in Butler's argumentation, she seems to leave the options open by using terms like *mime, theatricality of gender, hyperbolic gesture,* and *acting out.*[18] In any case, for me the etymological and homonymic overlap of *performative* and *performance* offers as persuasive a logic as psychoanalytic and deconstructionist hairsplitting. Thus, although I would like to focus primarily on *performance* in the sense of collaborative self-expressivity of a theatrical order—which henceforth I must theatrically indicate as "performance" to avoid confusion—I fear that I too shall still end up discovering "performativity" as well before the exercise is done. "Performance," then, as a primary aesthetic of seventies lesbian and gay documentary, a "performance" idiom that is ultimately politically, culturally, and affectively performative. . . .

Realism and "Performance": Public and Private

> "Ain't nothing like the real thing, baby."
> —song overlaid on climactic montage of anal penetration shots in
> *Erotikus* (Halsted, 1972)

> This film is about who lesbian mothers and their children *really* are.
> —prefatory credit, *In the Best Interests of the Children* (Reid, Stevens,
> and Zheutlin, my emphasis)

> In the field of documentary or *cinéma-vérité* . . . the index of reality is
> somewhat more reliable, and . . . we at least have the advantage of
> experiencing not actors impersonating gay types, but the real thing.
> —Lee Atwell[19]

What I would now like to show is how—songwriters, filmmakers, and critics notwithstanding—bent documentarists of the post-Stonewall famine did not rely on the real thing, the standard realist repertory of documentary performance that was available to them—the idiom that Nichols calls interactive. Like cinematic realisms of any period, interactive realism, a formulaic mix of interviews and archival footage joined by a mortar of observational vérité and musical interludes, was basically invisible to the audience of the seventies. Bent documentarists bent this realism out of shape. They evolved a wide spectrum of distinctive "performance" strategies, idioms of subject self-expression—verbal, dramatic, and sexual—that were both an answer to and an explanation of the invisibility that we felt.[20] Realist documentary, the medium of visualization par excellence, may have seemed adequate to visualize those other visible, fixed identities it would discover and cement in the seventies—worker, visible minority, Third World subaltern, above all woman—but it wasn't up to the job for a new political constituency characterized by both invisibility of social existence and fluidity and hybridity of identities.

For this invisible and hybrid constituency, the day's realism seemed to break down. Lesbian and gay documentarists seemed intuitively to prefer artificial and hyperbolic "performance" discourses that pushed through/ beyond the realist codes, that "[put] the referential aspect of the message in brackets, under suspension," as Nichols would put it.[21] The extent to which they did so and the particular "performance" formats they chose depended on whether the films treated public spaces of political mobilization, the semipublic territory of traditional social networks and sexual undergrounds, or the private spaces of relationships, sexuality, and fantasy. Many films would treat two or more of these domains in the same film, hence the tutti-frutti compendium of performance styles that characterizes so many of them.

Public Space: The everyday performance discourses of lesbian-gay *public* life as it emerged after Stonewall (marches, parades, demonstrations, press conferences, zaps,[22] electoral campaigns, concerts, raids, trials) were handily recorded intradiegetically through realist codes. Hence the parade/march genre, of which two pioneering 1972 films offer prototype glimpses: Kenneth Robinson's *Some of Your Best Friends* and Jan Oxenberg's *Home Movie*. Bressan's jubilant, sunlit *Gay U.S.A.* is the most fully developed example, and the angry nighttime demonstrations of Toronto (*Track Two*, Sutherland, 1982), Sydney (*Witches and Faggots, Dykes and Poofters*, One in Seven Collective, 1979), and San Francisco (*The Times of Harvey Milk*) effect a contrapuntal negative image. Most of the films of this genre couldn't seem to get over the novelty of visible queer public life, which after all had been unthinkable in the previous decade. When Pier Paolo Pasolini had made his documentary on sexuality in Italy in 1964, *Comizi d'amore*, he approached the *private* subject of sexuality primarily through that most *public* of documentary strategies, the "crowd-in-the-street" interview. No wonder that gays were entirely invisible, including queer Pasolini himself (and that street prostitutes, pushed into public visibility by the state closure of brothels and given a voice for the first time in documentary history, stole the whole film in the one scene Pasolini devoted to them).

Two decades later, *Before Stonewall* (Schiller, 1984), our attempt through the interactive compilation-interview format to retrieve the social history of the same period explored by Pasolini, came up with only one or two cinematic documents of public life—most memorably a dignified procession of New York drag queens into a paddy wagon and the lonely shots of the 1965 Mattachine demonstration in front of the White House—and otherwise relied on scarce home movies, snapshots, and print media to connote the rich reminiscences of private life recounted by interviewees. Also made in 1984, *The Times of Harvey Milk* is such an achievement in the queer history genre because of the wealth of audiovisual documentation of newly visible gay public life in the late seventies and early eighties, especially of mainstream electoral politics. These shifts from public invisibility to visibility also account for the staggering difference between *It Is Not the Homosexual*, shot *entirely* in "performance" modes in 1970, and *Army of Lovers*, shot several years later and now able to mix "performance" with strong realist inscriptions of the gay public life that had surged into U.S. streets.

Of *alternative* and *radical* politics in the same period, the resources of realism were less reliable. Political theater was sometimes captured intradiegetically through vérité realism (zoomy and swishy), as in an early zap of a convention of aversion therapists immortalized in *Some of Your Best Friends* (1971), or the famous pie-in-Anita's-face shots, which von Praunheim and several others recycled. Otherwise, von Praunheim's *Army* is probably typical in that, for the most part, the film's statements by movement radicals are self-consciously stagey and anemic, leaving the real vigor of radical gay liberation for self-consciously theatrical agitprop skits by Gay Sweatshop, who camp it up in front of the Meat Rack and undercut a political agenda of "700 leather bars and the right to serve in the army?" In *Blackstar: Autobiography of a Close Friend* (1977), Tom Joslin likewise turned to "performance" not only for vigor and camp but also for the utopian rhetoric of radical politics, letting his lover Mark Massi declaim a gay-lib manifesto alone in a wintry landscape long shot, a long take at once parodic and straight, literally from the rooftops. In one of Barbara Hammer's few films that deal with public space, the artist orchestrates a "performance" of excess, parody, and artifice: Amazon warriors in *Superdyke* (1975) take over urban space and assault its institutional and commercial fortresses (e.g., Macy's) on a rampage of street theater repossession. In short, realism was adequate for mustering ourselves as an electoral minority, but for *real* change (as we used to say), "performance" strategies were preferred.

Semipublic Spaces: For depicting the traditional semivisible social networks of bars and parties, and the coded male sexual underground of toilets, baths, parks, and street cruising, "performance" techniques were de rigueur—even with the advances in portable equipment and sensitive color stocks that seventies documentarists took for granted in depicting similar uncontrollable or unlit settings for other constituencies. Though the semipublic sites of community building, socialization, and political resistance are at the center of our histories (as recalled by the two nineties lesbian bar films, *Forbidden Love: Unashamed Stories of Lesbian Lives* [Weissman and Fernie, 1992] and *Last Night at Maud's* [Poirier, 1993]), they are zones fraught with tension and hypersensitivities—ethical, logistical, and technical. I can't think of a single bar scene developed through realist observational techniques in the entire corpus, although *We All Have Our Reasons* (Reid and Stevens, 1981) does construct a bar scene in well-rehearsed simulated vérité, and *Before Stonewall* stages a bar *reunion* of original participants whose intradiegetic "performance" of songs and rituals is a highlight of the film.

In *It Is Not the Homosexual*, von Praunheim sets up flamboyantly stylized "performance" scenes of parties and bars, only to denounce with his shrill contemptuous voice-over their undercurrents of self-hatred and complacency. The most appealing bar scene in the film, in a neighborhood hangout populated by drag queens, mixed-race couples, leathermen, and other salt of the earth who "don't feel comfortable in piss-elegant bars," is bursting with transvestite yodeling and other "performance" excess. But it is in this populist crossroads that the "desperate and lonely" allegorical hero meets his ideological prince, who leads him back home to his anarchist *Wohngemeinschaft*. In this urban commune the hero discovers the anarchist Alternative, and von Praunheim accidentally pastiches women's documentary and its consciousness-raising realism: a circle discussion of thirty-something longhaired nude chainsmokers lounging on pastel comforters, decrying both ghetto and underground, and climactically erupting in gay-lib slogans. But this realist vision of community is ultimately as "performed" as the garish scenes of alienation, simulated sincerity rather than high artifice.

The *ghetto sauvage* of parks, toilets, and bathhouses was even more of a challenge to documentarists than the bars. Sites of state terrorism and social violence, as well as sexual community, they obviously required highly contrived dramatization: *Some of Your Best Friends* reenacted police entrapment in a park, to which the victim's resistance and eventual vindication became a major realist thread and interactive denouement of the film; *It Is Not the Homosexual* dramatized queer-bashing in toilets; a decade later *Track Two* dramatized the infamous police raids on the Toronto bathhouse that triggered the community mobilization recorded for the rest of the film in vérité. But a much shorter film is the real gem of the underground subgenre: Michael McGarry's *In Black and White* (1979) abjured realist imagery *in toto* to encapsule the private space of the public toilet with abstractly visualized close-ups of carnality, terror, and resistance laid under a "documentary" montage of conflicting public social voices, a Vancouver version of Pasolini's crowd-in-the-street chorus.

Von Praunheim's queer-bashing scene is part of the fresco of creditable explorations of the sexual underground of both commercial baths and non-commercial parks in his work. In *It Is Not the Homosexual*, toilets, parks, and streets were the on-location settings for Brechtian agitprop and what the narrator calls "the tense choreography of men," at once austere and expressionist, all anchored in historical space through Rosa's run-on voice-over denunciation. In *Army*, von Praunheim, changing his tune as well as his continent, is now a nonjudgmental libertine, acting as on-camera guide to the underworld as the camera follows him cruising in Central Park, the Piers, and the Trucks; inspecting a Manhattan bathhouse (where not surprisingly the underground has been appropriated and commercialized in the Glory Hole Room); or accompanying John Rechy on a nostalgia-and-leather-decked fake-vérité prowl through some nighttime city, lamenting the loss of subversive undergrounds of yore. For me, the ideological evasions of voice and the complicitous voyeurism of this observational realist format have actually dated less well than von Praunheim's earlier high artifice.

Jan Oxenberg's *Comedy in Six Unnatural Acts* (1975) matches *It Is Not the Homosexual* and *In Black and White* in its 100 percent deployment of "performance" (not a flicker of documentary realism!). But Oxenberg was performing not subterranean debauchery but another kind of border zone between public and private: lesbian subcultural myths, fantasies, and appropriations of mainstream cultural baggage, from child molester stereotypes to romance. Oxenberg's skits are just as self-consciously frontal and theatrical as von Praunheim's, but her indulgent and affectionate humor effectively engaged communal approval rather than the almost universal outrage that *It Is Not the Homosexual*'s moralization sparked from gay audiences. *Comedy* became one of the few lesbian films of the famine years to attain genuinely canonical status at the time,[23] and when PBS balked at the intimacy of its subcultural circuitry, pretexting "amateurism," the corporation seemed stunned by the universal outcry.[24] In short, "performance" aesthetics may not have been an always reliable resource for exploring semipublic space—especially as regards audiences and broadcasters—but lesbian and gay filmmakers had few other choices in such uncharted borderlands.

Private Spaces: Consciousness-raising documentaries from the women's movement provided a language to post-Stonewall lesbian and gay documentarists for dealing with private life and the domestic sphere. But those who availed themselves of it were not all as successful as *In the Best Interests of the Children*, which became the most successful realist lesbian documentary of the period through its instrumentalist focus on the specific heartstring single issue of custody. Otherwise, trying to express "the personal is political" through realist codes was often a frustrating experience, especially with filmmakers unable to afford the shooting ratios of Wiseman, Kopple, and de Antonio. *Word Is Out* scored, thanks to its epic vision of cultural and class diversity, relying on the comprehensiveness of its interviews and animated by the feature-length confessional narrativity of "coming out" (see below). But by 1980 films of this nature were being disparaged and not only against the ideological checklists that constituted so much movement film criticism of the day. Pioneering lesbian film theorist Caroline Sheldon had already challenged "the assumption of film as 'pure' objective recording device" in 1977 (when as an afterthought she listed five documentaries that constituted a "start" for lesbian political cinema),[25] and Jacquelyn Zita took up the thread in 1981, lambasting "the pretended truth of objective documentaries," "the operatic confessionals of personal life, and the 'talking heads' of political documentary."[26] Quite simply, the antistereotype rhetoric of positive images, role models, and community enfranchisement didn't always fit an observational idiom, whether observational or interactive, that had evolved in order to communicate the texture of individual experience and yet were weighted with a liberal heritage of voyeurism and victim aesthetics. Films deploying collaborative and expressive "performance," including scripted dramatization and improvisation, seemed to surmount this problem, especially those dealing with the past or present private space of personal identities and relationships, with sons, daughters, and lovers. (The alternative families of *friends* are mostly missing from the period's documentary iconography, especially on the gay male side—perhaps they

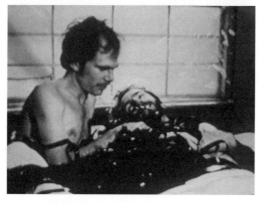

Susana (1979). In the studio with sister: performing open wounds. Frame grab from video version of 16mm film.

Blackstar: Autobiography of a Close Friend (1977). In bed with film: performing the invisible element in a relationship. Frame grab from video version of 16mm film.

didn't match the pre-existing cinematic iconography as readily as parents and lovers.)

Barbara Hammer's films, widely known throughout the seventies within the women's constituency to which they were then restricted and later by mixed audiences, were exemplary for conveying the give and take of sexual passion and exchange, relationships and rupture. They did so not only through the highly stylized editing and image processing she absorbed from her avant-garde mentors and peers, but also through the "performance" of bodily and facial acrobatics. *Double Strength* (1978) and *Synch Touch* (1981), for example, enact erotic vocabularies that are respectively balletic and gestural, based on a collaborative interaction by Hammer and her respective lover of the moment, "performed" intimately to the camera. Whereas a few of her films that deal with the public and semipublic space of lesbian collective politics seem trapped in their time and space—at least to my students, for whom "seventies West Coast" is pejorative critical short-hand for their stereotypes of lesbian politics of the period—the sex and relationship films are fresh and inventive.

Joslin's *Blackstar* bravely tackles not only connubial intimacy but also familial stress. Evasive father and controlling mother both give standard realist interviews on the origins of their filmmaker son's deviance (as we saw in my opening epigraph, where, significantly, Dad attributes it to the "performance" tendencies of the company kept by his son). But complicitous elder brother offers a fake-vérité monologue whose phony spontaneity is unmasked when the editor includes all three takes. There are more stiff theatricality and open wounds in Susana Blaustein's approach to similar territory, *Susana* (1980). The film lines up frontal declarations performed by the author-protagonist's sister, ex-lover, and parents; only the tearful, pleading sister, the sardonic lover, and brutal Susana ("No, Father, . . . You kept telling me to imitate my sister . . .") are actually visualized, whereas the parents are mercifully provided only in voice-over sound. If "performance" opens wounds in *Susana*, it heals them in *Michael, a Gay Son* (Glawson, 1980), which rechannels familial trauma by casting the protagonist's peers as his parents and siblings in role-playing improvisations of rejections and reconciliations.

As Hammer and Blaustein had demonstrated fully, lovers are generally more cooperative than parents. *Word Is Out*'s realist lovers perform indulgent smiles beside the narrator at the mike, cuddling on domestic sofas or lawns or obligingly walking hand in hand in sylvan settings. In contrast, Joslin's Mark Massi, literally in bed with his lover's film, is bristlingly aware of the inadequacies of cinematic realism for capturing the essence of his relationship with the filmmaker and fills the film with self-reflexive chatter about its uselessness:

> *Mark, cu:* What about us? I mean this isn't us, and I'm kind of . . . I feel bad that I'm afraid that we're not going to get us in the film.
> *Tom:* What is that?
> *Mark:* It's those seven years that we shared together, the love that held us together—you know the life and things we share.
> *Tom:* What's missing?
> *Mark:* This is a construction for a film. . . .

Tom: Yes, no, you keep saying, we keep saying it has to come out in dialogue because there's no way to do it visually. . . . And you keep saying maybe there's nothing between us because we can't find any
way of doing it visually and I think that's worth pursuing.

Mark: OK. Pursue. I'll follow.

Tom: Tell me Mark, do you think there's nothing between us?

Mark: There doesn't seem anything that we can do visually, that's for
sure, right?

Tom: There's nothing visible between us?

Mark: Maybe.

Tom: So there's something invisible between us?

Mark: Christ. Stop it. . . . I wanted just to show what we were like, and
that's where we ran into vacancy. . . .

   The crisis within the realist effort to render a private partnership—"running into vacancy"—is crystallized in the above wonderful bedroom dialogue in which the partners play with a "performance art" prop, namely a
spaghetti-like mass of outtakes that have come literally between them. And
when the couple finally agrees on "performance" ("planning something
out") as a means of expressing the invisible element of their relationship,
what to do? Sex is too highly charged to perform for the camera, except a little discreet cuddling under the sheets, and realist dialogue also went nowhere fast. Thus vaudeville banter and a two-minute disco pas de deux to a
Laura Nyro song, climaxing in a presentational pose and kiss for the camera,
was chosen to conclude this film, symmetrically framed in a long-take two
shot. This "performance" scene would be recycled in a similar place fifteen
years later in Joslin's posthumous *Silverlake Life: The View from Here* (with
Peter Friedman, 1993), summing up the relationship once and for all but
now in the before-and-after iconographical context of AIDS memorializa-
tion—the flashback of an artist who has just "performed" that most private
and visual act of all, his own death. In the nineties it looked natural for Joslin
to choose a hybrid interactive-observational video style to tell his last story,
but in the seventies, when private gay space was still contested, "performance" got the nod and defined what is surely the least seen and most underrated gay documentary of the seventies.

Coming Out, Cumming Out

> By the sixties, cocks were in and . . . [pause, as camera zooms out
> and narrator looks significantly at and continues pumping his now
> revealed erect penis] definitely on the rise.
> —Fred Halsted, *Erotikus* (1972)

> I'm coming out now, right? Here I am on television. Big white face
> on the screen saying, "Yeah, you know, I'm gay!"
> —Pat Bond, *Word Is Out* (1977)

The Stonewall generation's political ritual of coming out mixes private and public, "outs" the personal and thereby transgresses the social silence around sexuality and difference. Traditionally it had been the queen and the butch who had played this transgressive role in pre-Stonewall public life, as well as in representation (the sixties had been the great decade of queens on documentary, from Warhol to *Portrait of Jason* [Clarke, 1967]). However, in the seventies the transgressive role was to be played not by the queen, who was quickly shuffled offstage by the positive-image agenda of liberation politics (reappearing only in the eighties),[27] but by the assimilationist lesbian/gay who was by definition invisible and therefore required to *speak* her or his transgression, to come out like the Ancient Mariner by "the strange power of speech."

One might expect that realist modes were more appropriate than theatrical "performance" for capturing this confessional moment because of its premise of spontaneity, its revelation of inner authenticity, and indeed interactive realism is often the aesthetic strategy of choice. Yet this rote ritual is invariably *performed* and often "performed." I am referring not only to some of the most cinematic moments of the coming out repertory, where interviewees perform intradiegetically vivid gestural amplifications of their narratives, for example Pat Bond, swaggering through the role of worldly military dyke in *Word Is Out*, or butch Dorothy Hillaire in *Before Stonewall*, showing the camera how she literally booted harassers across a bar thirty years earlier. I am referring also to the ritualized, premeditated quality of the coming out performances, invariably delivered by a preselected (and in the case of *Word Is Out*, *pre-videotaped*) subject in close collaborative relationship with the filmmakers, moment and place propitiously chosen (usually beside a houseplant).

Not only does coming out require the interactive, presentational mode of interview and monologue by its very nature, but its confessional operation also requires the presence of the spectator, mediated by camera and crew. This operation thus posits performance but also performativity in the linguistic sense, *executing* one's identity of outness as well as *describing* it. It is performative also in Nichols's sense of performative documentary, making the viewer who is engaged by the on-camera confession the documentary referent, not only the speaker. This was assumed by Pat Bond in *Word Is Out*, who laughingly says, "I'm coming out now, right? Here I am on television. Big white face on the screen saying, 'Yeah, you know, I'm gay!' " and by Bruce White, whose voice on a sixties radio broadcast replayed in *Before Stonewall* says, not laughingly, that not only his family will find out, but "I'm quite certain that I will probably lose my job as a result of the program too. . . . I hope that through this means I can be some use to someone else other than myself." These two speakers of different periods know that they are signifying as well as enacting a relationship, cultural, affective, and political, with the viewer. They hold the listener like the Ancient Mariner, not only with bony hand and glittering eye but also with the strange power of speech, and transform him or her in the process. As Robin Wood says in his own coming out text, "gay" is both descriptive and effective: "Gay—not just the word and the fact it points to, but the word and fact asserted publicly: one who is conscious of belonging to one of society's oppressed minority groups, and who is ready to confront the implications of that for both his theory and practice."[28] The performance of coming out becomes the politics of performativity.

Coming out involved transgression of the public-private divide, as I said, but even its transgressive performative power became formulaic. Films such as the staid *Advocate* production *Who Happen to Be Gay* (Belden and Krenzien, 1979), for all their instrumentality in the political context of the 1970s, are also the ones most complicit in social invisibility and in the rote recapitulation of the interactive recipe (interview/snapshots/observational jogging or rock-climbing interlude/interview/workplace interlude/interview); the more these films began to pile up around 1980, the more they deserved Dyer's complaints about "hidden agendas," the erasure of "conflict, contradiction and difficulty," and "the quest for sameness," a concomitant sprawling and repetitiveness, an avoidance of both analysis and the problematization of representation and identity.[29]

Is it to escape these complicities of realism that there evolved highly theatricalized "performance" variants of the coming out formula, from Oxenberg's own cryptic juggling act in the "non-monogamy" sketch in *Comedy* to the explicit self-scripted and self-costumed monologues in *L'Aspect rose de la chose* (Chi Yan Wong, 1980), in which each character controlled his own identity "performance"? It is not simply a question of invoking the theatricality of the gay sensibility here—though there is a distinguished literature on camp and theatricality within gay cultures that is worth reclaiming, once we have separated the essential from the essentialist, as my inaugural epigraph from Jack Babuscio's pioneering essay attests (as well as more than a few tippy-toed stereotypes). Beyond such generalities, the style and substance of "performances" and their meanings in particular contexts must be situated and deciphered. In any case, the memorable queen who stole *Aspect rose* from her fellow collective members with flounces and fabrics was prophetic. For, as the effect of seventies positive images and realism wore off, coming out "performances" would become all the more prevalent in our nonfiction and would increasingly deploy not rock climbing but more and more of what Sedgwick calls "flaming" lesbian and gay "performative identity vernaculars": "butch abjection, femmitude, leather, pride, SM, drag, musicality, fisting, attitude, zines, histrionicism, asceticism, Snap! culture, diva worship, florid religiosity . . . activism."[30]

I would like to single out a particular tradition of coming out "performances" that is erotic. Evolving from the very beginning of the seventies was a whole subgenre of autobiographical sex "performance" films, recharging the power of coming out both as "performance" and as "performativity." In view of criticism already current during the seventies about the censorship of sexuality by documentaries, and my own echo of this criticism in the 1984 piece,[31] it is surprising to rediscover how frequent and brazen this self-erotic imagery of the decade really was. I have written elsewhere of the extraordinary achievement of Curt McDowell's diaristic *Loads* (1980), with its multipartner performance of erotic exchange and fantasy.[32] In fact Hammer matched McDowell's nimble on-camera authorial oral pleasuring four years earlier in *Women I Love* (1976) and one-upped him with a seventies-style lesbian reciprocality ("you-do-me-I-do-you") that Mc-Dowell's strictly "trade" partners wouldn't dream of. Hammer's extreme close-up labial diddling in *Multiple Orgasms* (1976) and *Women I Love* does more than rebut my students' stereotype that seventies lesbians hated sex—it also effectively symbolizes in retrospect the utopian moment of the entire post-Stonewall decade. McDowell and Hammer were far from unique, rivaled in their bravado by von Praunheim's sex acts in *Army of Lovers* (he performs a graphic blow job in a filmmaking workshop he is teaching at the San Francisco Art Institute and has midinterview sex in the Hollywood Hills with Fred Halsted, their telephoto encounter framed with flowers and liberation dialogue).

Halsted, author and star in another genre of seventies "documentary," hard-core porn, is sex "performer" in the porn milieu's own attempt at the docu-history genre, *Erotikus* (1972), where Halsted is on-camera narrator lazily masturbating for the camera as he steers us through the porn industry's lazily selective autobiography. Did we feel the load of representation back then! Chantal Akerman's *Je tu il elle* (1974) acquires a documentary aura around its stunning sex "performance" sequence because of the spectator's knowledge that the author is one of the inexhaustible acrobatic fuckers. There was plenty of soft-core competition, which sometimes seemed equally transgressive, and not only the obligatory "Hi Mom!" kisses for the camera in the parade/march genre. Abundant kissing permeated *Lavender* (Monahan and Jacobs, 1972), whose protagonists "embraced constantly," complained Andrea Weiss in *Jump Cut*,[33] and was the climax to *Blackstar*. *Home Movie* and *Susana* went further, the former with Oxenberg's touch-football pileup seemingly borrowed straight from the sixties with its surrogate substitution of sports for sex, and the latter with its sexy chiaroscuro insert stills and its dramatized shots of topless cuddling, faces obscured by long straight seventies hair.

Like all "body genres," the sex "performance" extrapolations of the coming out rituals executed a complex, even troubled, performativity. On-camera erotic behavior both described and enacted the confrontational track of identity politics, an in-your-face alternative to the assimilationist politics of invisibility. At the same time, the viewer's arousal was qualified by genre clash; documentary tact was scrambled by erotic exhibition and vice versa.

The spectator was engaged, linguistically, politically, and affectively, but also physiologically. Minority politics is not only asserted but "performed" as sexual exchange.

Shots from a Queer Canon

My conception of seventies documentary is not a monolithic or unitary one, far from it: famine or no famine, a rich diversity of aesthetic strategies and ideological negotiations resists efforts to reduce or generalize about this important moment in the history of New Social Movements in the West and its traces in *the* medium of social change par excellence. One can risk the following generalization however: those documentaries closest in organizational links or sensibility to gay and/or lesbian movement agendas were those that remained most anchored to the prescribed realist discourses of seventies documentary and were most visible in movement and community media at the time. Unfortunately many of these seem proportionally less important in retrospect, rightly or wrongly. In contrast, most of the prophetic "performance" films that stand up well in this retroactive view—autobiographical, experimental, and erotic, by Joslin, von Praunheim, Oxenberg, Hammer, and the others—had uneven relationships with the lesbian and gay masses who allegedly preferred positive images and realist convention. Self-indulgent or self-reflexive mannerisms were liabilities in the post-Stonewall political context of simultaneous mobilization and backlash. Even Joslin complained on-camera about "navel-gazing" vérité, and I for one moralistically seconded his prejudice in my own 1984 discussion of the relation of community fund-raising to the "eccentric subjectivism" of personal projects.[34] I now repent, of course, but such prejudices against autobiography and avant-garde practices did mean that much important nonfiction was undervalued or at the very least controversial and prevented from reaching its full potential audience.

Even without these cultural biases, as Nichols explains, performative documentary by definition always runs the risk of being misunderstood.[35] Part of the blockage is the way audiences are disturbed by shifting borders between fiction and nonfiction. And indeed the "performance" films I have privileged in this analysis necessitate a retroactive expansion in the definition of documentary. No doubt if anyone had thought at the time of a generic label for *It Is Not the Homosexual* or Oxenberg's *Comedy, documentary* is not the term that would have come to mind. But now the post-Stonewall generation's documentary image of itself cannot be separated from films that were then marginalized as experimental, weird, personal, short, fictional, politically incorrect, amateurish, divisive, pornographic, and inaccessible. In fact if Nichols is right in identifying performative documentary as the key mode of the nineties, the lesbian and gay "performance" documentaries of the seventies—and earlier (Warhol? Jack Smith?)—must be reclaimed not only as the key to our past but the key to the present.

Who says reclamation and redefinition says canon. My post-post-Stonewall queer students of the nineties who watched in stony silence the seventies documentaries I showed them were not only generational chauvinists (and admittedly the captive audience of a perhaps nostalgic and unimaginative teacher). They also saw themselves, I think, as canon busters, queer iconoclasts criticizing the legacy of Lesbian and Gay Baby Boomers. They may have been right, but busting a nonexistent canon—fragmented and fragile if it exists at all—may well be misdirected energy. Only a few documentaries from the seventies are available on video, and the texts that are constituting our cultural history, from *The Celluloid Closet* to *Queer Looks*, jump over this whole generation of artistic and political practice. (Vito Russo, for example, referred three times to *Word Is Out* but only in terms of content, never in relation to its own cultural importance as the antidote to *La Cage aux folles*, 1978.) For the sake of argument, a canon of post-Stonewall documentaries is exactly what we need. Challenging queer amnesia is not only a question of restoring our cultural history, our performances and our "performances" of the post-Stonewall years. Nor is it only a question of preventing young video queers in the nineties from reinventing the wheel. With the funding crises and political backlash of the nineties, the threat of famine is back, and glimpses of the resourcefulness, courage, energy, and erotic pleasure of our performances during earlier famines may show us how to tiptoe through the next one.

In Chris Holmlund and Cindy Fuchs, eds., *Between the Sheets, In the Streets: Queer/ Lesbian/Gay Documentary* (Minneapolis: University of Minnesota Press, 1996), 107–124

Notes

1   In Richard Dyer, ed., *Gays and Film* (London: BFI, 1977), 46.

2   Thomas Waugh, "Lawn Mowers and Harlequins: Two 'Trigger' Films, *Brad* and *Jenny*," *The Body Politic*, no. 63 (May 1980): 32.

3   Thomas Waugh, ed., *"Show Us Life": Toward a History and Aesthetics of the Committed Documentary* (Metuchen, N.J.: Scarecrow Press, 1984; rpt. 1988). The lesbian-authored short I included was *Heroes* (Barbara Martineau, now Sara Halprin, 1983).

4   This invisibility I discussed in "Gays, Straights, Film, and the Left: A Discussion" (this volume). The phenomenon has recently been analyzed by Michael Warner in his introduction to *Fear of a Queer Planet: Queer Politics and Social Theory* (Minneapolis: University of Minnesota Press, 1993), viii–ix.

5   Thomas Waugh, "Report on the 1979 Alternative Cinema Conference," *Jump Cut*, no. 21 (1979): 39.

6   Thomas Waugh, "Lesbian and Gay Documentary: Minority Self-Imaging, Oppositional Film Practice, and the Question of Image Ethics," in Larry Gross et al., eds., *Image Ethics, the Moral and Legal Rights of Subjects in Documentary Film and Television* (New York: Oxford University Press, 1988), 248–272.

7   I'm not sure why I didn't include some of the other early American works, at least two of which, *Lavender* (1972) and *Some of Your Best Friends* (1971), I must have seen—no doubt because of the critical distribution problems that prevented normal circulation of such works in the pre-video days. Distribution is certainly the reason I didn't include *Blackstar*, which I only was able to see in 1995 in preparation of this article, after having wanted to see it for seventeen years! The film is still unavailable, and, as with Artie Bressan and several other filmmakers whom we have lost to the Epidemic, Tom Joslin's estate is seemingly unconcerned about the problem.

8   To my knowledge, prior to *Framed Youth* (Lesbian and Gay Youth Video Project 1983) and *Orientations* (Richard Fung, 1984), the only titles in the corpus by directors or codirectors outside of the white Euro-American demographic mainstream were *Word Is Out* (Andrew Brown, 1977), *Public* (Arthur Dong, 1981), *L'Aspect rose de la chose* (Chi Yan Wong, 1980), and *Susana* (Susana Blaustein, 1980).

9   Richard Dyer, *Now You See It: Studies on Lesbian and Gay Film* (London: Routledge, 1990), 274ff.

10   "'Acting to Play Oneself': Notes on Performance in Documentary," in Carole Zucker, ed., *Making Visible the Invisible: An Anthology of Original Essays on Film Acting* (Metuchen, N.J.: Scarecrow Press, 1990), 64–91.

11   Bill Nichols, *Representing Reality* (Bloomington: Indiana University Press, 1991), 32–75.

12 My notion of performance as self-expressive behavior carried out in awareness of the camera, with either explicit or tacit consent and/or in collaboration with the director, needs to be distinguished from what Nichols calls virtual performance, the rich repertory of behavioral expression that constitutes social interaction in real life and has been recorded by the documentary camera as an unmistakable generic marker since its very beginning. Nichols's concept, apparently derived from sociologist Ervin Goffman's idea of the performance of self in everyday life, is articulated in *Representing Reality* (122).

13 The subject does *not* knowingly perform for the camera in the small subgenre of the hidden-camera espionage of unknowing subjects. This is not an irrelevant genre for gay film history, come to think of it, given the history of voyeurs with towel-decked home-movie cameras in locker rooms that began in the thirties and that of police surveillance of gay toilet sex that began in the fifties—but this exception is a Foucault-resonant topic for another day.

14 *Merriam Webster's Collegiate Dictionary*, 10th ed. (Springfield, Mass.: Merriam-Webster, 1993).

15 Judith Butler, *Gender Trouble: Feminism and the Subversion of Identity* (London: Routledge, 1990), 136, 141.

16 Bill Nichols, "Performing Documentary," in *Blurred Boundaries: Questions of Meaning in Contemporary Culture* (Bloomington: Indiana University Press, 1994), 92–106.

17 Eve Kosofsky Sedgwick, "Queer Performativity: Henry James's *The Art of the Novel*," *GLQ: A Journal of Lesbian and Gay Studies* 1.1 (1993): 1.

18 Judith Butler, "Critically Queer," *GLQ: A Journal of Lesbian and Gay Studies* 1.1 (1993): 17–32.

19 "*Word Is Out* and *Gay U.S.A.*," *Film Quarterly* 22.2 (winter 1978–79): 50–57.

20 Throughout this piece I use the politically incorrect first person plural to evoke the experience I lived as a (colonized Canadian) member of the heterogeneous (and no doubt hegemonic) discourse community of North American and European lesbian and gay filmmakers, critics, users, and specialized documentary audiences during the seventies . . . the eighties, and the nineties.

21 Nichols, *Blurred Boundaries*, 96.

22 "Zaps" were a characteristic gay lib strategy of public political theater in the early seventies, grafting camp and theatricality onto civil rights tactics like the sit-in, later to be reinvented and perfected by ACT UP–style AIDS activists.

23 Although my perception at the time was that there were more openly lesbian documentarists on the circuit than gay men, lesbians apparently did not share this feeling: Jacquelyn Zita's amusing footnote in the 1981 *Jump Cut* special section "Lesbians and Film," a sarcastic assurance to readers that there were indeed as many as three lesbian-identified filmmakers, probably reflects a widely held sentiment. (See *Jump Cut*, no. 24/25 [1981]: 29.)

24 Edith Becker, et al., "The Last Word: WNET Censorship," *Jump Cut*, no. 22 (May 1980): 39–40.

25 Caroline Sheldon, "Lesbians and Film: Some Thoughts," in Richard Dyer, ed., *Gays and Film* (London: BFI, 1977), 5–26.

26 Jacquelyn Zita, "Films of Barbara Hammer: Counter-Currencies of Lesbian Iconography," *Jump Cut*, no. 24/25 (1981): 27.

27 The major exception to this nonflaming hegemony within seventies "documentary" was the unique British TV film based on the autobiography of Quentin Crisp, *The Naked Civil Servant*. As with this film, Craig Russell's *Outrageous* had a nonfiction aura, based on Russell's persona, and was generally accepted by gay audiences and movement voices. Other gay-authored fictional queens of the late seventies, such as Albin in *La Cage aux folles* (scriptwriter Francis Veber), faced fierce debates in movement and community media, testifying to the delicacy of the queen's political presence. The token queen in *Word Is Out* was outnumbered and relatively restrained but, as with other types included in that presciently diversified film, was scrupulously representative.

28 Robin Wood, "Responsibilities of a Gay Film Critic," *Film Comment* 14.1 (January–February 1978): 12–17; rpt. Corey K. Creekmur and Alexander Doty, eds., *Out in Culture: Gay, Lesbian, and Queer Essays on Popular Culture* (Durham: Duke University Press, 1995), 12–24.

29 Dyer, *Now You See It*, 245ff.

30 Sedgwick, "Queer Performativity," 13.

31 Ray Olson, "Gay Film Work: Affecting, but Too Evasive," *Jump Cut*, no. 20 (May 1979): 9–12; I echoed this criticism in "Lesbian and Gay Documentary."

32 "Men's Pornography, Gay vs. Straight," *Jump Cut*, no. 30 (spring 1985), 30–36. Rpt. in Creekmur and Doty, *Out in Culture*, 307–327.

33 Andrea Weiss, "Filmography of Lesbian Works," *Jump Cut*, no. 24/25 (1981): 22.

34 Waugh, "Lesbian and Gay Documentary," 264.

35 Nichols, *Blurred Boundaries*, 97.

Archeology and Censorship

*   *   *   *   *

Giving birth to Hard to Imagine *was so traumatic that, like the Ancient Mariner, I had to tell about it. If struggles against censorship—both mine and others—have been a running motif of* The Fruit Machine, *this piece, written out of a combination of spleen and orgasmic release, takes the cake. It wrote faster than anything else I've ever written. That is not to say I understand any more about censorship than I did twenty years ago—I just have a lot more to say about it. This piece about writing, publishing, lawyers, and photos may well not quite fit a collection that is primarily about film, but in other ways it provides an ideal denouement for the book.*

"Archeology and Censorship" ran originally in a wonderful Toronto volume about censorship and the arts in Canada, with some anonymous man's sexy toes diddling bananas on the cover (or vice versa) and another John Greyson foreword inside, alongside fifteen dynamite artworks and think pieces by Canadian veterans and visionaries. It's a kind of end-of-century stock taking of where the politics and passions of art and sexuality stand in our mess of a country.

The Academy, Part I

Academics talk a lot about academic freedom, I mused last month when I received my twenty-year service ballpoint from Concordia University, but most of us don't often get close to what it's really about. That tenure has less to do with the unencumbered pursuit of truth than with "productivity," privilege, and corporate team-playing is something I already knew when this story all began, at my tenure hearings in 1981. Even though I was being red-baited by the department dinosaur (rather than queer-baited as I'd half expected), it was ineffectual, and I knew freedom wasn't even on the table.

At that time I was wrapping up a few years as occasional Montreal film critic for the legendary Toronto monthly *The Body Politic*. I felt underappreciated at TBP (they thought I was longwinded and inaccessibly academic, and I thought they never gave me enough space) and not really implicated in the rather glamorous political struggles the Collective had been waging one after another for years. *There* was where the real struggle over intellectual freedom was taking place, I thought from my safe and distant university environment. Well, it was a bit more complicated than that, I was soon to discover as I looked for my post-tenure research topic, confident in my tenured freedom and easing into what was then becoming entrenched as gay and lesbian studies, cultural history branch.

The topic was not long in coming, thanks to a New Left mentor friend of mine from Chicago. Chuck Kleinhans coedited the radical film journal where I had come out academically in 1977. *Jump Cut* was at that point becoming transformed by feminism (as was academia at large) and on the cutting edge of the porn wars. Chuck had been looking around the Kinsey Institute archives, one of the largest repositories of sexual imagery in the world, to check out their avant-garde film holdings and had come away bedazzled by heterosexual shoe fetish photos from the forties and by a 16mm New Jersey gay couple film from the fifties—experimental, accomplished, romantic, and way ahead of its time—that no film historian had ever heard of. There were a few other things there I might find worth looking at, he suggested, and not only six-inch heels. I got a little Concordia grant for an exploratory study of vintage gay pornography (academic freedom/privilege in practice) and headed down to Indiana for a few weeks of (wink, wink) Research.

Thus began my archeological odyssey in quest of traces of prehistoric desire, at Kinsey and soon elsewhere, and the more difficult, fourteen-year struggle to bring these traces to the light of historical understanding and print. This epic is finally ending in a few months (I hope as I put the final touches on this in the summer of 1996) with the publication of *Hard to Imagine: Gay Male Eroticism in Photography and Film from Their Beginnings to Stonewall* from Columbia University Press in New York City. My book, whose imminent appearance I have been announcing for at least eight years, may have robbed me of my youth—and my friends of their sanity— but it has taught me a lot about censorship and intellectual and artistic freedom: about visual representation of the body as a specially fraught field for the politics of desire and about historical research as a contested ground of power and truth, with the archives, the media and the arts, the publishing industry, and the law as its particular institutional arenas. This essay will follow the trajectory of my dig for desire and my run-ins with censorship in North America, run-ins that have everything and nothing to do with the stakes of academic tenure.

The Archive

The first thing that struck me about the Kinsey Archives was the formidable security apparatus: vigilant professional accreditation, steep fees, double locks and security passes, as well as the constant surveillance of all researchers. I understood the necessity: not only had the priceless collection been thinned out by kleptoresearchers in the past, but its very existence, publicly funded in the university system of Dan Quayle land, had always been precarious. The Kinsey Institute had been forced constantly to defend itself not only against the state legislature but also against the Rockefeller Foundation, which had defunded the pioneering Dr. Kinsey in 1954, when sex was getting too politically hot, and even against the U.S. government, which had challenged the very legitimacy of the scientific investigation of dirty pictures in 1953. In the nineties the New Right has been targeting sex research again, raking Dr. Kinsey's name over the coals forty years after his death with cooked-up accusations of child abuse and for all I know satanic cults. So only *legitimate scientific* researchers need apply to the archives that bear his name.

I got used to the security and paranoia, but what also took some getting used to was the way most of the visual materials in the Kinsey archives had been organized by biologists and anthropologists, so that behavioral data became the primary organizing principle. For example, two images with entirely different historical contexts and social connotations, say a 1960 American porn photo and a 1890 European art nude, would be filed together simply because the same gesture, such as kneeling, had been recorded in both. This intrinsic denial of the cultural and political valence of an image, however, I was able to compensate for then and in my subsequent two visits over the next years as I sifted through their visual treasure hoard of gay erotic history. This exploration entirely altered my sense of the queer past, not of its clinical and behavioral constellation, as the archivists seemed to want, but of the cultural and political role of forbidden sexuality in the growth of identities and communities, of the emancipatory thrust of its representation.

When I had to sign in blood that my use of illustrations from the collection was "for clinical or scholarly purpose," I should have got the hint that the artificial barrier between the clinical/scholarly and the political/cultural would need some organized assault.

The Press

I submitted to *The Body Politic* my two breathless feature-length reports on the Kinsey images of pre-Stonewall erotic history. The atmosphere in Toronto in those last years of the Ontario Tory regime was tense: both the paper and the community were battered but defiant in the face of court battles and escalating police persecution (the latest in a series of major bathhouse raids would happen in April 1983). My editors hesitated about a series that celebrated hard-core imagery as our gay cultural heritage and, even worse, defiantly illustrated it. But we finally took the plunge in January 1983 with "A Heritage of Pornography," a cover feature on the vintage erotic movies I had unearthed. Convinced of the historical interest of the material, which dated largely from the twenties and thirties, and reassured by the antique patina of the images, the paper was willing to affront several then-current taboos with this first piece: the frame enlargements showed frontal nudity, albeit fuzzy and postage-stamp sized, and even fellatio and anal penetration, albeit well draped. The first installment went okay, and the cops seemed not to notice.

But when it came to the second piece on the more statistically significant collection of erotic still photographs, both commercial and amateur, some members of the TBP collective suddenly got cold feet. Now, much sharper and larger views of the same activities would be presented, this time fully undraped, plus mutual masturbation, autofellatio, and teenagers in heat. Someone suggested black dots over offending anatomy and activity, which I promptly vetoed on principle. An internal memo debate ensued at the magazine, fanned by the battles about pornography and racism that were being waged in the pages of the magazine that year (the collective was in deep shit for running an ad for Vancouver's Red Hot Video outfit and a classified expressing a non-p.c. racial fantasy, respectively). The controversy over my porno piece wasn't helped by the fact that the famous "Men Loving Boys Loving Men" case was still languishing in court, six years after the initial charges and four years after the first acquittal.[1] No wonder the magazine's lawyers, Charles Campbell and Clayton Ruby, both strongly opposed running a piece that was "certain" to be charged by the intransigent Project P, the joint task force of the Ontario Provincial Police and the Metropolitan Toronto Police, which had been running its own antipornography Inquisition since the sixties. "If I were to choose an article on which to test the legality of showing erections and blow jobs, it wouldn't be written like this one," declared Campbell (lawyers always say no, I would soon learn, for they are trained in "protection," not in fairness or morality, and certainly not in artistic freedom). David Rayside, a fellow academic who headed the Free the Press Fund, was equally adamant, for an exhausted readership would not back up the paper for "picking a fight" with the state in this way. Rayside also inaugurated, in the memo debate, a theme that would echo through the subsequent struggles, in fact through most modern debates about censorship, that pictures were somehow intrinsically less important than words: "TBP supporters are more likely to criticize a printing of photographs or drawings which elicit prosecution than they would prose. . . . This particular slice of our community's history is not so critical to our lives or our political struggles that we will suffer greatly without it."

Interestingly, MLBLM defendants Ken Popert and Gerald Hannon (who years later would learn more than he wanted to know about academic freedom when he was fired from the Journalism Department of Ryerson Polytechnical University for an up-front sideline in sex work) were my most ardent supporters, making principled arguments in favor of the paper's responsibility to discuss pornography in the light of specific examples of it:

> The time and the issue seem particularly well suited to publication of this piece, and many like it. . . . There's no doubt pornography is on the public agenda, both for movement sorts and the general public. . . . Pornography *is* under attack, both ideologically and legally. If we want to create a larger space for it, or even keep the public space it once had,

now's the time to fight for it since there are forces afoot intent on constricting that space. We shouldn't wait, hoping that things will get better or blow over, so that we can publish such pieces without fear of reprisal. They won't and we won't.

And they didn't. At a hot August meeting, the Collective killed the piece.

But three weeks later the second acquittal of the MLBLM three was upheld on appeal, and when the Tory Crown Attorney declined to appeal yet again, the political tension began to abate. In March 1984 "Photography: Passion and Power: Tom Waugh on the Kinsey Still Photo Collection" finally graced TBP newsprint, with kissing World War II sailors on the cover, cropped of their upwardly snaking penises of course (the sailors would become famous because they were pirated a few years later onto the Queer Nation "Read my Lips" T-shirts, still cropped), but a ³/₄ page cocksucking layout on the lead page was luminously uncropped.

Once again the cops didn't even notice. I doubt if the editors shared my twinges of disappointment that my groundbreaking analysis of the historical role of erotic images was not recognized by state power as a threat to the heterosexist capitalist hegemony. In the succeeding months there would be more cover stories on porn and censorship, but the Epidemic was demanding more and more room on TBP covers, and by the time the Tories were finally booted out of office in the spring of 1985, the porn-and-censorship wars seemed to be over. Little did we know that the days of the best political community paper in North America itself were numbered, victim of a kind of economic censorship: TBP would sign off in February 1987, taking its brave, principled, and unprofitable (and often academic) style of community journalism and intellectual debate with it into history.

Meanwhile back in 1984 I had begun to think for the first time about a book-length version of my research but had settled back into the routine of academia, spicing it up a bit with the new special topics course on erotic film genres that my academic tenure now allowed me to get away with.

The Law, Part I

Then the Kinsey lawyer's letter came. I remember the bottom falling out of my stomach in October 1984 as I read the stiff reprimand for having published my research and illustrations in a "magazine such as *The Body Politic*" and for having revealed that one of my illustrations had been donated in 1950 by a certain metropolitan police department (which I had innocently named because of its historical interest). I was ordered to return a signed confession along with all materials and to cease and desist. Ironically, the attorney was the same Manhattan civil liberties expert, the now elderly Harriet Pilpel, who had successfully defended the Institute against the feds back in the fifties, which somehow added hurt feelings to injury. More significantly, since my initial visit, the Institute helm had passed from Paul Gebhardt, a laid-back anthropologist disciple of Kinsey, to a strong-willed psychologist known for her research in biomedical determinations of gender-based behavior, June Reinisch.

Having by now developed an even clearer idea of the shape of my book project, and having grown up pretty strong-willed myself, I could not tolerate either this rejection or this command to back off. In a letter to dozens of scholars in sexology, gay and feminist studies, film studies, and related disciplines, I identified the issues at stake: I was being denied rights to the archive materials because of inappropriate assumptions about the boundaries and constituency of "clinical and scholarly research," and this was "a serious threat to . . . any other scholars who wish to pursue nontraditional historical work at the Institute." Furthermore, "those of us working in the area of sexual history and culture, whether feminist, gay or radical, must be free to develop analyses that may not be popular with Kinsey or any other institution and must be free to address non-traditional scholarly forums." Basically the question was this: who owned the archive materials that Dr. Kinsey had painstakingly collected from a whole generation of gay men, clinical scholars or the gay community?

I think Reinisch must have been surprised when a truckload of letters from such luminaries as Jeffrey Weeks, Martin Duberman, Ruby Rich, Richard Dyer, Dennis Altman, Jonathan Katz, and the president of the Society for Cinema Studies landed in her ornate gender-determined pink office, using tact, logic, pleading, flattery, sarcasm, and outrage to pull off the legal intimidation of my research. I thought I was winning when June consulted her "scientific advisory board" and finally agreed implicitly to let me proceed. But she'd also consulted lawyers, who devised many new hoops I would have to jump through before my book would see the light of print, exorbitant new fees ($250 a picture at first), and worst of all, the right to approve the manner and context of my use of any photos. With this attempt to control my *interpretation* of the images in addition to their publication setting, a new phase had been entered in my relationship with Dr. Kinsey's legacy. Negotiations got so complicated and drawn out over the next seven years that the details sometimes obscured the essence of what was really happening—an arbitrary and bureaucratic exercise of power, a refusal to allow records of historical bodies and desires to be used, not for clinical evidence but for community affirmation and, God forbid, pleasure. In retrospect I laugh thinking of those straight white Dan Quayle lawyers sitting there looking at the photos I had requested, trying to decide whether to veto one sizzler or another. Why was this 1930 commercial photo of an interracial hetero-homo daisy chain refused while a similar all white homo shot with similarly recognizable faces from a few years earlier got the okay? If the faces were the problem, why the veto on this wild but discreet 1952 New Year's Eve party shot of one sailor simultaneously fucking and sucking another, whose flailing nautical limbs filled the frame? Why the 1951 bumfucking close-up I'd chosen simply because a condom was visible but little else? And why another bumfucker from the same period, no condom, no faces, and an amazing angle from the pillow: was it the tasteless flowered drapes in the background?

The three major legal issues that were the vehicle and camouflage of these caprices of power, issues that would chill the remaining production and distribution of the book and increasingly also the whole field of cultural production in Canada and elsewhere, gradually became all too clear:

1. *obscenity*: still contradictory and unsettled territory, but centered on a hysterical consensus forbidding the representation of under-eighteen bodies. Reinisch refused outright any of the Institute's unique collection of turn-of-the-century teenagers, whether in the arty nudes by Baron von Gloeden that are on every bookstore art rack or the irreplaceable, stagey fuck photos starring mustachioed young men in vintage brothels.

2. *civil liability*: The pretext that the individual identities of proud, horny, and recognizable faces captured forty, fifty, sixty years ago needed protecting. Dr. Kinsey's fastidious confidentiality protocols

may have been necessary during the McCarthy era but need updating in an era when gay people display publicly and proudly their social identities and gay bodies. (For example, for the Institute to maintain the shroud of confidentiality over two George Platt Lynes thirties nudes of Jean Cocteau's lover Marcel Khill, dead for over fifty years—his identity a matter of published historical record—while glibly naming the sitters in Lynes's portraits of clothed intellectuals and artists, is erotophobic, homophobic, classist, and pedantically antihistorical).[2]

3. *copyright*: Archives around the world are increasingly jittery about copyright as artifacts of the cultural past become increasingly marketable, and as historians are increasingly being blocked by individuals commandeering the collective past. But the fear that anonymous producers of underground noncommercial and unpublished photos of generations ago, rights holders who could never be traced, would come back from the dead to sue the archive or publisher that had dared let them out into broad daylight was clearly one more unreasonable restraint on my historical research.

The cruncher that would supposedly protect the Institute against all of these paranoid scenarios and one that would come back to haunt me, was that "You AND your publisher must provide a written document holding The Kinsey Institute harmless and *indemnifying* it and its employees from any claim arising out of the publication of the materials you have selected."[3] And by the way please provide your publisher's name and address before any photographs can be released. . . .

The Book Industry

It was the late eighties, and it all seemed a vicious circle. How could I write if I couldn't get a contract from a publisher because I couldn't get the Kinsey go-ahead without a contract from a publisher, and couldn't write anyway because I couldn't finalize what pictures I was writing about? When the going gets rough there's always the Canada Council, and in fact the nonfiction creative writing program provided me with a nice little grant in 1988 that was as important as a symbolic morale booster as it was a ticket to more archives in Europe and California to look for the images that Kinsey wouldn't let me have. The council officer, Robert Richard, was indeed supportive and suggested I look at another book that had just been published in Paris on vintage turn-of-the-century erotic imagery, prefaced by a hotshot French pomo theorist. There was just one hitch, my local gay bookstore, L'Androgyne, couldn't get the book, and when I tracked down the Canadian distributor I learned they *could* import it but *wouldn't* for fear of prosecution: a book depicting heterosexual vanilla sex from seventy or more years ago! Not a good omen of the courage and commitment of the publishing industry that I was beginning to get into bed with.

Now, as for finding a publisher, a few tentative inquiries with Canadian firms confirmed my expectations that I would be wasting my time. Aside from the volatile legal climate, mine was a large book, all the more expensive because of my plan to run four hundred photos, and with only a small proportion of Canadian content (queer cultural history overflows national borders, not only because of its anonymous, unrecorded, and clandestine structure but also because, where pictures were concerned, our ancestors were inveterate smugglers and cross-border shoppers). Besides, having been led on for years on my previous book on radical documentary film, similarly transnational in scope, by sympathetic but marginal and underfinanced Canadian publishers, I preferred to be led on by the hopefully better capitalized Yanks.

In those days, New York's St. Martin's Press had one of the richer gay lines in the marketplace, thanks to the commitment editor Michael Denneny (who also provided the *New York Native* column on gay porn under the pseudonym Mingus, which I thought was promising). But Denneny was pretty clear in his first polite rejection letter of 1985 that no contract could happen without a manuscript or a breakdown of the illustrations so that legal issues could be examined. So I began to publish a few preliminary extracts of the book in Canadian arts mags like *Parallelogramme* (1986) and *Cineaction!* (1987) and came up with a first chapter on the nineteenth century. Denneny's on-again-off-again courtship continued (I even got my first literary lunch out of the process, at the swank NYC Gramercy Hotel!) before he gently but definitively let me down, partly because of the cost, partly because of my "theoretical prose" (too much Foucault in chapter 1!), partly because only a portion of the manuscript was still on hand, and mostly (I gathered) because "St. Martin's (and any other commercial publisher, as well, I would think, any university press) would simply not be able to publish the 'illicit' photos (sucking and penetration—even erections would be very iffy). I could understand if you considered these photos absolutely necessary from a historical and theoretical point of view—but I think this would give most publishers a great problem." Lunch or no lunch, erections weren't all that iffy because every newsstand was now showing them in the *Blueboy* rack. Gay Men's Press, the exciting new outfit in London, meanwhile, expressed interest in the book but not in a contract, while British Routledge was next with a tactful assessment that "given the level and nature of the illustrations in particular, I think it's too far beyond our normal style for me to feel that it would fit easily into the list."

The book that was now called *Hard to Imagine* was getting harder and harder to imagine. Despite having since acquired an agent (at 15 percent!), I was still getting rejections fast and furiously: Columbia, Crown, Grove Weidenfeld, and Chicago all politely declined (the last named inviting resubmission of substantially more manuscript). Harvard spat it back out in one icy sentence by return mail, and Minnesota enthusiastically begged for the proposal and then didn't have the courtesy to reply. The worst insult came from Sasha Alyson, the commercial Boston publisher of nonacademic gay fiction and nonfiction (and incidentally one of Customs Canada's favorite victims):

> I have no patience for the verbose, jargony style of writing that is so common in academia. Waugh's piece in *The Body Politic* was suitable. On the other hand, if I got a manuscript written in the style he uses for *Cineaction* or *Jump Cut*, I'd get it out of the office as fast as possible. Nobody has yet proven that pomposity isn't contagious.
>
> Did Waugh write the BP piece himself, or was it extensively edited by someone else? If the latter, then I doubt he could produce a manuscript I'd want to see. . . .

Then there was the nibble from The Haworth Press, Inc., known for the uneven and idiosyncratic though sometimes useful *Journal of Homosexuality*, which churns out special issues sold as expensive hardcovers to university libraries. Paradoxically it was Haworth who came up with a weird suggestion to de-gay the title to *Male Eroticism in Film and Photography* with the word gay only in the fine print: "The word-phrases 'gay male eroticism' immediately imply pornography. This is sad and regrettable but it is reality. We want to be able to sell the book to *both* film and photography professionals who have gay interests, and those who do not but would be open to reading about your thesis. The best way, from our experience, is this main title/subtitle approach—sort of like the good cop/bad cop method of getting a confession out of the academic brain tissue." Aside from not getting the simile, I found this unacceptable on principle (not that I had many principles left) because "male eroticism" reminded me too much of the furtiveness of sixties coffee-table books. Still I was willing to call the book chopped liver in exchange for a contract. But despite Haworth's profession of "excitement" and "enthusiasm," they continued dancing excitedly around the table and enthusiastically avoided the signing.

Meanwhile Columbia University Press had come back into the picture. Under Ann Miller's leadership, Columbia had been publishing a growing series of gay and lesbian studies books, called "Between Men, Between Women," spearheaded by Lillian Faderman and my old friend Larry Gross (the "out" communications anthropologist from Penn). I didn't really care if there were a few bad smells around Columbia as well: most ominously, the previous series editor, gay philosopher Richard Mohr, had recently stomped out, slamming the door, reportedly over the press's veto of his own book in the series, related to his raunchy illustrations by Tom of Finland, Robert Mapplethorpe, Rex, and others. This book, *Gay Ideas: Outing and Other Controversies*, was to have an ominous Canadian link as well: after being turned down by nine university presses, it was brought out by Beacon in 1992 and favorably received, but the Canadian distributor, Oxford University Press, refused to handle it because of the illustrations, which Richard contextualized not as art but as sex. This one more example of corporate complacency led OUP's Canadian agent Bruce Walsh to resign in protest and become a "Censorstop" activist. Then distributed by the late lamented Inland Distributors, *Gay Ideas* would be detained repeatedly by Customs Canada, and was the book that straight Canlit superstar Pierre Berton analyzed on the stand in the Little Sisters trial,[4] opining that reasonable people would need two minutes to determine that it was a scholarly work and not porn but that customs officials might need an hour. But all this is another story.

So I explained to Ann all about the Kinsey complications around the indemnification, all about my rejections on the grounds of the illicit images and cost, and told her to back off if she wasn't really interested. For it was now 1992, I had another humongous chapter on physique culture ready, and I didn't want to be jerked off one more time. This seemed cool, and she explained the various processes of sending the existing texts out to anonymous readers and vetting the project through various levels of corporate and academic approval. The package sailed through these stages (interestingly the two selected academic assessors were both straight), and the editorial committee only suggested a more "accessible" "trade-oriented" style (did they want butch hustlers to be able to read the book?).

The Law, Part II

Next came the legal approval: the press's lawyer had a look at groups of representative illustrations as well as my legal rationales for the "sensitive" chapters, along with my exhaustive breakdown of legal implications for each classification of photo, from "anonymous amateur photos, no info about photographer or rights holder" to "commercial photo, photographer's authorization obtained." I proposed a 1930 cutoff point before which we could be relaxed about model identification and civil liability: after all my strapping schoolboy posing with a hard-on in 1929 (clearly "eighteen years old" of course) would be in his mid-eighties by the time the book appeared, a reasonable risk to be incurred, I thought. The Columbia lawyer, Mary Luria, seemed to think the 1930 idea was OK, and to my surprise thought s/m was a nonissue, no doubt based on the recent Mapplethorpe vindication in Cincinnati.

However, the lawyer had "serious reservations" about some of my other arguments. She effectively vetoed using post-1930 private (i.e., noncommercial, personal) photos showing any identifiable figures, regardless of previous publication history or nonsexual poses, because of "the risk that such an individual is still alive and *might consider* being depicted in a book of this nature libelous and/or an invasion of privacy, as the inference is easily raised that all those pictured in a book on homosexual imagery are homosexual." No shit. I add the italics above because I still can't believe that the *fear* of *possible* suits, rather than the conviction that one could successfully fight such a suit, routinely provides the basis for decision making in the publishing—and academic—world. Recommending bars over figures' eyes (why was I beginning to hum this tune in my sleep?), Luria went on to suggest that the eighteen-year-old limit be strictly imposed for all models in nude poses of any kind, sexual or not, indicating that no exemptions could be assumed for artistic or scientific or literary or medical reasons. The von Gloedens that I'd carefully scrounged after the Kinsey veto had to go, and even one of Magnus Hirschfeld's 1920s medical illustrations of adolescent hypospadia was out of the question. Most damaging of all, Ann believed the lawyer implied that the context of my book's theme of eroticism changed the legal meaning of my images, so that von Gloedens that everyone else was publishing (including Columbia's own 1992 book *The Homoerotic Photograph*, whose glossy paper and ostentatious layouts I am jealous of to this day) under the name of "art" would be seen as kiddy porn in my book because I refused the usual artistic alibis and called them erotic. After a few months of screaming I eventually won the battle for the von Gloedens and even for the hypospadia.

After more months of haggling, a contract finally arrived with a special added clause threatening that Columbia would pull out and demand all their money back if I didn't comply with future legal directives. The next twenty-one months involved the intense creative activity of actually thinking and writing about my subject, an exquisite torture, and the intense bureaucratic activity of writing hundreds of letters requesting prints, permission, and discount rights fees for my four hundred illustrations. Many rights holders, collectors, and above all the few surviving image makers were generous in view of the nonprofit nature of the enterprise (unless, like the gracious Paul Cadmus, they had a greedy Manhattan dealer, who squeezed a whopping $220 U.S. out of me for my single Cadmus, or, like Cecil Beaton, a greedy estate [Sotheby's], who extorted the same amount for each of two Beatons). Money wasn't the only kind of censorship in play: one elderly Philadelphian nixed my use of a 1929 erotic self-portrait by George Platt Lynes (with hard-on), which he had inherited from his ex-lover, the long-dead Museum of Modern Art founder Monroe Wheeler, who was in turn one of Lynes's exes, simply because he didn't want to "out" the long-dead, long-outed Wheeler with the current MOMA Board! Another elderly artist, Edmund Teske, yanked his thirties photo out of my "erotic" book after a bad experience with Columbia's 1992 homo "art" book: he'd been sloppy with releases for a 1972 frontal nude of a flower child with long hair and a short dick—whose real name was the photo title—and who, twenty years later as a New Jersey dentist, started hassling Columbia and confirming their worst paranoia about civil liability. One New York gay millionaire collector deserves a special place in hell (alongside dentists and lawyers). This personage had cornered the world market in vintage homoerotic photography at outlandishly inflated prices, literally one step ahead of me as he bought up every collection that surfaced in Europe and North America, and wouldn't give me the time of day. Still, the rich queer hoarders were fun compared to the other shit that would hit the fan as soon as I exhaustedly plunked my magnum opus on Ann's desk in March 1994.

The immediate blow was that, after two years of gently nurtured hope, Luria finally and irrevocably vetoed any idea of indemnifying Kinsey for the photos that were so crucial, especially to my perhaps most original chapter about illicit imagery. In fact it seemed that Columbia had never seriously considered the idea. Whether or not Luria had gone to the same law school as the faceless Dan Quayles at the other end, it was a bitter pill to swallow that a decade of research on priceless icons of past private lives should be swept away so casually by high-paid heterosexual lawyers playing poker with each other.

Larry agreed to try to mediate with Kinsey and get them to back off on the indemnifications, and it actually turned out to be easier to get at least partial concessions out of them. Reinisch was gone, and in response to Larry's expert badgering, the Institute's new interim director agreed to forget about the indemnifications for all of the categories except fourteen anonymous illicit shots produced since 1940, none of which had identifiable faces. I was a bit relieved, but it was still a fond farewell to some icons that I had grown sentimentally attached to over the last decade, several that had appeared in the original 1984 TBP piece: the immortal military blow job that had illuminated the lead page; the 1944 portrait of two big-cocked lovers from New York, nipples to knees, who had told the photographer that the one on the right was the masculine one; the bacchanalian 1950 cock bouquet. Good-bye also to others from the thirties, forties, and fifties that I'd assembled since and would not be able to share with gay readers of the nineties: an array of historic hard-ons by an elderly picnicker, a guy in silk panties and black nylons, a TWA steward with sock garters, a motorcycle fetishist in jeans and goggles, not to mention the masked sixty-niners; the African American threesome, hands on asses, sauntering away from the camera, fully dressed; the nude piggybackers at the beach; the pre-Mapplethorpe African American music student who let it all hang out of his boxer shorts on New Year's Eve 1950. I swallowed hard and made the necessary second-rank substitutions.

Luria was not finished. Tooth-combing my entire manuscript, she came up with some more exciting and original ideas. She insisted that names of models be dropped in post-thirties photos, even in the case of physique photos where bodybuilders had been proudly showing off their hard-earned muscles in non-nude poses: another reclosetting of a subculture that was defiantly unashamed. As for the fanatical eighteen-year-old taboo, good-bye to my teenage sailors bumfucking their hearts out in turn-of-the-century Europe and to two of my clerical series from the same period about a horny priest and his altar boy (leaving only the one that had been recently published in a German history of the photographic nude—thank God for small mercies).

But worst of all, Luria was most het up about a dozen or so post-1930 non-commercial photographs in which the subjects were allegedly identifiable (by what authority the lawyer decided that the faintest glimmer of an eyebrow on a tiny blurred face seen in total shadow constituted identifiability and decreed that a 1931 couple posing proudly in berets on a Dutch nude beach posed a greater threat than the 1929 schoolboy hard-on is a subject for future research).

For me, as a gay cultural historian, individual identities are an inextricable part of my research orientation and the texture of history itself. The historical closet has no place in historiography. I've never forgotten my revulsion at the 1981 CBC documentary *Sharing the Secret*, which actually tarted up its documentary protagonists in fake goatees and glasses to "protect" their identity. In my own research, by and large, respondents seemed happy to disclose their identity to my readers. There had been only a few exceptions, a couple of angry ex-bodybuilders who had hung up on me (one, now married, who had been described in one fifties diary as the biggest slut in New York) and a couple of elderly former artists whom I had easily talked out of their shyness. But not everyone shares my slant on naming names: no doubt there are class and gender aspects to attitudes around identities, but disciplinary factors may be the most important: anthropologists and sociologists seem trained to slap a pseudonym on anything that moves and art historians to name the author of anything that doesn't move. As for historians, only half of George Chauncey's seventy interviewees in *Gay New York* had requested pseudonyms, only one-third of Allen Bérubé's sixty interviewees in *Coming Out Under Fire*, and only two of Becki Ross's almost fifty in *The House That Jill Built*. In *Boots of Leather, Slippers of Gold* Madeline Davis and Elizabeth Kennedy produced brilliant groundbreaking work and no doubt had a research process inflected by the gender, class, and race of their narrators from the pre-Stonewall lesbian bar scene in Buffalo. But I felt that their solution to the issue of identifiability was less than satisfactory:

> We have chosen to use first name pseudonyms in identifying people throughout the book. Most narrators wanted to be associated with the project in this manner. But a significant minority of narrators spent their entire lives refusing to hide, and therefore were not completely satisfied with our decision to use pseudonyms. In these acknowledgments it seems appropriate not only to thank the narrators in general but also to specifically mention those who are able to be visible.[5]

My profound discomfort at this recloseting of proudly out people deepened when I noticed that Davis's and Kennedy's photos had been tampered with, invaded by the body snatchers. Rather than the eye bars and silhouettes, which are at least blatant, the authors had opted for the more subtle practice of digitally grafting fake real faces onto every nonpermitting or unidentified person in the casual snapshots provided by the respondents. What was worse in my mind, Davis and Kennedy had only incompletely disclosed this practice, and spectators more innocent than I were no doubt unsuspecting that the face of history had been lifted.

Well, said Ann, if I wanted to use my dozen problematic photos and refused the eye bars, it was Davis's and Kennedy's example I would have to follow. Although I feel strongly about the digital fakery and image manipulation that constitute a critical issue in contemporary media ethics (from the skin darkening of O. J. magazine covers to the dubious fetus of the *Operation Rescue* video), I meekly agreed to have my faces lifted, insisting only that full disclosure of the practice accompany every altered photo.

Anonymous Dutch frolickers (ca. 1950s) before and after face grafts.

Ann and I managed to reduce the number of photos to be doctored down to nine (I angrily went at a couple of the eyebrow-glimmer ones with a magic marker, so absurd was the idea of grafting stranger's faces on tiny, unrecognizable patches of shadow). When I finally saw the completed facelifts fait accompli, no negotiation possible, many of them were okay; a couple looked too old, had face twists, or insufficient tongue effort; and I thought it was funny that Ann's hired digitalizer had reportedly grafted his wife's face onto the body of my grinning Italian teenage masturbator and that it actually worked. In any case I found myself too numb at that late stage to really care anymore, even if there had been any point, provided the disclaimers about the tampering were in every single caption.

One final stipulation by Luria that had completely "blindsided" even Ann was the advice not to distribute or licence my book outside of the United States and Canada because of the potential for copyright and civil liability and obscenity complexities in so many jurisdictions. Farewell to potential readers in the huge English-language Commonwealth market, as well as in such hotbeds of English-reading gay cultures as Western Europe, a geographical area covered extensively in my research. Once again, however, I was too numb to react to one more heartbreak, perhaps because I had the assurances that Canadian distribution would not be affected. So I didn't pay much attention as Ann sent off the manuscript and illustrations to a Bay Street law firm in order to vet the Canadian distribution oĸ. I should have known, for the true North strong and relatively free was going through another censorship crisis, thanks to Catherine Mackinnon, the Supreme Court, and a man named Butler.[6]

The Press, Literally

It has been clear almost since the invention of photography that the most efficient locus of state control over the subversive image has been the printer. When the photo cartels like Kodak took over the amateur photo trade, they turned out to be the most vigilant agents of the state in controlling perverts who wanted to make dirty pictures. And what totalitarian state doesn't attempt to control printing presses and photocopiers? Some of the most interesting queer cultural research in the last decade has had trouble seeing the light of print simply because the printing firms, purported hotbeds of white male blue-collar masculinity, would not countenance images of queer bodies and genitals. Bad Object Choice's anthology *How Do I Look?*, for example, had to be printed in Germany because no American printer was willing to print the tiny little safe-sex illustrations. Richard Mohr's *Gay Ideas* was nixed by twenty-three U.S. printers, including R. R. Donnelley, which had just brought out Madonna's *Sex*! Closer to home, Sylvie Gilbert's forthcoming Banff volume *Arousing Sensation*, essays on "Much Sense: Erotics and Life," the 1992 sex show at the Banff Centre (that almost single-handedly ended arts funding in Alberta!), ran into similar roadblocks with Canadian printers until I agreed to drop the illustrations for my own contribution, which had intended to juxtapose current feminist videos and films with vintage illicit iconographies.

Though neither Columbia nor I expected smooth sailing in the printing department, we were reassured when the job was contracted out to a Hong Kong firm that had done good low-cost (and probably nonunion) work on several of the press's previous photographic books, including the glossy 1992 homo art book. So the press was very upset when the news came in April 1995 that the printer had just backed out:

> We cannot print this book for you. It is due to the law in Hong Kong which might be passed in the next couple of months that will prohibit all printers from printing any sexually related subjects. The Hong Kong legislative party is working out a new law which will be completed and passed some time in June or July 1995. Then, it will be illegal for any printer to print projects consisting of sexual matter, unless we want to apply for a special permit each time we do this kind of book. I don't however feel that this permit is easy to obtain, especially with the type of atmosphere presently in Hong Kong.

At least this time I could blame Beijing. Eventually, I understand, Columbia found a mom-and-pop printer somewhere in upstate New York, but I won't believe that it's actually happened until I have the book in my hand.

And then there will be bookstore sales to think about as a potential site of censorship. At the very last stage of the editing, I learned that the Columbia CEO, already skittish about this queer porno book under his nose, had personally vetoed the use of any image whatsoever on the cover, an odd strategy in marketing a photo book one might think. *Hard to Imagine* will be pretty hard to see in the bookstores. Furthermore, pricing will also apparently be part of this sudden damage control, for the book is to be not only prohibitively expensive ($60 U.S., perhaps defensible because of all those darn photos) but also disadvantageously discounted for community-oriented retailers, entirely a judgment call (when the manager of Montreal's queer bookstore L'Androgyne learned of the discount, her face fell). Was this to be censorship by careful neglect—a censorship strategy we are familiar with in Canada thanks to the National Film Board—despite the enormous investments Columbia had made?

The Law, Part III

The final bombshell came in January 1996 in New Delhi, where I was on a film festival junket, thanks to that great academic perc, the sabbatical. Ann's fax said that the Canadian legal opinion had finally arrived. John Wilkinson of Weir and Foulds, Barristers and Solicitors, First Canadian Place, had alerted the press to several risks, arising most critically from the new post-Butler definition of obscenity as, in his words, the depiction of "explicit sex that subjects people to treatment that is degrading or dehumanizing or which involves violence." Three photos were "open" for a Canadian court finding of obscenity. Ann therefore had no choice but to give me an ultimatum: cut the three offending photos or forgo Canadian distribution. The three photos were indeed naughty but in fact had been originally selected for their relative tameness:

1. a century-old French image of a man pissing into the mouth of his supine, masturbating buddy; badly reproduced (in fact a bad photocopy of a picture that had been snapped up by the greedy hoarder, above) but clear enough to see that the golden stream was a length of string;

2. a campy single figure study from the mid-fifties, a nude hunk in a cowboy hat and boots tied to a tree and looking matter-of-factly down at his erection; made by Richard Fontaine, a pioneer of gay cinema and one of the principal participants in my research, and now recycled as a comic gay greeting card;

3. a moody romantic duo that had been part of Mapplethorpe mentor Sam Wagstaffe's bequest to the J. P. Getty Museum; one of a narrative series, c. 1960, of a GI tricking with a civilian in jeans, of which I had wanted to run two panels: the offending item showed the couple in bed in their underwear, one with hands tied behind his back, kissed tenderly by his newfound Master.

Wilkinson decreed that anything flavored however slightly by water sports and bondage was so extreme that none of the normal legal safeguards applied. Once again I'd become sentimentally attached to these three wonderful glimpses of arousals long past, but that was not all. It was not only the arbitrariness of the choice (other equivalent images had been deemed acceptable, confirming my low impression of the semiotic skills learned in law school). It was that I had been struggling for all of my professional life against censorship in Canada and had viewed publishers and artists who had buckled to state censorship as beneath contempt. Here I was being induced to betray every principle I held as a gay man, a scholar of culture, a Canadian, to betray *The Body Politic*, the Peterborough three, Glad Day and Little Sisters, Eli Langer, and everyone else who had stood their ground to maintain freedom of expression in this country.[7] Martyr at last, I abjured forever the right to distribute among my own community this labor of love and told Columbia what vile cowardly worms they are. This hurt Ann's feelings, and she calmly and rightfully reminded me that only Columbia had had the courage to publish my book in the first place. . . .

By the time I got home, the Little Sisters judgment had come down; this mixed decision (Yes Customs Canada has the right to intercept bad things, and Yes they do so in a discriminatory way) hardly sent an encouraging signal to Columbia, but it at least confirmed their sense that they needed to be less afraid of customs seizure (I wasn't so sure, since *Gay Ideas* had been extremely popular in the Fort Erie border checkpoint, but kept this to myself) than of obscenity prosecution. For tactical reasons I tried to stay calm, offering arguments why Wilkinson's advice was inappropriate and more ambiguous than Columbia had inferred: that only one of the photos included was explicitly sexual according to contemporary conventions; that the lawyer himself acknowledged that the law judges images or text "against the entire work, and in the context of the book's theme"; that "the undue exploitation of sex must be the dominant characteristic of the publication for it to be found obscene"; and that not a single book of this kind or of any other kind had been prosecuted for obscenity, successfully or otherwise, within the last generation (which is why customs was so necessary to keep filth like Marguerite Duras novels out of Little Sisters). The other strategy was simply to point out the masses of books more risqué than mine comfortably ensconced in the Canadian marketplace, from Madonna's *Sex* to Columbia's own 1992 homo art book, replete as it was with piss scenes from Mapplethorpe and anal rape fantasies from Arthur Tress. I was not the only one arguing, for the Columbia representatives in Canada also flooded the head office with sex books bought at random from legit bookstores in Toronto and Montreal, from *Bob Flanagan: Supermasochist* to *New York Girls*.

Buried under an avalanche of filthy American books re-exported from Canada and facing pressure from editors and sales people, Columbia finally capitulated, opening the door to huge Canadian profits.

The Academy, Part II

A Pyrrhic victory? I wonder what the unique lesson is in all of this and why *I* had to learn it. I wasn't the first person to discover that the circulation of cultural meanings and artifacts is severely impeded in our civilization by commerce, greed, legalism, cowardice, amnesia, erotophobia, bigotry, and complacency, and in Canada in particular by a fatal mixture of vestigial colonial-mindedness, prudery, liberalism, and politeness. Nor was I the first academic to be squeezed between the contradictory demands of academia and community accountability, the corporate marketplace and the pursuit of knowledge, the current vogue for queer culture and its erotophobic legal context. And I certainly wasn't the first image producer to discover that structural and institutional means of control can be more effective silencers than outright violence; that cowardice, threats, and self-censorship are often more the problem than full legal sanction. Nor am I, unfortunately, the first academic or image maker to make use of the alibis of academic and High Cultural legitimacy to sanitize the danger of radical images and ideas and to panic when the house of cards starts to tremble. And ultimately does one more imported "academic" commodity on the Canadian marketplace participate in a strengthened ecology of freedom, or is it profoundly beside the point? I knew all these questions before I even got started, but I guess I was surprised by all the terror over the few iffy weenies uncovered by my archeologist's shovel.

Why are images from the past so frightening? Beyond the strategic importance of the battles against bigots and censors, of the inclusion of silenced voices, why is it ultimately so urgent and necessary to unearth the visual artifacts of historic desire, to analyze, contextualize, and share them with this and future generations? Censors obviously have unexamined assumptions about their importance and danger, but it behooves us to examine ours. The value of the traces of our ancestors' forbidden and invisible fantasies is more than academic or historic. Does it also have something to do with the pursuit of what Foucault called an *ars erotica*, a pursuit of truth in desire, a reclamation or reinvention of the body's capacity for pleasure, community, resistance, and transformation . . . , a capacity that industrial and consumer utopias have withheld and that sexual and feminist revolutions have fallen short of but that transgressors of yesterdays and elsewheres have maybe glimpsed?

Whatever the answers to these persistent questions, it is clear that a free-lance visual artist or independent community researcher could never have asked them in the same relative sustained luxury as this tenured academic. Nor could a photographer or filmmaker creating work today equivalent to my brazen blow jobs and hard-ons of the paleolithic past, whatever that might be, invoke the artistic and academic alibi as easily as Columbia University Press. The proximity of the Eli Langer and the Little Sisters trials has reminded us that books and pictures, academics and artists, are out there together at the front of the struggle against censorship, in different but in inextricably dependent ways, and must shun the isolation and alibis that are so easy.

Meanwhile, still safe in academia, now promoted and now buoyed up with a CUP book on my c.v., I am looking for a postbook research topic. Any ideas?

In Lorraine Johnson, ed., *Suggestive Poses: Artists and Critics Respond to Censorship* (Toronto: The Riverbank Press and Toronto Photographers Workshop, 1997).

Notes

1 *The Body Politic* article "Men Loving Boys Loving Men" (by Gerald Hannon, December 1977, called MLBLM by insiders) described in nonjudgmental terms several relationships between adult men and their partners below the legal age of consent. For another historical take on the epochal 1978 charges against the magazine, see Beck Ross, *The House That Jill Built: A Lesbian Nation in Formation* (Toronto: University of Toronto Press, 1995).

2 As the institute did with two unidentified "Male Nudes" (1936; nn. 21 and 26) of the touring exhibition of a selection of the Kinsey Institute's Lynes bequest, originating at Grey Gallery, New York University, 1993.

3 All quotes from letters to the author are unpublished and in the author's possession, available on request.

4 Little Sisters, the Vancouver lesbian and gay bookstore, sued the federal government for years of unconstitutional harassment through Canada Customs. As of this February 1999 edit, the bookstore's appeal of the mixed judgment has just been ac-

cepted for hearing by the Supreme Court. Inland Distributors' business in handling American small-press books and alternative magazines in Canada, a mainstay of the queer bookstore circuit, was effectively killed by customs interference.

5 Elizabeth Lapovsky Kennedy and Madeline R. Davis, *Boots of Leather, Slippers of Gold: The History of a Lesbian Community* (New York: Routledge, 1993), xxi.

6 In 1992 a Winnipeg video-store operator named Butler saw his name given to the Supreme Court judgment upholding his obscenity conviction. The judgment transformed obscenity jurisprudence in Canada, enthroning U.S. right-wing feminist Catherine Mackinnon's subjective criterion of "harm" into our criminal code (she who had failed in her effort to do so south of the border) and effectively setting in motion the systematic scapegoating of lesbian and gay periodicals and bookstores that has continued until this day.

7 The Peterborough Three had been convicted of exhibiting an experimental film without the Ontario censor's approval in the early 1980s; Glad Day is the Toronto queer bookstore convicted in the first post-Butler verdict of distributing U.S. lesbian magazine *On Our Backs*; Toronto painter Eli Langer went on trial for his nightmarish paintings evoking child abuse but was eventually acquitted.

Selected Additional Works

*   *   *   *   *

Books

Hard to Imagine: Gay Male Eroticism in Photography and Film from Their Beginnings to Stonewall. New York: Columbia University Press, 1996. 470 pages, 376 illustrations.

"Show Us Life": Toward a History and Aesthetics of the Committed Documentary. Metuchen, N.J.: Scarecrow Press, 1984. 508 pages, illustrations. Reprint in paperback 1988. An anthology of twenty-five articles edited by and including two essays by Thomas Waugh.

Articles

"Queer Bollywood?: Patterns of Sexual Subversion in Recent Indian Cinema," forthcoming in "Sexualities and Third Cinema," special issue of *Journal of Film and Video*, 2000.

"Cinemas, Nations, Masculinities," *Canadian Journal of Film Studies* 8.1 (spring 1999): 8–44.

"Good Clean Fung," *Wide Angle* 20.2 (1998): 164–175.

"Posing and Performance: Glamour and Desire in Homoerotic Art Photography, 1920–1945." In Deborah Bright, ed., *The Passionate Camera: Photography and Bodies of Desire*. New York: Routledge, 1998. 58–77.

"'Effigies de nos Adonis en quête d'immortalité': La photographie homoérotique à Montréal, 1950–1965." In Frank Remiggi and Irène Demczuk, eds., *Sortir de l'ombre. Trajectoires des communautés lesbienne et gaie montréalaises depuis les années 1950*. Montréal: VLB, 1998. 53–80.

Review of *Another Fine Dress: Role-Play in the Films of Laurel and Hardy*, by Jonathan Sanders. *Journal of the History of Sexuality* 7.4 (April 1997): 621–624.

"Cockteaser." In Jennifer Doyle, Jonathan Flatley, and José Esteban Muñoz, eds., *Pop Out: Queer Warhol*. Durham, N.C.: Duke University Press, 1996. 51–77.

"Beyond Queer Alibis and Labels: Thoughts on the Fruit Machine and Little Sisters." *Parallelogramme* (Toronto), winter 1994–95, 46–57.

"Cultivated Colonies: Notes on Queer Nationhood and the Erotic Image." In *Canadian Journal of Film Studies* 2.2–3 (fall 1993): 145–178.

"The Third Body: Patterns in the Construction of the Male Body in Homoerotic Photography and Film." In John Greyson et al., eds., *Queer Looks: Perspectives on Lesbian and Gay Film and Video*. London: Routledge, 1993. 141–161; rpt. Nicholas Mirzoeff, ed., *The Visual Culture Reader*. London: Routledge, 1998. 431–447.

"'Learning to Play Oneself': Notes on Performance in Documentary." In Carole Zucker, ed., *Making Visible the Invisible: An Anthology of Original Essays on Film Acting*. Metuchen, N.J.: Scarecrow Press, 1990. 64–91.

"Les Formes du discours sexuel dans la nouvelle vidéo masculine." *Communications* (Québec) 9.1 (spring 1987): 44–66.

"The Sexual Anxiety of the Boys' Club." *Copie zéro* (Montréal), no. 24 (June 1985): 7–9.

"Men's Pornography, Gay vs. Straight." *Jump Cut*, no. 30 (spring 1985): 30–36. Reprinted in Corey K. Creekmur and Alexander Doty, eds., *Out in Culture: Gay, Lesbian, and Queer Essays on Popular Culture*. Durham: Duke University Press, 1995. 307–327; and in Susan Dwyer, ed., *The Problem of Pornography*. Belmont, Calif.: Wadsworth, 1994. 142–161.

"The Death of Camp?: Tom Waugh on [Demetrios Estdelacropolis's] *Mother's Meat and Freud's Flesh* and [Bachar Chbib's] *Or d'ur*." *The Body Politic*, no. 108 (November 1984): 33–34.

"Uncovering a Forgotten Canadian Gay Film—from 1965 [on David Secter's *Winter Kept Us Warm*]." *The Body Politic*, no. 83 (May 1982): 36.

"Gays Set the Record Straight [on the CBC's *Sharing the Secret*]." *Cinema Canada*, no. 73 (April 1981): 32–33.

"Nègres blancs, tapettes et 'butch': Images des lesbiennes et des gais dans le cinéma québécois." *Copie zéro* (Montréal), no. 11 (October 1981): 12–29.

Index

* * * * *

Thomas Waugh is Professor of Film Studies at the
Mel Hoppenheim School of Cinema at Concordia University. In
addition to his many published articles and reviews, he is the author of the
award-winning book *Hard to Imagine: Gay Male Eroticism in Photography
and Film from Their Beginnings to Stonewall.*

* * *

Library of Congress Cataloging-in-Publication Data
Waugh, Thomas. The fruit machine : twenty years of writings on
queer cinema / Thomas Waugh ; foreword by John Greyson.
p. cm. Includes bibliographical references and index.
ISBN 0-8223-2433-4 (alk. paper). — ISBN 0-8223-2468-7 (pbk. : alk. paper)
1. Homosexuality in motion pictures. 2. Homosexuality and
motion pictures. 3. Gay motion picture producers
and directors. I. Title.
PN1995.9.H55W38 2000
791.43′653—dc21 99-27252 CIP